Studies in the Psychosocial Series

Edited by
Peter Redman, The Open University, UK
Stephen Frosh, Centre for Psychosocial Studies, Birkbeck College, University of London, UK
Wendy Hollway, The Open University, UK

Titles include:

Stephen Frosh
HAUNTINGS: PSYCHOANALYSIS AND GHOS⁻

Uri Hadar
PSYCHOANALYSIS AND SOCIAL INVOLVEMEN⸏
Interpretation and Action

Margarita Palacios
RADICAL SOCIALITY
Studies on Violence, Disobedience and the Vicissitudes   ᴜelonging

Derek Hook
(POST)APARTHEID CONDITIONS

Gath Stevens, Norman Duncan and Derek Hook (*editors*)
RACE, MEMORY AND THE APARTHEID ARCHIVE
Towards a Transformative Psychosocial Praxis

Irene Bruna Seu
PASSIVITY GENERATION
Human Rights and Everyday Morality

Lynn Chancer and John Andrews (*editors*)
THE UNHAPPY DIVORCE OF SOCIOLOGY AND PSYCHOANALYSIS

Kate Kenny and Marianna Fotaki (*editors*)
THE PSYCHOSOCIAL AND ORGANIZATION STUDIES
Affect at Work

James S. Ormrod
FANTASY AND SOCIAL MOVEMENTS

Jo Whitehouse-Hart
PSYCHOSOCIAL EXPLORATIONS OF FILM AND TELEVISION VIEWING
Ordinary Audience

Bülent Somay
THE PSYCHOPOLITICS OF THE ORIENTAL FATHER
Between Omnipotence and Emasculation

Julie Walsh
NARCISSISM AND ITS DISCONTENTS

Wendy Hollway
KNOWING MOTHERS
Researching Maternal Identity Change

Studies in the Psychosocial Series
Series Standing Order ISBN 978–0–230–30858–9 (hardback)
978–0–230–30859–6 (paperback)
(*outside North America only*)

You can receive future titles in this series as they are published by placing a standing order. Please contact your bookseller or, in case of difficulty, write to us at the address below with your name and address, the title of the series and the ISBNs quoted above.

Customer Services Department, Macmillan Distribution Ltd, Houndmills, Basingstoke, Hampshire RG21 6XS, England

Also by Wendy Hollway

SUBJECTIVITY AND METHOD IN PSYCHOLOGY: Gender, Meaning and Science

WORK PSYCHOLOGY AND ORGANIZATIONAL BEHAVIOUR: Managing the Individual at Work

MOTHERING AND AMBIVALENCE (*co-editor*)

CHANGING THE SUBJECT: Psychology, Social Regulation and Subjectivity (*co-author*)

DOING QUALITATIVE RESEARCH DIFFERENTLY: Free Association, Narrative and the Interview Method (*co-author*)

THE CAPACITY TO CARE: Gender and Ethical Subjectivity

Knowing Mothers

Researching Maternal Identity Change

Wendy Hollway
The Open University, UK

First published 2015 by
PALGRAVE MACMILLAN

Palgrave Macmillan in the UK is an imprint of Macmillan Publishers Limited, registered in England, company number 785998, of Houndmills, Basingstoke, Hampshire RG21 6XS.

Palgrave Macmillan in the US is a division of St Martin's Press LLC, 175 Fifth Avenue, New York, NY 10010.

Palgrave Macmillan is the global academic imprint of the above companies and has companies and representatives throughout the world.

Palgrave® and Macmillan® are registered trademarks in the United States, the United Kingdom, Europe and other countries.

ISBN 978–1–137–48122–1 hardback
ISBN 978–1–137–48125–2 paperback

This book is printed on paper suitable for recycling and made from fully managed and sustained forest sources. Logging, pulping and manufacturing processes are expected to conform to the environmental regulations of the country of origin.

A catalogue record for this book is available from the British Library.

Library of Congress Cataloging-in-Publication Data
Hollway, Wendy.
   Knowing mothers : researching maternal identity change / Wendy Hollway.
      pages   cm. — (Studies in the psychosocial)
   ISBN 978–1–137–48122–1 (hardback)
   1. Motherhood—Psychological aspects.   2. Mother and child.
   3. Mothers—Psychology.   4. Identity (Psychology)   I. Title.
   HQ759.H722 2015
   306.874'3—dc23   2014028126

In memory of Cathy Urwin, who died on 3 June 2012

Contents

Part I   A Psycho-Social Research Project Example: Introducing Principles, Methods and Practices

Part II   Three Psycho-Social Perspectives on Knowing and Becoming: Psychoanalytically Informed Theorising in Mothers' and Researchers' Knowing

Part III   Analysing the Politics of the Maternal Psycho-Socially

In Conclusion

Illustrations

Preface

How do women experience the identity changes involved in becoming mothers for the first time? When this is the question posed by an empirical research project, it sets a methodological challenge: how can research bring to light such experience; how can identity change be documented, conceptualised and written about? This book revolves around these methodological questions, addressed throughout via data from the 'Becoming a Mother' project. Nineteen women's lives populate this book, as they become mothers for the first time, each unique and all having much in common amidst the diversity of East London.

I initially wrote this preface in Oslo, where – just ten minutes' walk from where I lived – Gustav Vigeland's sculptures inhabit the park like a huge community, all naked and, at that time of the year, capped and shawled in snow. The mother image that I photographed and chose for the book cover expresses a theme that had been brewing in my mind for several years: the ineffable in maternal experience. Ineffable has two allied meanings, both coming from the Latin root [in]ex – fare, to speak out. The first is 'incapable of being expressed'; the second is 'not to be uttered'. What is her wordless experience as she sturdily plants herself on all fours, with two children on her back? Her face is almost impassive. A conventional reading of the scene would be that she is playing a game with the children and indeed on one of the websites I found, this image is called 'mother plays horse'. But I don't find her expression playful, nor – to my eyes – is it resentful. Perhaps the children are playing horse, especially the boy on the front who is gleefully using her plaited hair as reins, complete with the part that works like a horse's bit. The girl behind looks slightly askance. What imaginative world is their mother enabling them to inhabit? Perhaps she looks a little resigned, her body grounded in the present moment while her gaze is also somewhere else, looking forward, not down, into the middle distance ahead. Like most of Vigeland's adults, this mother is huge, with arms and legs as thick as pillars. Her back is not straining under the children's weight; her hands are grounded like strong roots; her belly and breasts full and firm. In the background are other images of fecundity: the ant-heap of children and another, smaller number who look as if they are rooting for the mother's nipples like a litter of piglets under the sow.

The feature of this maternal figure to which I am recurrently drawn is the tress across her mouth, not quite a horse's bit ('bite') because it is not inside her mouth; more like a loose-fitting gag, with which she cooperates to keep it in place, cooperates in being wordless in her act of maternal bearing. This is the feature that suggests maternal ineffability to me. To the extent that ineffable means incapable of being expressed, I must acknowledge that such aspects of the maternal will remain outside the scope of this book. To the extent that early maternal experience has been ex-communicated, I am motivated to extend the available language and methods of knowing to make it more accessible. Loosely based around the idea of wordlessness, then, I pattern the two interdependent themes in this book: maternal knowing (how – in what modes – do mothers know their pre-semantic infants?) and research knowing (how do researchers know about this partly ineffable maternal becoming?). In practice, how did we, the research team, learn about the mothers participating in our project?

Qualitative psycho-social research has largely been based upon what participants say, while this project recorded new mothers' words as well as observing them in the wider context, often of family. Both interview and observation methods have gradually drawn me towards what is not said. The not-said manifests in many ways, each challenging researchers to ask if, when, how and how well we know. So the ineffability of maternal experience calls into play a parallel in the researchers' experience in which the ineffable must be transformed so that it can be meaningfully communicated. If it is to some extent beyond words, how can it be researched and validated? What methods do I have for grasping the maternal ineffable and what words and concepts might do justice to it? Has it got lost in discourses and representations of the maternal, with what consequences? Do maternal discourses also reflect what is not to be uttered (what is taboo)?

Not everything about maternal experience is ineffable: mothers, like all human beings who have entered language, use language to make sense of their experiences and to communicate; researchers likewise. What these 19 mothers say in the research setting forms a considerable part of the information on which this book is based. However, words act on many levels, and this book is also about what exists on, behind and beyond the borders of language and symbolisation; that exceed it and escape it, and yet are communicative and co-exist with it. This is the unthought known, residing initially in embodied affect, or emotional experience, through which the excommunicated can be made available to language. Throughout this book, I illustrate how a different research methodology, underpinned by a psychoanalytically informed epistemology, can transform our understanding of the early foundations of maternal identity.

Acknowledgements

The original research idea about first time mothers' identity transition was hatched within the Open University Psychology Department's Discourse and Psycho-social Research group. It was worked up with Ann Phoenix, Yasmin Gunaratnam and Cathy Urwin. The Economic and Social Research Council funded the project. Heather Elliott, appointed as researcher, was central in putting the proposal into action. The 20 participants in that project welcomed us into their homes at a time of considerable upheaval and, apart from one, stuck the course. Others, including a pilot interviewee, contributed data. Six observers, Monika Flakowicz, Sandy Layton, Elspeth Pluckrose, Judith Thorp, Ferelyth Watt and Sarina Woograsingh, generously committed many hours of their demanding working lives travelling weekly to six participants' homes, observing, writing notes and attending the weekly observation seminar. Cathy Urwin took responsibility for recruiting them and led the weekly seminar at her home in London. Her wisdom and experience were crucial to the success of the observation side of the study. She continued to develop infant observation as a research method, in many ways that have informed this book, until her death in 2012. Her approach was an inspiration for this book; an inspiration only magnified by the loss and my wish to do justice to her memory.

Harriet Bjerrum Nielsen and Hanne Haavind invited me to the Norwegian government-funded programme at the Centre for Advanced Study in Oslo where I took case data to work with the group in one of four eight-week sessions. A scholarship funded (again) by the Economic and Social Research Council enabled a period of digestion and further analysis without which the book would not have resembled what has emerged. The intellectual climate and growing post-graduate research culture of psycho-social studies in the UK has provided me with a lively network within which to situate my work.

Several psycho-social colleagues have read and commented on recent drafts or parts of this book: thank you to Peter Redman, Yasmin Gunaratnam, Ann Phoenix, Heather Elliott, Jette Kofoed, Griselda Pollock, Tony Jefferson and Rachel Thomson.

I am grateful for this multi-faceted support.

Part I

A Psycho-Social Research Project Example: Introducing Principles, Methods and Practices

1
Knowing Mothers, Researching Becoming

This book's exploration of identity transition, specifically the changes involved when women become mothers for the first time, is framed by a methodological perspective: it asks how researchers know what we know from empirical data. It is based on the data from a funded research project.[1] 'A focus on mothers shifts our epistemological, political, social and psychic horizons' claims Petra Bueskens (2014, p.4). Indeed, research into new mothers' changing identities has shifted my knowledge horizons: it poses epistemological questions and methodological challenges because the experiences of women as they become mothers are partly beyond words. It is these challenges that provide the structure of the book, and it is in this sense that this is a book not only about new mothers' knowing and its relation to their becoming, but also about methods adequate for researching such a topic.

I start by offering you, the reader, the example of one new mother's experience written in rough verse, based on the words, observed practices and situation of Juhana (not her real name), one of the 19 mothers in our sample in Tower Hamlets, East London. Juhana was one of six within the research sample of first-time mothers who participated in weekly observations at home, as well as in three interviews extending, in her case, over 16 months, starting before her baby was born. My aim in using this method is to provide scenes that change over time, to give a lively overall impression, replete with emotion-laden meaning deriving from Juhana's words and actions, in order to convey – while necessarily using words – more than the literal meaning, through rhythm, cadence, association and idiom. I call it 'rough verse' after the term used by poet Ted Hughes, referring to its capacity to preserve 'the fresh simple presence of the experience' (see Chapter 6). It is a form of data which

3

I hope takes you, the reader, to the heart of the fieldwork involved in the project. The idea of scenes, like the theatre curtain opening on successive acts, is here used to afford images of Juhana in her family and local context in its complexity, conviviality, generosity and constraint. I include practices and situate them within circumstances: for example, feeding and bathing the baby, how Juhana, her baby and husband live, spend their time and sleep in the context of her husband's position as the financially responsible eldest son, Juhana's overcrowded family home and her relationship to the block of council flats in which she has grown up, where she feels comfortable. I discuss in Chapter 6 how this approach reflects my methodological choices and how I approached the composition. At this point, I hope that you simply let the verses wash over you and pause long enough to reflect on how you feel and what you might know as a result.

Mum's over the moon[2]

Scene one. Living at the in-laws

Mum's over the moon
Their first granddaughter (That's on both sides.)
My hubby and me, we wanted to name her after me.
She's like the queen, all her needs are served.
I always wanted a little girl.
It's like a little you. I love that about her.
Me, the eldest sister too.
I love dressing her up.

I live with hubby's family.
He's the oldest son and his parents need him.
When we were engaged he asked me to come and live
    here so I did.
Our families are from different sides of Bangladesh.
I don't like my mother-in-law's ways.
My husband wouldn't like me saying this
But I don't really like living here, I don't get on with them.
They're weird.

Dad comes round to see me all the time but not Mum.
I'm like, Mum you probably don't love her as much as Dad,
You don't get round to coming to see us.
She's like, No I do all the housework, cook the food,
for everybody else to come home.
So she's a bit stressed herself.

I didn't think much about the pregnancy, it all went well.
I was tiny and I was misleading from the back
because you couldn't see the bump until I turned round.
I knew she was there inside, it was a perfect feeling.
When I stopped work I went to stay with my Mum.
I stayed about two weeks, that was really good I just
    totally unwind.
My Mum was great she did all the cooking and all I did was
    put my feet up.

I didn't take it all on board how it was going to be
I hadn't actually looked into it.
You have to be ready to be a Mum.
She wasn't planned so it came as a shock to me and hubby.
But I was happy, I was very happy.
We've been married for three years and going out for another two.

My mother-in-law wants me to go back to work
So that she can have her all to herself
She wants the baby to sleep with her.
She thought I shouldn't go out for 40 days after the birth
but my Mum thinks that's silly.
I won't go back to work at 24 weeks although they want me to.
I'm too glued to her.

I've got so much help when I'm at home.
All my sisters know how to look after her.
Here I keep myself to myself.
Hubby leaves early and won't be back from the bank till later.
I hope she goes to sleep so I can too.
She kept me awake most of the night wanting my breast.
Hubby says he'll help but he doesn't wake up.

Scene two. Back at home
My father-in-law gave me permission to come and stay at Mum's
to support her while Dad's back home in Bangladesh.
I sleep with Mum while Dad's away and baby's carrycot
Just fits beside.
I'm the one getting up in the night to feed, up and down all night.

I never go out any more. I shop online or my sisters get what I need.
It's the feeding that's the problem.
I've been out once to get my eyebrows plucked.
Mum kept her but she won't take a bottle.

How has being a mother changed me?
I think I've started to *age* since I've had a baby
'Cos the way my parents talk to me
Oh she's a mother now
It seems like they all think I'm a bit more grown up
I don't like it but.
I don't like it.
You know, I'm still the age that I was
I'm still young.
Before it was like Yes Mum, that's what I wanna do
And that's what I'm gonna do.
Whereas now I've got to think about *her* before I decide to
    do anything
I really don't like it.
Well, I'd like them to treat me the way they used to before.

In the evenings when my sisters are back I don't see my daughter.
I sometime wonder if she even recognises me.
I can have a bath in peace
And get properly dressed for the first time all day.
Mum has a bath for her and it has dolphins.
I love dolphins and I told Mum to get her one with dolphins too.
My sister says that's no reason why she'll like them.
I'm too scared to bath her though.
I might get water in her eye or drop her.
So Mum does it.

I can't wear my hoops and stuff like that, she pulls it off
    and it *really* hurts.
And if I stop her she starts crying
So I let her do what she wants basically.
Mum is sure she knows I'm her proper Mum now
I went out for two hours last week and none of them could
    stop her crying
But she stopped straight away when I got back.

I really miss my Dad. We went to see him off at the airport.
All that way and he didn't kiss me goodbye, only her.
I asked him why and he apologised, hadn't thought about it,
Said when you had a grandchild that's how it was.

Scene three. Staying put where she's at home

They want me back there again, the in-laws.
I did go back for a bit.

It wasn't right for me to be here again so soon.
When they were missing her growing up.

But that house is a disaster zone,
I thought No I'm going back to my Mum's
And this is where I'm staying.
They're very disappointed.
'Cos they thought, now that she's born,
They want her to be brought up in their house.
But I've totally said no, I don't want her round there.

Hubby's in depression anyway, he doesn't know what to do
    with his brother.
His Dad's retired so hubby pays the mortgage.
He's hardly ever there, though, just to sleep.
He visits here morning and evening,
Here I'm more relaxed,
It's my Mum, I know everybody.

I've seen all my little younger sisters grow up
And I was always here to support my Mum,
So I love exactly what she does
And I think that's the perfect way of doing it
'Cos she raised all of us.

I'm glad I don't have any brothers
Because we're all very close to each other
And if we had a boy it would change everything,
He's probably Daddy's little boy and my Dad loves me
And I'm the first and I'm the most loved
And I wouldn't want to change that.
If I had a little brother, he would probably want to take my place
And I'm not too keen on that.

Scene four. Exhausting daily demands
I spend all my days feeding her and changing nappies
She drinks for five minutes and then she stops.
She starts talking, looking around or she falls asleep
And then in another ten, fifteen minutes she's hungry again
Milk again. Madam wants her milk.
Because I'm only on the breast.
I might start changing to the bottle to get some rest
It takes a lot of time and it's just wearing me out.

When she's asleep, my Mum's like Go on,
Try and get some sleep
But I'm like, Mum,
I've got shitloads of things to do.
Make the bed, tidy up
Wash her clothes, wash mine
Have a shower.
I can't even go into the bath any more because she keeps crying.
Sometimes I'm about to dip myself in and I'm like
Oh no, come out again, she's crying
Hubby tries to keep her but it's just like, she's more with me
So I know how to calm her down
Whereas him, he only gets to see her at the weekend
And late in the evening when she's sleeping.

I don't get time to myself any more, I don't.
Whereas before I had all the luxury of -
I never thought -
I had all the time in my hand.
But now I don't even get around to wearing my favourite clothes
Don't make the time for anything anymore
Even phone calls.
I used to be on the phone all the time.
Whereas now I look at my bill and think, wow, how did I do that.
It's really boring every day to day.

All I want is my own place.
I hope the council will find me one before Dad gets back.
Hubby's stayed here for three nights running
But he won't be able to do that soon.
The health visitor suggested I see my MP.
I went to stay with my Aunt for a while.
It's just that here we take up too much space.

Dad's back.
Now he knows about what's going on at the in-laws.
We didn't tell him when he was away because of his blood pressure.
He's sleeping on the living room sofa.
He's alright with it
But he keeps moaning about not being able to find his stuff
This place is so cramped.
There's three in one bedroom, two in another.

Our Dad's Mum has the little bedroom to herself.
She needs somewhere quiet to pray.
My sisters and me, we don't pray like my parents do.
Let's say, my sisters we're all very westernised.
I so need my own space.
I hate leaving things around the house, I'm a tidy freak
And anyway when relatives come round
I don't want them to think I'm making myself too
   comfortable here.

Yesterday I decided I'd had enough of her wanting my breast
   milk all the time
I waited till she was 6 months old because SureStart said.
She kept spitting out the baby rice so I gave up
But watch this!
There, one spoonful after another, quick
She likes vegetables too
There you go, Mom, smack your lips it's so good.
The health visitor recommended a high chair
I was trying to feed her on the bed because where else.
Things are going better.
I actually had a decent night's sleep
And I feel as if I know what she wants.

Scene five. Managing with family help

I'm sooo tired.
Mum's having to do everything for me and I feel bad about that.
Today I felt dizzy in the park
Came straight home to lie down.
My hair's been falling out and I've lost too much weight
I wanted to get back down to seven stone but now I'm nearer six
The health visitor thinks I might be anaemic so
I'm going to the doctor tomorrow.

Shhh. I haven't told Mum yet, but Soraya knows.
I'm pregnant again. It's been months, they say.
And I really wanted to go back to work when she was a year old
But now there wouldn't be much point.
I daren't tell them at work.
I hope they'll hold my job open but
I'll probably have to start from the bottom again.
I was just looking forward to getting my life back.

First thing I did was phone hubby
He was shocked too.
He says we can do it. He says we can have two together
And get it over and done with
And then I can go back to my career
And stop stopping and starting.

I don't know how I'm going to manage
It's hard enough with her.
She won't stay in her buggy and screams
And she'll be jealous too.
And it'll be more stress on Mum and Dad.
My gran's due back so there'll be more people anyway
And hubby won't be able to stay at weekends.

Dad insists on me sleeping in his room with Mum
But the doctor says he shouldn't be on his own
He's got so many illnesses.
Mum's had an operation on her varicose veins
But she's always on her feet there's so much to do.
We have to keep up the pretence that Mum's ill to the in-laws
So she needs me here.
It's the best way to keep them off our backs.

Hubby keeps out of it.
They gave him a really hard time at the beginning
But now they're OK.
They're saying that their granddaughter would be walking by now
If she lived in their house.
There's not much space for her here, but she's beginning to crawl.

They'd all miss her so much if we left and
Mum's worried that I'd neglect her once the new baby arrives.
But I said no, the new one will just sleep all the time
and she'll be demanding my attention.
Hubby says she'll always be number one with him.

She adores my Dad
She'll choose him over me any day
Sometimes she won't even go to Mum.
He takes her to every room where she points
Looking at everything that attracts her attention.
She always gets her way
She's a little madam, just like a firstborn.

It's awful when she coughs
Look, it's waking her up
Hello Mom, hello Mom.
I don't know why we call her Mom
I think my husband started it
I caught on and now it's stuck.

We've moved into my sisters' room
I needed to give Mum and Dad more space
I started to feel like I was breaking up the couple
With Dad always sleeping on the sofa.
The only way I'd get housed is if Mum and Dad threw me out
And they'd never do that.
They'll take all the pain.
I can't do this on my own.
I want to be able to manage on my own but I know I need Mum
    nearby.

I like it round here.
Where the in-laws live it's all Asians
And there seems to be a little bit more fight and gossip
Whereas here we've got a mix.
All the whites blacks Asians they're all mixed up
I mean we all speak to everybody in our building.
I was raised up in this borough and I'm happy to raise my daughters
    here.

Scene six. Coping with two

It wasn't planned, number two
To be honest, I was really upset
It was really hard for me.
I was planning to go back to work, I was due back.
It took me ages, it must have been four weeks after the news
That I got to terms with, you know, going ahead with the pregnancy.
I was going through a depression.

My husband was really excited like the first time.
I thought he might think ohhh not just yet
Whereas my family everyone was ohh you'll find it really difficult
And they knew I wanted to go back to work
But then Mum and them, they were like Noo,
Other people do it, single parents could do it
And you've got all of us

My sisters were really excited, they'd forgot what it was like
To have a baby at home.
I dunno, it's a blessing I guess.

The past two weeks on Saturdays -
That's when we go out in the car -
Just hasn't been nice
We've had to head back
Because the kids were doing our heads in
And we think OK just leave them with Mum and Dad
They're more than happy
They're like Why don't you leave them with us.
That's when we'll go to Nandos
Just spend some quality time.

My parents, well to be honest it's really sad
But they don't go out.
Mum was doing a childcare course and she dropped that
It was just too much with the two little ones
I'm coming in her way
Because she really wanted to do something for a change.

This one is not taking solids.
I had to see the health visitor for that.
It helped for a little while then she's gone off again.
She's totally on breast milk that's all she's surviving on
She even spits out chocolate.
So she wakes up two or three times every hour
And that's not me exaggerating.
It's taking a lot out of me.
The new one's totally on bottle milk, mum's feeding her now.
It's not really fair, I mean
The midwife is sort of encouraging me to breastfeed
But I just can't do it I just can't feed another one.

My health? I think I'm quite fine, yeah
I'm looking after myself more
And I've got my Mum to look after me.
If I was alone I would probably have found it extremely difficult.

Mum's taken over the baby
I bath the little one once in a while
But Mum usually does both

Cos I find it more simple
I feel like she does it better than me.

My husband, he's happy with the new one,
you can see he's got a strong bond with her already
and I'm quite happy with that.
I'm just waiting till I can hopefully pass my driving test
and then go back to work, get on with my career
I just need to prove to them at work that I can go back on management
    level.

Scene seven. About becoming a mother

You want to know what I would say about motherhood?
I think every woman should be a mother
At least once
It's a great feeling, um
And it gives you something to do as well
For all women who are just at home
And not really doing much, it's nice
To be um looking after a baby and see them grow
And that's what I'm going to do um till a certain age
Motherhood's nice, it's a good feeling
I used to say no I never want a baby
But when I did have her
Wow you know it's lovely
Seeing her call me Mummy today.

It was nice to have someone visit, someone to talk to
I don't get to talk to my Mum about being a mother.
It did make me think about it a lot more
Because you don't actually think about being a mother,
You just do your role play, your role
And that's it.

Is it possible to extract some preliminary insights about identity change
from this plethora of impressions? The following stands out as I (re) read
this portrayal.

Juhana's initial presentation of the new baby is through her mother's
delight ('Mum's over the moon'), the importance of the baby in both
families, then the shared wish of the parental couple to name the baby
after her (an explicit continuation to the next generation, 'like a little
you', made all the more satisfying to Juhana because of the continuity

of the position as well: eldest sister, implying there will be more, which soon occurs). Her pre-eminent position in her family of origin and all the support she can rely on is apparent throughout, from her early confession that she dislikes the 'ways' of her husband's family, to the long-running negotiation of reasons to remain with her own family, despite a common cultural practice in which she is expected to live with her husband's family. She and her family proceed to reinvent this rule in the context of the two families' unique situations (overcrowding in hers and a 'disaster zone' of infectious disease and potential violence in his), the setting of contemporary London and its housing policies, and of the power that Juhana can exert in her family to get her own way. She reflects on feeling ambivalent about the desired, successful outcome: 'it wasn't right to be here [at her parents' home] so soon/ when they [her in-laws] were missing her growing up'. Her ambivalence is underpinned, but not determined, by a cultural practice translocated from Bangladesh. The difference between the two families appeared, at least partly, to be not just one of 'different sides' of Bangladesh but also potential conflict arising from how traditional they are, for example, her mother's and mother-in-law's different opinions about staying at home for 40 days after the birth.

In her family of origin she nonetheless feels uncomfortable with changes in the way she is positioned. Her daughter threatens to take her place as the indulged focus of love and attention as, for example, when her father forgot to say goodbye to Juhana at the airport ('when you had a grandchild, that's how it was') and the generational shift affects how her parents treat their eldest daughter, expecting her to be more grown up. She repeats that she doesn't like this, and forlornly claims 'I'm still the age that I was/ I'm still young'[3] (she is 24). She continues, in her own free association, to the nub – the rub: before she could do whatever she wanted, whereas she now has to consider her baby daughter first. At this point she repeats 'I really don't like it' and segues back to the theme of how her parents treat her, as if it is their fault she has to think of the baby. Perhaps a new baby recalls the times when her four younger sisters were babies, when they were not her responsibility. In the wider data, we see that Juhana's daughter gets assimilated into the line of 'daughters' (her youngest sister was only eight when Juhana became a mother). The continuity of generational cycles is indexed also by the baby's nickname 'mom'.

On the other hand, there is evidence of Juhana wanting to be recognised as her baby's 'proper Mum', distinguished from the plenitude of females (six if the great grandmother is included) who are available to care for the baby. Despite (or perhaps because of) this shared family care, it matters that the baby knows who her real mother is. This theme too extends across the sample: a baby's singling out of their mother supports the mother's developing feelings of being the mother. It is her own mother who can reassure Juhana that 'she knows I'm her proper Mum now'.[4]

In these details, ordinary conflict (ordinary in the sense of being mundane and a feature of typical lives) seems inherent in the transition that Juhana is making, as a married woman (a conflict in where she lives) and, at home, in the move from favoured daughter to mother as well. Even the welcome support of her sisters and mother involves the negative facet (she has to be reassured) that perhaps her baby does not know the difference between these different female carers. Elevated to a general principle, we could propose that life experiences involve simultaneous pleasure and frustration or anxiety, and that the balance of these varies depending on the quality of events. A psychoanalytic ontology is based on the idea of dynamic internal conflict as an inevitable feature of experience and subjectivity and especially so for the demands of coming to terms with a maternal identity: 'Psychoanalytic thinking is particularly relevant to understanding emotional investment in a present social reality, and the difficulties in dealing with change' (Urwin, 2007, p.242).

There are also minor details providing evidence for Juhana's emotional investment in her prior identity as an autonomous young woman and its conflict with the demands of motherhood: she can't wear her hoop earrings, and doesn't get around to wearing her favourite clothes; she 'never' goes out (but does prioritise going to get her eyebrows plucked) and no longer spends hours talking to friends on the phone. She can't wallow in a bath and spends 'all my days feeding her and changing nappies', which is 'really boring every day to day'. These build up to a considerable practical conflict between time to herself ('I don't get time to myself any more'; now she realises the luxury of 'time in my hand') and the non-negotiable demands of early motherhood ('Madam wants her milk', 'oh no she's crying', 'I'm the one getting up in the night to feed, up and down all night'). A binary between mothers' needs and babies' needs has dominated feminist discourse (see Chapter 8).

Being a mother is still a huge strain, despite the support she has once she returns to her family of origin (the sisters know how to look after the baby; Juhana's mother always baths her and then the next baby too; when the children are 'doing our heads in' on a Saturday out, they park them with her parents who are 'more than happy').

It would be impossible to do without her family ('I can't do this on my own ... I know I need Mum nearby', 'I've got my Mum to look after me'). Juhana comes across as still harking back to when she was a carefree teenager.

However, Juhana comes to feel bad about the effect on her parents' life. Her mother's postponed career has been dropped ('I'm coming in her way') and her father should be in the marital bed, with his things around him, especially because of his health problems ('I started to feel like I was breaking up the couple/ with Dad always sleeping on the sofa'). These conflicts are contingent on the family's material circumstances, the severe overcrowding ('it's just that here we take up too much space') in the context of Juhana's stubborn reluctance to return to live in her husband's family home ('I've totally said no'), and the long waiting list to be housed by the council (her requirements reflected her needs but were unlikely to result in an allocation).

Soon after her first daughter's birth, Juhana felt 'too glued to her' to imagine returning to work at the end of her maternity leave. However, when she became pregnant again, the prospect of not being able to return to work precipitated a depression ('just looking forward to getting my life back'). We can almost hear the encouraging voices of her family as she reels at the news and her ambivalence as she tries to see the second child as a blessing. Her older daughter reverted to breast feeding only (when things had just improved through weaning and Juhana could get some uninterrupted sleep) and so the new baby had to be bottle fed from the start, a job that could therefore be taken over by others, notably Juhana's mother ('Mum's taken over the [new] baby'). The conflict between maternal, domestic life and following a career intensified ('I'm just waiting till I can hopefully pass my driving test and then go back to work, get on with my career/I just need to prove to them at work that I can go back on management level').

In the final scene, between the lines of a conventional but notably faint endorsement of motherhood (recommended for those, unlike herself, who do not have work outside the home), her conflicted feelings about becoming a mother remain apparent. The research period covered the passage back into employment of many of the participants and provided information on the conflicts involved at the level of childcare, money and time, but also their identity investments as autonomous working women and, often conflictedly, as mothers of babies. Juhana's satisfaction with pregnancy is related in terms of 'not being able to see the bump' from behind and the 'perfect feeling' of her being 'there inside', features of pregnancy that did not impinge on her working life.

She acknowledges her reluctance to envisage the impending change ('I didn't take it all on board') and the difficulty of her unreadiness emerges from the sequence 'I hadn't actually looked into it. /You have to be ready to be a Mum.'

The final verse acts as a reminder that the researchers (observer and interviewer) are present and suggests that the research has provided a unique reflective space for Juhana. In an interchange immediately preceding this verse, Ann, Juhana's interviewer, asks 'did being part of the research change the way you felt about being a mother at all?', to which Juhana replies 'no but it did make me think about it a lot more, 'cos I get to speak about it so I get to actually think about it. Let's say you're gone now, I'll think about everything I've said and it just makes me think about being a mother a bit more than I would.' It was quite common within the sample that the research visits afforded a space to reflect, especially among the six observed mothers, who had almost weekly visits.

In contemporary Western cultures, becoming a mother – psychologically speaking – is rarely easy. In this prose poem, I wanted to do justice to the upheavals that Juhana went through in the seismic identity change involved in becoming a mother for the first time and to the importance of her family in helping her cope. I wanted to convey the complex mixture of pleasure, frustration, boredom, loss, worry, exhaustion, satisfaction and pride that she felt and the continuity of generations. I wanted also to convey the clamour of conditions – spatial, relational, cultural, material, biological, ideological, discursive, group and institutional – within which the experience of becoming a mother achieves its meanings. These, in the present, past and future tense, are the conditions of possibility of becoming a mother – becoming in the sense of an identity transition.

Becoming mothers in Tower Hamlets: Project design in brief

The project on which this book is based was part of a programme funded by the British Economic and Social Research Council entitled 'Identities and Social Action'.[5] It was led by me, as Principal Investigator, and Ann Phoenix; we recruited Heather Elliott as primary researcher. Following a pilot interview, 20 women (one later dropped out) were recruited via general practitioners (GPs) and antenatal classes in the London borough of Tower Hamlets. We aimed to reflect the diversity and changing class patterns of the borough (while limiting our sample to English-speaking participants).

The population of Tower Hamlets is ethnically mixed. At the time of the fieldwork 51% was White, from a variety of ethnic groups, with Bangladeshi-heritage people constituting the largest ethnic group (at 33% on the 2001 Census, in comparison with 0.5% overall in England and Wales). Most are Muslim by religious background (with 36% of the Tower Hamlets population enumerated as Muslim, ONS, 2001). A growing number of young professionals, largely White, live in the newly developed areas close to the City, the financial district of London (Dench and Gavron, 2006). Information at the time of the fieldwork described Tower Hamlets as an area

> unique in terms of its physical and socio-economic geography. It is ranked in the top 5 most deprived local authorities in England in terms of its residents. It includes the office district of Canary Wharf and therefore receives large numbers of relatively affluent incomers daily. At a neighbourhood scale it is a complex mosaic of small pockets of recently developed affluence in close proximity to areas of high deprivation. Pressure on land for development is high so the urban landscape is dynamic.
>
> (Instant Atlas, 2007)

Our sample consisted of nine Bangladeshi heritage women, seven White (of whom four were English, two were originally from continental Europe and one from South Africa), two African-Caribbean heritage and one West African. Three interviews were conducted with each participant: the first during the third trimester of pregnancy (or in several cases as soon after the birth as possible), one four to six months after the birth and the last 12 months or more after the birth. These were recorded (except in one case where permission was not granted and detailed notes were made). On occasion, a recording failed and we depended later on notes. Recordings were transcribed in ordinary speech fashion. Participants were offered a copy. Six of the interviewees were also recruited to the observation sample: two Bangladeshi, two White (English and South African), one African-Caribbean and one West African, and visited up to once per week for one year after the babies' births by trained infant observers.

Our approach was psycho-social, an attempt to go beyond the dualism of psychology and sociology that has afflicted research into identity, using and adapting psychoanalytic ways of thinking to tap not only those aspects of identity accessible through discourses but also those residing in unthought modes – unconscious, preconscious and embodied. We used two psychoanalytically informed methods: an evolving form of the free association narrative interview (Hollway and Jefferson, 2013), which can elicit from participants free associations alongside more consciously crafted accounts, and a form of observation based closely on infant observation (Urwin, 2007). This observation method was designed to access the more unconscious, taken-for-granted, intersubjective, affective, embodied and practical aspects of the new mothers' experience.

Our psychoanalytically informed epistemology also provided a model for noticing and thinking about the impact of the participants' changing identities on the researchers and of researchers on participants. This led us to produce a reflective form of field notes (Thomson, 2009a) that use the researcher's subjectivity as an instrument of knowing. Field notes provided a vehicle for interviewers to reflect on the co-construction of interview accounts and, as the fieldwork progressed, on our own subjective responses, what this meant about the participant and our own insights and blind spots (Elliott, 2011; Elliott, Ryan and Hollway, 2012). They enabled us to learn more about that intersubjective relationship, the identity differences that are suggested and how these have necessarily affected the talk and behaviour produced as data.

Cathy Urwin, from the Tavistock Centre, led the observations, recruiting trained observers and leading the once-weekly seminar, attended also by the interviewers (Heather Elliott, Ann Phoenix and me) (Urwin, 2007). We adapted Esther Bick's (1964) 'infant observation' method from a training method to a research method and from observing babies (in the mother–baby couple) to observing mothers (usually in that couple). The relation of mother and baby was therefore a primary object of study (as opposed to the idea of the mother as a separate individual). However, since observers followed the baby (if the mother was elsewhere or with others), we accessed many other family members too. The research design remained faithful to the original infant observation method in most respects: a weekly visit at a set time, a friendly but non-participatory presence, not using mechanical recording devices but writing up detailed notes after each session. As in the traditional method, these notes formed the basis of the observation seminar, whose purpose is to help the observer and the group as a whole to process their experiences. Different responses among the seminar group help enlarge thinking. The infant observation method is central to this book's exploration of a methodology that is sensitive to uncognised knowing and affective communication, using them in a rigorous way to aid reflection.

The methods we adopted and adapted to gather data, to make sense of it as researchers and to write about what we found were in one sense in place in the funding proposal preceding the research, but in another sense they emerged during the process of the research. The book's narrative aims to present the process, emphasising the experience of wondering and uncertainty, as well as finding out, making links between ideas and finding coherence in the daunting, messy particularity of information we collected about 19 women's becoming mothers for the first time and the research team's relationships to these data.

Identity and identity change

Since it became a core area of social science research in the 1950s, the study of identity has been approached through many disciplines (psychology, sociology, anthropology, geography and history, and the already interdisciplinary areas of cultural, feminist, disability, ethnic and organisational studies). Its study remains, in the words of Margaret Wetherell, the director of the Identities and Social Action programme, 'slippery, blurred and confusing (...)[6] notoriously difficult to define' (Wetherell, 2010, p.3) and many have dismissed it as being an unworkable concept for empirical research, with 'no analytic value or purchase' (ibid.). The study of women's transition into being mothers is probably the most elusive topic possible to research and highlights the dynamic features of identity that are more often emphasised in current debate. Recent theory, often framed in terms of 'subjectivity', rather than 'identity', emphasises fluidity, process and ongoing dynamic change (Blackman et al., 2008; Wetherell, 2010). This applies especially to maternal subjectivity because 'one is always chasing the tail of [it] (...). It involves relations with a particular and peculiar other whose rate of change is devastatingly rapid, who is always, by definition, "developing", shifting changing...' (Baraitser, 2009, p.22). Stuart Hall described identity as 'the unstable point where the "unspeakable stories of subjectivity" meet the narrative of history and of a culture' (1988, p.44). This nicely illustrates two of my purposes in relation to identity (subjectivity) theory. The first is my psycho-social intentions (history and culture are always there in the way that participants are situated and narrate; therefore within which they feel, act and make meaning). The second is that I aim to make visible the 'unspeakable stories of subjectivity' via the project's methodology.

Our initial project title, 'Identities in process: Becoming African-Caribbean, Bangladeshi and White mothers', reflected our emphasis on dynamic process and our wish to avoid a normative approach based on White middle-class mothering. It also reflected a sampling approach which often gives rise to a comparative research design where groups of mothers, predefined by ethnicity and class, are compared on various dimensions; an approach we modified considerably. We soon dropped this title, recognising among other considerations, that we did not want such a heading on every piece of information that went out to potential participants and health professionals in Tower Hamlets, positioning mothers so saliently according to their ethnicities.

My approach to identities research is guided by the wish to focus on subjectivity as the total, substantive, acting, thinking and feeling, embodied, relational being,[7] or more pointedly, in Simondon's phrase, 'the becoming of being' (cited in Venn, 2014, p.43). Research and theory in qualitative social science was dominated for decades by the prioritisation of language and discourse and the rather deterministic tendency to see identity as the sum total of positions in discourse. Lisa Baraitser explained as follows her wish, in talking of 'maternal subjectivity', to go beyond what has been conceptualised through the lens of maternal identities:

> When I talk of 'maternal subjectivity' however, I am attempting to point towards an experience that resides 'otherwise' than or is excessive to maternal identities, thought of as emerging at the intersections particularly between gender, class and 'race'. Paradoxically arising, I argue, out of the mundane and relentless practices of daily maternal care, maternal subjectivity presents us with particular philosophical and ontological conundrums, not only in terms of the pregnant and lactating body that is both singular and multiple, disturbing notions of unity and the bounded self, but also because maternity is an experience that I maintain is impossible to anticipate in advance.
>
> (Baraitser, 2009, p.22)

I wish to embrace these connotations in my inquiry, whether termed subjectivity or identity. To write of a phenomenology of motherhood, Baraitser chose to use vignettes from her own mothering, creatively using a version of anecdotal theory (Gallop, 2002), and acknowledged that as a result 'I am speaking from the most narrow and particular location one could conceive' (2009, p.23). We aimed rather to select a group of first-time birth mothers – within the constraints of a sample size consistent with our in-depth methods – for diversity and variegation, based on the dimensions of ethnicity and class.

To study maternal becoming is a way of studying a dynamic change of identity that is – after babyhood – the most inaccessible to language. It is first experienced through pregnancy (all our sample were birth mothers) when there is no clear distinction between the 'me' and 'you' of what will become mother and baby. Then, after birth, mothering involves responding appropriately to the needs of a pre-semantic baby whose now external and becoming-separate life depends primarily on her. This is why, at the heart of the question about identity change, I came to focus on how new mothers find a way of *knowing* their babies that involves engaging (actually re-engaging, because we all started out there) with non-symbolic, non-cognitive, non-conscious elements in themselves and in between them and their babies.

Knowing mothers

The word play in this book's title brings together researchers' knowing and mothers' knowing. Psychoanalytic epistemology and methodology, often clinically based, is illustrated mainly through the work of Wilfred Bion and Bracha Ettinger (with others, especially Donald Winnicott and Alfred Lorenzer, in support roles). They provide a way of conceptualising knowing which originates with mothers. Concepts that illuminate uncognised knowing that I find useful are Bollas' 'unthought known' (my favourite for clarity and pithiness, Bollas 1987), compassion (Ettinger), reverie, containment and communicative projective identification (Bion), transitional space (Winnicott) and scenic understanding (Lorenzer). These approach the ineffable quality of new mothers' experience, a puzzle which, in a way, motivates this book. Ettinger's matrixial theory focuses on the pre-maternal/prenatal space in which the rhythms and resonances that characterise matrixial 'joint eventing' lay the foundations for the earliest form of communication, a transsubjectivity based in com-passion (literally 'feeling with', 'an originary joint event', Ettinger, 2010, p.6). Bion locates the origins of knowledge in the earliest postnatal form of communication between infant and mother, a communicative normal form of projective identification in which the infant, as yet without the mental apparatus to think thoughts, lodges indigestible emotional experience in the mother (if she is available to receive it) who contains the disturbing material. She processes it through her 'reverie' (unselfconscious uncognised knowing) and returns it through her actions in a bearable form. This capacity, internalised, becomes the basis for 'learning from experience', which Bion (1962a, 1967) distinguished from the kind of knowing[8] that increases one's stock of knowledge but does not change the knower. Lorenzer's scenic understanding is holistic and initially affect-based, embodied. For Bion, Ettinger and Lorenzer, these pre-symbolic, non-lexical, embodied forms of communication do not disappear in adult communication, although they do get overlaid to some extent. Key concepts – trans-subjectivity, com-passion, containment, learning from (and thereby being changed by) experience, becoming – will inform my treatment of mothers' and researchers' knowing. It requires researchers finding ways to modify our dependence on cognitive, conscious, language-based styles of knowing and tune into our bodies, to decipher our affective responses. In both cases – mothers and researchers – we are straining against a long history of formation as rational autonomous adult subjects, in which, more recently, women have been included. For these psychoanalytic traditions, intuitive kinds of knowing change the knower, which implicates identity change, a trans- or intersubjective process that is the motor of becoming.

Influences and resources

In addition to the two tranches of funding by the Economic and Social Research Council (ESRC),[9] for which I am profoundly grateful, there are four aspects of my life, which in combination made this research possible. Chronologically, first occurred my training in methodology as a psychology student, a paradoxical influence because it was through my profound dissatisfaction with the scientific paradigm that gripped psychology at the time (late 1960s) that my intense interest in alternative ways of doing psychology was formed. Next (mid 1980s) came my transformative experience of becoming a mother. Continuing as my daughter grew up, it fed into my understanding of the questions I wanted to ask of identities research, and thus, from 2000 on, into the discussions with Open University colleagues (in the Discourse and Psycho-Social Group and Centre for Citizenship, Identities and Governance), which culminated in a research proposal to the ESRC 'Identities and Social Action' programme. Finally, my formulation of an alternative way of knowing could not have happened without psychoanalysis, which enticed my interest over many decades. It has contributed to the way I theorise subjectivity and gradually came together with empirical research to inform this alternative epistemology and methodology.

There are several reasons why it is difficult yet important to reflect upon the way that knowledges of mothering are produced and on the way that we produced it in the research project that forms the basis for this book. Broadly speaking these are as follows. First, knowledges about mothering are all around us; indeed in the social sciences they are commonly viewed as ideologically freighted sets of knowledge (Urwin, 1985; Rose, 1990), both because of the importance of mothering in social reproduction and psychological wellbeing and because of the gendered power relations involved in their construction. Second, everyone has an intimate experience of being mothered – whether good, bad or a mixture, whether in its absence or presence – and this relationship is only partially accessible to conscious thought. The earliest experiences of a relationship with mother and mothering reside in the 'unthought known', embodied, never erased by access to language and self-consciousness. Third, the difficulties are reflected in the differences and disagreements that abound in formalised approaches to mothering, in the various social and human sciences and in the humanities. Fourth, the methods available to social scientists are likewise compromised (notably by their reliance on what is available to participants through language) and liable, in my view, to produce and reproduce depleted images of motherhood. All these reasons underline the importance of what methods we use: how researchers' subjectivities can be used with awareness as instruments of knowing about mothering, how we strive for what has been called objectivity, and our sampling frame, in empirical research, which guides who we find as exemplars of becoming mothers. Together these considerations mean that our research practices are steeped in ethical challenges, as we shall see.

Representations of mothering emerge through and into a world characterised by strong (often deeply buried and taken for granted) investments in certain images of mothers, by professional dogmas and ingrained habits, institutional and personal defences and ideological differences across fault lines of class, ethnicities and religious belief. How do we represent the conflicts of motherhood, the strivings for something else? Amongst this clamour how do we represent the delights and the joy without romanticising or idealising these? How do we embrace the multiple forms of good-enough mothering that abound in the London borough of Tower Hamlets? How do I, in this writing, recognise and respect the travails of each woman whose experience I represent here, keep faith with the particulars of their lives, and at the same time protect the privacy that is their due and forms the basis of their consent to be a part of the study? In what ways have I encountered them and are these adequate?

To return to Juhana as an example: I met her face to face, briefly, at a get together for the participants with the research team after the end of the study and feel as if I have come to know her only indirectly through our data. Heather Elliott recruited Juhana and the other women into the study. Ann Phoenix conducted her three interviews with Juhana over the course of 16 months. Sarina Woograsingh, one of the six observers, visited almost every week for a year (Woograsingh, 2007). Cathy Urwin[10] led the weekly observation seminar group (of which I was a member, as were the other interviewers), which studied each of the observers' detailed notes. Through sharing our impressions we began to process the effects on us of the observed mothers and how they were changing over the course of the year. The research team met in various groupings to think about the data. I have poured over Juhana's words, yes, but also opened myself to her voice, as it was recorded in interviews (Hollway, 2013c). I know something of her body's expressions and have a sense of how she affected those whom she met, through the observation notes and reflective interview field notes. My knowledge of Juhana (and of the others, including those whom I interviewed) is mediated, therefore, not only through the methods used and my taken for granted knowledge and fantasies about who she was, but also theirs and their relationships with her as these evolved over the year. Such mediations are true of any research method, however 'scientific'. Throughout this book, I want to ensure that, since these are inevitable, their uses are rendered visible rather than covered up and reflected upon in the service of good data analysis.

The shape of the book

I try to maintain bifocality in this book, and in two respects. I have explained the dual focus on mothers and researchers and have articulated this as mothers' and researchers' *knowing*, across which – according to contemporary British psychoanalysis – there is considerable similarity, for example in the concepts of reverie and containment. However, the empirical project on which this book is based is about *becoming* – becoming mothers. So my bifocality also embraces the *relation of knowing to becoming*, where both mothers and researchers are concerned.

   Part I introduces the book's purposes and themes: in **Chapter 1** I have outlined both the theoretical and methodological foundations of the book; in **Chapter 2**, I ground these in the specific research project – empirical, qualitative, psycho-social. My aim in **Chapter 3** is to illustrate the changes in my theoretical repertoire which enabled a psycho-social data analysis.

I started this chapter by launching readers into a direct experience: a case study in rough verse, a format designed to preserve the affect and the participant's idiom, through the content and form of her language including rhythm, cadence, intonation and associations. (Consider for example, Juhana's wish to 'stop stopping and starting', a phrase whose jerky lack of flow and reverse ordering conveys powerfully her relation to the interruption in her working life occasioned by bearing children.) By asking readers to reflect on their experience of reading, to 'pause for thought' (reflection takes time), I hope to make greater space for emotional experience in the process of meaning making.

Only then did I outline the project. If emotional experience is the weft of meaning, the milieu in which it has been generated constitutes the warp. There are many facets to this social and material milieu; in respect of research, I covered the intellectual and funding context of identities research, the two psychoanalytical approaches to knowing on which I primarily draw, and the biographical resources I bring to the topic of maternal becoming. In **Chapter 2,** I start by providing detail of the research project itself, always in the context of the principles guiding the design of a psycho-social project. The main focus then sets out, under the label of 'psychoanalytically informed methods', the core epistemological principles guiding the methodology on which the project was based. I describe the practices and principles involved in the parallel use of free association narrative *interviewing* (FANI) and infant *observation* (IO) and discuss two themes which address practically some abiding questions about the trustworthiness of research knowing: using the support of other minds and the value of triangulating interviewing and observation to go beyond the limitations of singular perspectives and methods. In **Chapter 3** I use a single case study, Jenny's, to illustrate and explain the shifts in my usage of concepts and approaches that dominated critical qualitative research – construction, positioning, social identity categories, power relations – towards a psychoanalytically informed psycho-social approach (still informed by the above) which takes into account agency, the flow of becoming and the strain of facing reality. The chapter pays attention to key binaries in dominant academic knowledge – knower and known, internal and external, objectivity and subjectivity – and situates my intellectual project in this wider context.

Part II consists of three chapters, illustrating three diverse psychoanalytically informed approaches to the unthought known (inspired, respectively, by Ettinger, Bion and Lorenzer). I build conceptual resources for a research epistemology and methodology, and, by extension, an ontology centred on becoming. In each chapter, I use examples to demonstrate my data analytic approach, illustrating how I factored in the interview relationship, the observer's use of their own emotional responses, the containment of anxiety and ethics based on feeling with the other. Each approach shows how psychoanalytic methodology can be used outside the clinic. **Chapter 4**, uses the matrixial theory of Bracha Ettinger, which takes prenatal experience as the model and origin of uncognised knowing, thus casting a radical further light on maternal knowing and maternal co-becoming. Using data examples, I describe how matrixial concepts provided new insights into the prenatal data and into both maternal and research ethics. My core topics of identity change and knowing inevitably require interpretation (neither topic presents as such in raw data), and enable me to explore the value of psychoanalytically informed interpretation, which has been contentious in psycho-social studies. This is where I begin in **Chapter 5**, taking the example of how I infer anxiety in a specific case. In the course of the case analysis, I develop the concept of anxiety through concepts that link mother–infant relating and research knowing: projective identification, containment, reverie and learning from experience. Bion's theory of thinking transcends several entrenched binaries in Western thought: mind/body, cognition/emotion and individual self/trans-subjective connectedness. **Chapter 6** introduces the German psycho-social tradition, using Alfred Lorenzer's concept of scenic understanding to inform data analysis and case writing, using extracts from Jenny's observation. The data analysis, using my scenic composition based on observation notes, follows Lorenzer's injunction to use the 'provocations' in the text and demonstrates how through scenic understanding it is possible to access the embodied societal-cultural and bring it to symbolisation.

   Part III uses single cases to open up socio-political themes, especially the status of the maternal and gender difference in discourses, including feminist discourses, and also the status of discursive positioning in identities research. Matrixial theory's alternative to the phallic model of gender difference creates space for thinking beyond the current model of gender equality. In **Chapter 7**, I draw further on matrixial concepts, in particular 'fragilization', to explore in detail the case of Arianna, who experienced extreme conflict about becoming a mother, diagnosed medically as postnatal depression. Intrapsychic conflict is well conceptualised by many strands of psychoanalysis. Here, through a psycho-social analysis, I make precise links between Arianna's internalised conflict and the larger socio-political culture in which her identity as a self-governing autonomous career woman has been formed. In my exploration of the matrixial feminine, I draw out implications for contemporary feminist discourses on mothering. In **Chapter 8**, the themes of conflict and binaries are extended in the case example of Justine. I juxtapose the egregious effects of a cluster of binaries – motherhood versus career, mothers' needs versus children's needs, gender equality according to a masculine model versus maternal–feminine difference, social versus biological, separation versus clinginess – with the possibility of learning from experience and tolerating ambivalence. I analyse examples of three facets of Justine's relation to becoming a mother: the discourses, the actualities and the echoes of a previous generation, facets that are expressed together in her experience of the ordinary conflicts in becoming a mother.

The **concluding chapter** notices and resists the fantasy of bringing it all together, and of including everything left out. I focus on how the shape of the book emerged over a long period, in tandem with changes wrought in me by the research and writing. I discuss what happened to whole-sample analysis and make some overarching remarks on mothers' becoming and mothers' knowing derived from patterns in the data that show up through the sampling categories we used.

2
Empirical Psycho-Social Research: Design and Psychoanalytically Informed Principles

Introduction: The quality of psycho-social knowledge

The quality of knowledge that research can produce is fatally shaped by its methods, methodology and epistemology. Easy to state now, but what a long, reiterative journey that discovery has been for me: always the need to examine critically another implicit assumption, to unsettle the convenience of established social scientific principles, to expand sterile terrain (for example, the conventions of writing up findings). The value of using psychoanalysis to inform an epistemology as well as methodology was boldly stated by Georges Devereux back in 1967: 'one may postulate that psychoanalysis is, first and foremost, an epistemology and methodology. This is the chiefest of its permanent contributions to science.' (Devereux, 1967, p.294). I read that book in the early 1970s, but it took me the intervening decades to 'know' it as a researcher.

The identity change involved when women become mothers for the first time is probably the most inaccessible to language. If researchers can offer only language and cognitive analytic understanding in relation to such an inquiry, we would fail to go beyond what is already available, and which – this is my thesis – distorts and oversimplifies, leaving pregnant women and new mothers ill-equipped to makes sense of what is happening to them. Yet I must rely on language throughout: a contradiction I hope to turn into a productive paradox by my attention to the place of affect or emotion in uncognised knowing. Nonetheless, I did not expect to have to rethink the theory on which knowledge is based (epistemology), nor travel so far outside established research practice in qualitative psychology and sociology to satisfy myself that I can inquire into new mothers' identity changes without just reproducing the dominant thought known (in participants and researchers). This was only possible because others were on a similar path, perhaps because mothering research is so horizon shifting.[1] In this chapter I systematically show how I apply this questioning, within a psycho-social framework, through the various stages of an empirical project: design and sampling, field work and data analysis. Writing from data and ethics are central themes of later chapters.

Criticism of psychoanalytically informed psycho-social research is often based on the worry that 'the social' will be neglected. In a discussion of this tension in psycho-social research, based on a commentary by Sasha Roseneil, Tony Jefferson and I endorsed Roseneil's statement that

> the sphere of personal life – intimacy, sexuality, love, friendship, parenthood [here, becoming a mother] – is *both* socially patterned and constructed, varying cross-culturally and historically, *and* that it has a life of its own, that it is experienced as beyond the control of reason, as inherently individual, internal and as particular to specific relationships.
>
> (Roseneil, conference presentation, cited in Hollway and Jefferson, 2013, p.x–xi)

Our sampling principles – the single geographical location, the multicultural sample, the diversity of family, partner, housing and employment circumstances – afford due attention to the settings within which new mothers experience and live their 'becoming'. However, a psycho-social perspective depends on analysing participants' *relation to* aspects of their setting (a relation infused with biography and changed through the workings of imagination), and reflecting on our – the researchers' – *relation to* our encounter with them.

Roseneil comments that 'in attending to the social construction of intimacy, sociologists have neglected their equally important shaping and constitution from inner life and have failed to address the psychodynamics of biography' (2006, p.847). This accounts for my emphasis on dynamic inner and intersubjective life. Failing to find sufficiently complex and convincing accounts of these in psychology, I turned to psychoanalytic thinking. When researchers focus on participants' relation to objects in their worlds, the researchers' relation to that participant in their world is the means through which meaning is made of their experience: again therefore, epistemology and methodology appear at the centre of a psycho-social approach. During this project I discovered how psychoanalysis, as well as affording theoretical insight into being and becoming (an ontology), could afford the required alternative epistemology, an embodied, affect-based way of knowing which could inform my research practice and was consistent with new mothers' ways of knowing.

Psychoanalytically informed methods in psycho-social research result from a dialogue with clinical psychoanalysis, not an application of it (Hollway and Jefferson, 2013, p.149ff). Two key consequences are both based on the principle of the combined use of emotional impact and reflection. Psychoanalytically informed methodology expands the way that 'reflexivity' is understood in qualitative research, in the unconscious intersubjective dynamics in field (and later data analytic) encounters, and demonstrates the value of other minds to aid reflection. Without reflection, supported and recursive where necessary, responding to emotional impact can result in the indulgent exercise of one's preferred view of the world and imposition of one's own belief system in the service of a wished-for certainty that does not reflect the complexities of what is observed. The use of the researcher's subjectivity as an instrument of knowing (Hunt, 1989; Hollway, 2008) requires reflection if it is to go beyond subjectivity in the old sense of emotion-led bias, where it contains all the derogatory implications of being constructed in a binary with an idealised and split off notion of objectivity (Hollway, 2013b). Reflection in the psychoanalytic sense is not just another word for cognitive activity; it requires keeping an open mind and that, as Bion's theory of thinking explains (see Chapter 5), is a supremely emotional process.

Social scientists are wont to dismiss the possibility of this open-minded kind of objectivity. They usually base their rejection on the constructionist principle that a partial perspective results inevitably from the socially situated construction of the researcher. This principle is well founded and it is now recognised that data are never free from the observer's worldview, which reflect, among other things, differences in cultural and class position. In qualitative research, the term 'reflexivity' has opened the way for the necessary developments of a research stance that is open to examination (Henwood, 2008; Thomson, 2009) because 'without examining ourselves, we run the risk of letting our unelucidated prejudices dominate our research' (Finlay, 2003, p.108). Psychoanalysis offers some tools to help researchers continue to examine the ways we make meaning throughout the research process.

Design of a non-ethnographic study begins with the basics of sampling – numbers of participants and what they need to represent – and so I begin this chapter with discussion of the criteria we used, followed by our purpose in using the two psychoanalytically informed methods together. A description of these, interview and observation, picks out what distinguishes them from typical qualitative social research. I then examine extracts from both methods produced within the same week, to see if and how the interview and observation methods afford different images of the same mother, Zelda.

Sampling and numbers: Nineteen soon-to-be mothers in Tower Hamlets

Our goal for total participant numbers was reduced from 30 to 20 (which became 19 when one mother dropped out after six weeks), partly because it would otherwise have taken too long to recruit and finish fieldwork. Also it became clear we had ample data and sufficient variety for the kinds of analysis we planned. There remains a strong tendency in qualitative research to assume we need greater numbers than is actually necessary: the initial decision to recruit 30 participants might have been a hangover from sample sizes needed in statistical data analysis, which paradigm affects what researchers bidding for funding worry that assessors will require. Deciding about sample design and participant numbers is just one example of the need to rethink every aspect of research design, both to continue reframing the methodological basis of qualitative psycho-social research and to tune the design to the particular question and theoretical approach. If theoretical extrapolation can work from one case, qualified psycho-socially, then new understanding can be achieved by building on links found between and amongst cases and groups of cases, and similarities and differences reflected upon conceptually. The limitations and strengths of a sample are then to be addressed in terms of the optimum variety (diversity) that can be built into a sample, within its defined goals. In practice, this meant identifying a field location incorporating class and ethnic diversities and lifestyle variegation – Tower Hamlets. It also involved selecting for diversity on other psycho-social dimensions, such as mothers' family and housing arrangements and employment status, which were highly relevant to their experience of the transition into motherhood.

In summary, the sampling frame derived from several considerations:

> *Sampling for diversity.* To avoid reproducing normative knowledge about white middle class mothers, as if they represented some universal condition, in recruitment we prioritised two dimensions of social difference, class (classified impressionistically in terms of level of education and job type) and ethnicity.
>
> *Reflecting the population of Tower Hamlets.* Chosen for its diversity, we tried to recruit in proportion to the borough's main ethnic groups and reflect the mix of middle and working class. We excluded

from the study women who were not English speakers. All the Bangladeshi-origin participants, referred to for short as 'Bangladeshi', were British born and educated.

Feasibility. We recruited pregnant women through health professionals in contact at antenatal classes and GP visits and needed to communicate the above criteria of diversity to them. Heather Elliott was in close touch with them and followed up each contact if, after an initial mention from the health professional, the pregnant women expressed interest in the study. This was a time-consuming procedure and was partly responsible for reducing sample size from 30 to 20.

The participants: An introduction to our sample of becoming mothers in East London

All names are pseudonyms and, where there are two, they reflect the different pseudonyms used by the interviewing and observation teams (they remain here to facilitate cross-referencing). Occasionally pseudonyms were changed again later. Listed publications refer to use of the specified case example, usually as a single case.

Six mothers both interviewed and observed

Adowa/Martina

Aged 34, West African born and raised, followed by time in the USA, she came to UK aged 30 to join Salif, originally her childhood sweetheart. They both worked shifts in the food retail industry. They appeared isolated, their only contacts being one aunt and the church community; eventually they relocated to a part of southern England with a larger support community. Adowa suffered from not being at home and cheered up notably when her mother visited. A major problem was how they would arrange childcare, without family support, when Adowa returned to work, which she was keen to do: their attempts at alternating night and day shifts produced many difficulties.

Thorp, J. (2007); Urwin, C. (2012).

Azra

British born of Bangladeshi heritage, aged 24, Azra lived in her father's house after her mother died and during the early period of her father's remarriage and the birth of two half-sisters. During a visit to Bangladesh, her father introduced her to a man who she subsequently married there. Two years later he joined her in London and very soon after their baby was born, they moved into a high rise flat. Azra had been closely involved in the childcare of one of her nephews; she visited her father's house almost daily, where her siblings and their children congregated. She planned to resume work as a retail assistant but after a short period in work when her husband was unemployed returned to family-based childcare. She missed her mother palpably (felt by both researchers) and came to depend on her father.

Azra's data provided the case study with which the group at the Centre for Advanced Study, Oslo, worked during an eight-week session in 2011. Two jointly authored publications based solely on her data resulted.

Layton, S. (2007); Urwin, C., Hauge, M-I., Hollway, W., Haavind, H. (2013); Thomson, R., A. Moe, B. Thorne and H. Nielsen (2012).

Jenny/Calise

Living with parents and three younger brothers, Jenny, of African Caribbean heritage, discovered she was pregnant at the end of her GCSE school year and was 17 when she gave birth. Her boyfriend and she both continued into college, but she postponed, due to the baby's ill-health and for fear her grades would suffer. He continued living with his mother and six siblings, visiting every day. Looking back at the end of the first year, Jenny said that the advantage of being a young mother was how much help you got. Her parents and younger brothers were involved with caring for the baby who brought new happiness into the household.

Watt, F. (2007); Hollway, W. (2011); Hollway, W. and Froggett, L. (2012); Hollway, W. (2013a).

Juhana/Amina

Juhana, living with her Bangladeshi family of parents, paternal grand-mother and four younger sisters, worked as a front of house hotel manager and had been going out with her boyfriend for two years when they got engaged. He worked in the financial sector. She moved into her in-laws' house on marriage, but gradually contrived to spend more time back with her family of origin, where she eventually stayed, despite overcrowding, on the grounds of the threat of disease and antisocial behaviour in his home. Her father-in-law acquiesced in this. Her husband continued to live with his family, given his financial and other responsibilities as the eldest son. Juhana acknowledged she could not manage without her mother and could only move out if it were close. Her first baby's feeding and sleeping patterns depleted her energy. By the end of the year, she had two daughters, felt the second pregnancy as a setback in resuming her career, and looked forward to getting back to work.

Woograsingh, S. (2007); Hollway, W. (2013c).

Charlotte/Laura

A primary school teacher, of white English heritage, Charlotte was living with her boyfriend of several years. In her early thirties, ready to start a family, she was delighted to be pregnant. Her boyfriend worked in IT and they had two marriage ceremonies after their baby's birth: one in the Far Eastern country where his parents originated and one in the North of England, where her parents had recently moved. Charlotte returned to work briefly and the couple moved out of East London to the city where Charlotte had been a student and soon after the end of the study had a second baby. She felt uncomfortable not having an independent income.

Flackowicz, M. (2007).

Zelda/Jane

A primary school teacher of white English African heritage, born and raised in South Africa, Zelda, aged 25, had come to London with her boyfriend, also a teacher and of Afrikaans heritage. They married during a return visit to South Africa to visit their families. She resumed teaching at the end of maternity leave, finding a young woman relative of her husband, on a gap year in London, to look after the baby at home. Just before the end of the year, they returned to South Africa, instigated by her husband arranging a job. Zelda was impatient to have another baby, but also arranged a teaching job to take up on arrival. Zelda had two traumatic pregnancy-related health problems. She coped with her baby's feeding and allergy problems.

Pluckrose, E. (2007); Hollway, W. (2009).

Hafna

Withdrew from the study after three months, following a visit to Bangladesh to visit her husband's family.

Interview-only participants

Arianna

Arianna, 35, lived with her long-term boyfriend; both had professional jobs. She originated in southern Europe, where her parents remained. Arianna felt very ambivalent about becoming pregnant. She loved her work and dreaded the impingement on it her baby would require. She disliked changes to her body with pregnancy and the idea of breast feeding. After the birth she felt she had lost touch with herself and life. She had considerable support from her husband and parents during this period. Returning to work felt like a crucial step in re-finding her identity.

Hollway, W. (2012a).

Becky

Becky, white British and aged 20, was living with her family of origin, including twin sister, when she became pregnant and immediately stopped working in a nightclub. This occurred soon after a 'heartbreaking' miscarriage. She had a 'horrible' birth, culminating in a caesarean, and blamed the medical staff for not listening to what she knew to be the case. She soon moved into her own council accommodation and graduated later to a two-bedroom maisonette, throughout remaining in a visiting/informal live-in relationship with her boyfriend, with whom she had been for four years before getting pregnant. Her life revolved around mothering her baby; she was consistently critical of expert advice, convinced that the Mum knows best and close to her family of origin.

Fareena

Fareena was in her mid-twenties, of Bangladeshi heritage. When she married, she gave up her job as a primary school teacher and moved from the North of England where she grew up, to her in-laws' home. Marriage, she says, has 'de-spoilt' her, from being the youngest, favourite child to looking after others. She enjoys mothering at home, as well as the support she gets from living with her in-laws, and has no plans to return to work. Faith and prayer are frequent themes and guide her practice as a mother. They are on the waiting list for council housing but want to remain in the borough to stay close to her husband's family.

Hannah

Hannah is 18, white English, living with her family of origin at first, continuing in the previous pattern of her relationship with the baby's father. They both belong to close-knit families and most of their time is spent with family visiting, staying over at her parents' house three or four times a week: her mother never wants her to leave. She started a photography course but gave up after two months because she was missing her baby, looked after by his two grandmothers. By the second interview, she was living in a three-bedroom flat, a confident mother who enjoyed her situation. When her baby was six months old, she fell pregnant again.

Justine

Justine, aged 24, of African Caribbean origin, was unemployed and living with her mother and younger sister when she got pregnant, after an unsettled year when she had lived with her boyfriend's family, quit her PA job after falling out with her boss, and had a miscarriage which upset her for months until she sought out counselling. By the time her baby was born, she was in emergency accommodation and moved into a cramped studio council flat, where her boyfriend visited. She enjoyed introducing her daughter to educational experiences and the two were inseparable. She wished she had a career to return to and found it difficult to arrange work because of her daughter's 'clinginess'. She hoped her boyfriend would move in with them but he preferred living with his mother, further outside London where he grew up.

Hollway, W. (2010a).

Leanne

Leanne, aged 20 from a white British family of Irish Catholic origin, was left pregnant by her boyfriend (who turned out to be in a relationship, with a child already, and never saw the baby). She quit her part-time job in a night club. When her baby was born, Leanne remained with her parents and younger brothers until she acquired nearby council accommodation. She was careful not to call on her parents' help too often (they were both in employment) and stoically coped with little money or help, keeping her friends mainly at arms' length. The idea of having another boyfriend felt like just someone else to look after, but she regretted not having the father there to help share the child care load. She kept intending to start a course, but did not, and wanted to move outside the borough, which she regarded as an undesirable place to raise a mixed-race baby. Leanne attends mass and baptism classes, not because she enjoys them but because it has to be done. She did not trust offers of childcare from her church contacts. She commented that, although she felt like Daniel was her son, she didn't feel like a mother.

Liyanna

Liyanna, a Bangladeshi graduate aged 30, was pleased to leave her training job in late pregnancy, partly because of her chronic health problems.

She had a turbulent relationship with her parents, who did not attend her wedding when she married outside the Bangladeshi community, even though her husband converted to Islam. They became reconciled once she had her baby. Her relationship with her sister was close and they were constantly caring for the children together, sometimes with a few women friends who constituted a support and Islamic study group together. She breastfed until her daughter was nine months old, when the baby stopped accepting the breast.

Hollway, W. and Elliott, H. (2014).

Nila

Nila, Bangladeshi, aged 22, had moved into her husband's huge family home, did not go out to work and was fully occupied supporting the large family domestically. During pregnancy, she had 'all the symptoms', but it was 'fine'. Her family of origin was hardly mentioned and Nila thought her mother would be away in Bangladesh at the time of the birth. The baby was born after a long and difficult labour, her mother arriving home just in time. Her marriage produced complications because it was a love marriage. Nila was still breastfeeding at six months and enjoyed the closeness and exclusivity. After nine months, she and her husband moved to a temporary council flat, where she found it much harder because she had no help on hand.

Elliott, H., Ryan, J. and Hollway, W. (2012). (One of three case examples.)

Rabiya

Rabiya, Bangladeshi, in her mid-twenties, was a graduate and administrator, her husband a teacher. She had moved into her husband's family home on marriage and took four years to get pregnant. The birth was long and difficult, resulting in a caesarean. She pursued her intention to breastfeed her baby exclusively, with her husband's support, despite being under pressure from the community and family who advised that she should be mixed feeding. The couple were looking to buy a house, but her husband's obligations as older son create pressures to remain, a situation which had advantages because of all the support she got. She found it difficult at first to return to work. Although she left the baby in the care of her mother-in-law (she enumerated five childcare options), she felt obliged to make up for her domestic duties by working extra hours, leaving no time for herself. The baby also became more difficult when she went back to work.

Sarah

Sarah, 29, was born in southern Europe but lived most of her life in the UK with her parents. She and her boyfriend lived together in a privately owned flat, both working long hours. She prepared very fully for the birth, using many sources of expert advice. Sarah found it difficult to avoid work completely after her baby was born and also made space for the small enterprise she had making craft goods from home. She had a successful birth but felt she had failed at breast feeding and had got her life back only when she switched to bottle feeding and found childcare to permit her to return to work. She remained in control of all the arrangements for her baby, such as when her partner could take the baby to visit his parents at weekends and how often the grandparents were invited round.

Elliott, H. (2011); Elliott, H., Ryan, J. and Hollway, W. (2012). (One of three case examples).

Sharmila

Sharmila, aged 27, a Bangladeshi teacher, had agreed to an arranged marriage which had quickly failed, such that the couple were splitting up immediately after their baby was born. She worried about the effects on her son. A traumatic birth left her convinced that she would never have another baby. She felt her life had ended. She was unhappy with how her body had changed and felt she looked older. She had no further contact with her husband and by the end of the year was planning to marry again, Sharmila had serious health problems during pregnancy and quickly started retraining for a different career. Although she owned her own flat, she spent a great deal of time back in her parents' home and they provided total childcare and support. She changed from planning to buy a large house so that they could live with her to craving a bit of peace. She planned a wide range of activities for her son and talked about enjoying how she can 'do everything', living in London.

Silma

Silma, Bangladeshi, aged 25, lived with her husband's family (where her sister-in-law also lives). She wanted to become a mother at age 25 and went to the doctor to get information about how to conceive, which she relayed to her partner (as she always referred to him). She stopped her job in a department store when she started having debilitating nausea during pregnancy and had no plans to return to work, not least to ensure being at the centre of her son's care with so many people around to look after him. She attributed the straightforward birth to her mother's active presence and she continued to see a lot of her mother and younger sister, who lived close by. She comments how much more she is 'around family' now she is a mother and how it has even affected her choice of clothes.

Elliott, H., Gunaratnam, Y., Hollway, W. and Phoenix, A. (2009).

Sylvia

Sylvia is a white English woman who worked in the private sector and had been told that due to chronic health problems she would not be able to get pregnant. At 29, when she became pregnant, she and her partner were thrilled. Because she did not expect it, it was nine weeks when she found out. Despite wanting a natural birth, Sylvia had a caesarean after two failed inductions. She wanted to breastfeed and felt a failure when she could not do so. The pregancy and birth of her daughter set in train a re-evaluation of her career investment and her relation to her family, which had been difficult, following traumatic events in her teenage years. Having a family of her own was a key part of the identity change that she so welcomed.

Elliott, H., Ryan, J. and Hollway, W. (2012). (One of three case examples.)

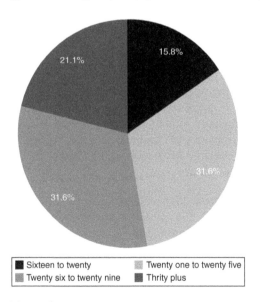

Sixteen to twenty | Twenty one to twenty five
Twenty six to twenty nine | Thrity plus

Chart 2.1 Participants by age group

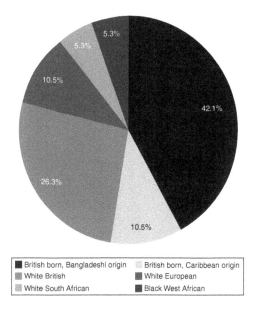

Chart 2.2   Participants by ethnicity and/or nationality

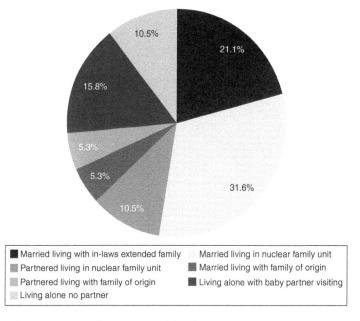

Chart 2.3   Participants by partner and family status

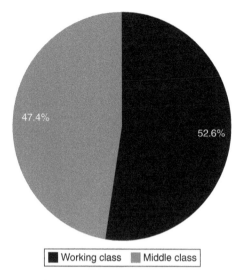

Working class   Middle class

Chart 2.4   Participants by class

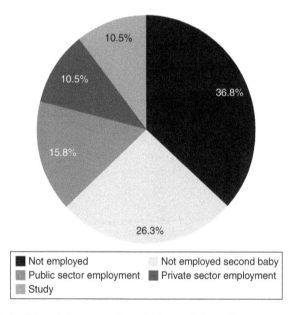

Not employed   Not employed second baby
Public sector employment   Private sector employment
Study

Chart 2.5   Participants by occupation at 12-month interview

Evolving two psychoanalytically informed methods

The first of our two methods, the FANI method, had been developed in the context of research into fear of crime (Hollway and Jefferson, 2013) in order to steer interviewees away from well-worn responses dominated by readily available discourses. It aimed to elicit participants' experience in a form dictated as little as possible by the protocol of questions and introduced the idea of a 'defended subject' to take into account the effects of defences against anxiety on participants' actions and the accounts they give of these. Although the FANI method is usually capable, through free associations, of eliciting the kind of experience-near accounts that afford psychological depth within particularised social settings, the method necessarily relies on language and elicits a mode of communication that is to a significant extent under conscious control. There is a tendency to reproduce the image of a rational, unitary, language-based subject, a premise on which interview methods were traditionally based (Hollway and Jefferson, 2013, Chapter 2).

To address this weakness, we adapted the psychoanalytic, infant observation method, originally designed as part of professional training for those working with children and families (Urwin, 2007). We had as a result one interview-based and one observation-based method, both psychoanalytically informed. Together the two methods had the potential to complement each other, overlap and to achieve a kind of triangulation that would support the validity of both:

> The observation method was intended… to enable us to see identities that are less the product of conscious, intentional production through narrative, more sensitive to affect, to unconscious intersubjectivity and to embodied aspects of identity. This broadly turned out to be the case. However, it is worth pointing out that words spoken in an interview do not only provide semantic information. (…) In a similar way to how interviews can provide information that goes beyond discourse, so observations are often bursting with talk, including information of the kind that is likely to be provided in interviews.
>
> (Hollway, 2007, pp.334–335)

The FANI method

In the following short response to a FANI question (not untypical of a semi-structured interview), Silma's account of her return home from hospital with her new daughter stayed close to her experience, while not eschewing generalisation. Her response provides information about her relation to various aspects of her experience, information that affords a psycho-social focus. She had just been asked 'can you tell me about that first day [home from the hospital], how did it go?' We could learn about her practices as they were imbued with her feeling about them (without which meaning is depleted), helped by her narrative style, especially about her preoccupation with feeding, when she got home.

> When I was coming out the car, yeah, they were all at the door. (. . .) And then um (.) [softer] then I was thinking, 'What shall I do?' I was a bit nervous. Then I had to make her milk, and then I fed her, changed her nappy, changed her clothes and put her to sleep. [louder] And then I used to like look at the clock every time, it was like [softer] three hours [louder] every three hours. But then she's drinking little by little bit, so it's like every two to two and a half hours actually.
>
> (Elliott et al., 2009, p.25)

The interview questions (see below) were designed to encourage narratives and allow free association to emerge, reflecting the emotional underpinning of participants' remembered experiences, such as 'feeling a bit nervous'. Transcription conventions aimed to contribute to this information, but were not expected to obviate use of the audio recording, which holds a further level of information derived from the voice.

In the original fear of crime study, there had been no longitudinal design involved and so a pair of interviews, two weeks apart, had provided all the data. Narrative analysis, especially in its biographical form and combined with a repeated interview format, has contributed to a perspective on processes over time, but 'The existence of two accounts does not in itself resolve the problem that interviews are constituted through stories that are told about life, rather than the life as it is lived' (Thomson 2007, p.572). Research about 'becoming' requires the adoption of specifically longitudinal methods and we were fortunate to be in close contact with a sister project, 'the Making of Modern Motherhood' (MoMM), exemplary in this respect (Thomson, 2009; McLeod and Thomson, 2009). For a start we needed to extend our data points to cover whatever key period in the process of becoming we could include in our fieldwork. This represented a shift *from* an expectation that the participants would talk about their own changes (by implication already processed, known and registered), *towards* an emphasis on eliciting, over time, participants' immediate experiences. Three interviews had to suffice (given time and budget constraints), starting prenatally because of the importance of pregnancy as psychological preparation for becoming a mother (Raphael-Leff, 1993). In the event, we managed to interview only ten of the sample before they gave birth; in the remaining cases, the first interview was rearranged as soon as possible postnatally.

Shaping FANI questions

In this method, questions are designed to be open ended, to elicit experience-near stories arranged according to the participants' associations and meaning frames and to discourage the kinds of opinion-based generalisations often elicited by why questions (Hollway and Jefferson, 2013, p.32ff). Subsequent interviews are guided by previous ones in the selection of appropriate and salient questions, so each interview will proceed uniquely, rather than in a manner that follows a schedule mechanistically. The questions are not devised to be asked word for word, as written, but to define an area of interest that can be asked in whatever manner the interviewer finds appropriate in the moment. Even small details like this were rethought: the idea of a standardised delivery to all interviewees derives from an experimental scientific framework and is antithetical to our emphasis on co-meaning making and intersubjectivity.

The 'becoming' focus of our research suggested a chronological structure and so our first interview questions aimed to elicit the story of the first, second and third stages of pregnancy; how body and bodily change is experienced; how the birth is anticipated; the relationship with, and support from, important others:

Can you tell me the story of your pregnancy?
Can you tell me about when you first knew you were pregnant?
Can you tell me about how your body has been changing?
Can you tell me about when you first felt the baby moving?
Tell me about getting ready for the birth.

We asked 'Can you tell me about the birth' at either first or second interview, depending on whether the first interview was post- or prenatal. The difference in accounts was noticeable, between the freshness (sometimes traumatic) of a recent birth experience and the birth as it was remembered four or five months on. This reminds us how influential time lapse is in narrative accounts.

The development of the FANI method was based on a critique of the assumption, common in qualitative research, that interviewees are sufficiently transparent to themselves to provide adequately full accounts (Hollway and Jefferson, 2013, p.3). In research on identity change, the transparent subject assumption is especially inadequate, both because it constructs a view of identity as what can be told through language and because it assumes that change is accessible for the telling during the research process. The FANI method initiated a focus on the 'defended subject', but in the earlier study the reflexivity of the researchers was scarcely in view in terms of intersubjective dynamics and what Rachel Thomson called the 'defended researcher' (see Hollway and Jefferson, 2013, p.xi for an autocritique and discussion of new methodological developments). Therefore a further innovation in our use of the FANI method was not only to be fuller and more systematic in our use of field notes for recording ethnographic detail, but also to use them to reflect on the emotional impact of the interview encounter, how it left us feeling and what it might say about our relationship to that interview at that time. The idea of reflective field notes was borrowed from the MoMM sister project (Thomson, 2007). Over the course of fieldwork, these were further influenced by the note-taking skills evident on the observation side of the project, with which the three interviewers (Heather Elliott, Ann Phoenix and myself) had weekly contact through the observation seminar.

The following example, from Heather Elliott's reflection on a part of one of her field notes provides a rich example. In her second interview with Nila, she notes that it 'felt like an interview which had not worked' (Elliott, Ryan and Hollway, 2012, p.5), but went on to use a later part of the field note as follows:

> However, I do note a moment when I am able to identify with her. Nila has left her baby at home and he is unhappy: her phone started buzzing almost as soon as we started. She checked her phone and ignored it; then took two or possibly three calls. For a while she looked like the essence of torn and juggling. Telling her story with an eye on the phone. I said she must take the calls and do whatever she needed to do. Writing up my notes I think of dropping off my younger son with his childminder this morning, the need to go and the need to stay. Never being entirely in one place. The feelings around getting calls from home on the mobile. These moments of connection help me recognise the challenges Nila faced in negotiating the complexities of her life as a

new mother and her responsibilities within an extended family. I also recognise, with hindsight, that the arrangements I had offered to make our meeting easier may have made things more difficult for her.

(ibid.)

The fact that Heather was also a mother of young children was helpful in this com-passionate identification. In addition to the dynamics of identification, we see how she is using an association ('writing up my notes, I think of...'), the extension of her reflection over time ('I recognise with hindsight'), and the ethical access through her own experience, so that instead of being irritated at the disruption of the interview, she can see a mother who 'looked the essence of torn and juggling'. This passage was also part of an exploration of the role of a form of supervision, neither academic nor clinical, which provided a space where reflection could be supported by another's thinking (Elliott, Ryan and Hollway, 2012).

The infant observation method

Because the infant observation method evolved as a training in infant and young child development (Bick, 1964), trained observers become very good at noticing non-verbal, embodied aspects of communication and mental states. The method was therefore consistent with our aim to go beyond the consciously aware, talk-based methods of finding out about identity, wishing to pick up a range of other levels, from the unsaid to the unthinkable; that is those that reside in and are expressed affectively through the body. In other words, our use of psychoanalytically informed observation aimed to go beyond an exclusive methodological focus on text towards a focus on practices and embodied, affective expressions of states of mind and relationship as they are enacted.

The six observers were all trained in infant observation as part of child psychotherapy training (most at the Tavistock Centre), in which training they had learned a psychoanalytically informed style of observation pioneered by Esther Bick at the Tavistock in the 1950s (Bick, 1964). Each observed one of the larger sample of mothers, once per week over the course of the first year of her baby's life. For six of the mothers in our sample (two Bangladeshi, one English, one African-Caribbean, one West African and one white South African), we therefore have all types of data: interviews (recordings and transcripts), interviewers' field notes, observation notes and observation seminar notes.

Observers make notes only after the session has ended, at the time paying detailed attention to the baby and mother. We followed the psychoanalytic training tradition, in which the observation is combined with a weekly seminar, where the group of observers meets throughout the observation period, led by an experienced psychoanalytically-trained observer (in our case, Cathy Urwin), to process together the impact of the developing observation. They were not seminars for the purposes of applying theory to the data: 'The weekly observation seminars were deliberately devoid of theoretical discussion, both to avoid the tendency for theory to lead or blind observation and because of the assumption that new theory may be required' (Urwin, 2007, p. 249). Notes are made of these proceedings too, so that the observation notes and seminar notes represent different layers of reflection, the former being a type of raw data. Judith Edwards (2008, p.61) specifies the three opportunities afforded by this method to experience the observation and reflect on it: in the actual observation setting, during note writing and via the seminar. A great deal of learning can be achieved in the process of this layered, structured experience (Groarke, 2008, p.317), not least because it is not always an isolated activity. The processing of observers' emotional responses in the seminar group affords the triangulation of others with different feelings and thoughts about what seemed to be going on in the notes. To some extent this shared processing precedes the ascription of meaning to the data. As we saw above, the principle of layered reflection applies to field note writing. It was important for the team to have access to reflective field notes, so that further processing and the triangulation of other minds could take place. In a longitudinal design, it is important to remain open to what has not yet occurred, to resist premature theorising.

The observer's stance in infant observation is based on making mental space for processing the emotional impact of the experience:

> knowledge, theory, etc are set aside during the acts of observing and recording in favour of allowing the experience to make its impact (...) a new concept of the observer is being employed (...) here the truths which interest us are emotional truths. The observer cannot register them without being stirred (...) correctly grasped, the emotional factor is an indispensable tool to be used in the service of greater understanding.
>
> (Miller, 1989, p.2)

It turns out that 'allowing the experience to make its impact' and 'the emotional factor' are key tenets of a psychoanalytic epistemology and clinical method which, when put into practice in psycho-social research, go beyond old principles of objectivity (Hollway, 2013b; 2012b) and afford different approaches to grasping meaning. However, researchers' use of the emotional impact of participation in a research encounter is only the start; in order to 'correctly grasp' the emotional factor, it must be reflected upon. This is the principle governing group work in the observation seminar (See Urwin, 2007, p.244ff), which we applied to our emerging field note style, our use of group data analysis and the resource afforded by supervision. Raw emotional experience must be reflected upon (digested, symbolised, processed; in Bion's terminology, transformed into alpha function, 1962), if it is to be used helpfully.[2]

Support of other minds: Psychoanalytically informed supervision and group data analysis

As we have seen, the method of infant observation (Miller et al., 1989; Urwin and Sternberg, 2012; Urwin 2011) builds in a weekly observation seminar where observers can process the inevitably emotional experience of being with vulnerable and dependent infants and their carers and think about their notes with a group. This puts into practice a psychoanalytic principle emerging out of Bion's theory of the intersubjective origins of thought, summed up memorably by Thomas Ogden as 'it takes two minds to think a person's most disturbing thoughts' (Ogden, 2009, p.91). More than two minds adds further strengths. We extended this practice into group data analysis, using many different configurations to encourage analysis (confidentially) of data extracts from multiple viewpoints. The disadvantage of short group meetings is that 'the whole' of a participant example cannot be shared within the time span. When an opportunity existed to consider the interview and observation data of one participant with a group over the course of six intensive weeks,[3] I realised the value of both the group and the time to achieve a depth of analysis never previously attained (Thomson et al., 2011; Urwin et al., 2013).

Heather Elliott, who undertook half of the interviews, was in a situation close to the new mothers she interviewed (Elliott, 2011), as we see above. She gives an account of how she worked with both the negative and positive features of her identifications with participants and of her use of external sources of support. A small sum was budgeted for 'non-clinical supervision' for Heather, during fieldwork, a model quite close to therapeutic work supervision. The supervisions took place with Jo Ryan, the supervisor, at Heather's instigation. This kind of supervision followed a psychoanalytic model in that it provided a confidential space separate from the main team where all aspects of researcher subjectivity could be thought about and explored for their meaning and relevance (see Elliott, Ryan and Hollway, 2012, for detailed examples). Heather gives an example of one interviewee, Sylvia, whose 'unruffled' account held some disturbing themes:

> Here supervision helped process the disturbing effect of the interview, allowing me not to act on my immediate reactions, but consider what they might mean. This material is an example of how the anxiety arising from emotionally charged issues for the mother (own mother's death, her health problems, which she feared would affect her unborn baby) can be projected into others, with varying consequences but allowing the mother to remain seemingly unruffled. This is an example of how the unconscious aspects of emotional communication are as much part of the emotional work of research as the more conscious ones. My fieldnotes as well as discussion in supervision allow us to see how this happens, to detoxify its impact, and forestall any unhelpful reactions. Disentangling the various strands allows me to see the mother in a more separate and thus more objective way.
>
> (Elliott, Ryan and Hollway, 2012, p.4)

Our use for research of this form of supervision, for which we were aware of no pre-existing model, attempted to address a wider ethical set of questions too: How does one become sufficiently aware of oneself in the fieldwork process to work in this way? How does one make reflexive data available to others? And, importantly, how can the emotional work involved in undertaking reflection be acknowledged and supported? (Elliott, Ryan and Hollway, 2012, p.2).

Comparing interview and observation methods

I chose Zelda's case study on which to base a methodological comparison because I concluded, after my first full encounter with the data, that she came across differently in the two methods. There is plenty of overlap, but the differences were consequential, I thought, for a view of her identity change, especially within the terms we had set out in the research proposal, namely that we wanted to tap the affective, embodied, relational and practical aspects. Zelda's case would therefore be instructive to look at in detail to find out how different productions happened. The interviewing and observation methods have different strengths, but they also overlap: verbal accounts are plentiful in observations (Zelda was notable for her volubility), although accounts are not elicited by interviewer questions, and interviewers make observations which, adding to how they may get recorded in an interview, form a part of field notes. Babies were often present during interviews, therefore much was happening that was not in direct response to interview questions.

I compiled a list of factual information afforded by each method and looked for patterns, but at this level of told information, nothing was notable, except that, predictably, the interview method – even the free association narrative version that resists asking lots of direct questions – is better for gathering specific information.[4] In consequence there is more about Zelda's family of origin, their wedding, the extra scans that were occasioned by the pregnancy scare, Zelda's mother's arrival and the details of the birth. Through the interviewer's direct questions, we know that Sharon, Zelda's housemate and close friend, was the first to know about the pregnancy and also that she was there at a critical time during the pregnancy when Zelda needed to get to the GP surgery. It was clear from both methods, largely through Zelda's explicit assertions to both researchers, that friends were a very important feature of her life in London.

The observation method never involves the observer in initiating topics and getting answers, but records whatever is witnessed. In this way it practices abstinence in relation to what is sought by the researcher. The detail of what Zelda says during observations therefore reflects – we can assume – what is on her mind and what is meaningful in the context of that day and her developing relationship with the observer. This is illustrated in the following comparison, which takes explicit statements about what it was like becoming a mother. One extract is derived from each method, produced within days of each other (interview first), so there are bound to be links between them.

Sometimes you're *exhausted* obviously, and you're really tired. And when- when they're sick you feel helpless sometimes, and everything. But it's just (.) *oh* if he just smiles at	She spoke about a friend in South Africa who is pregnant ... and this led into reflections on what a massive change having a baby had made to her life (...).

(Continued)

you or whatever, you forget everything and you just (.) it's *so* rewarding. I don't think there's anything better *ever* than being a mum, it's just fantastic, yeah it's great. And like I say, all the changes don't make a difference, 'cos they (.) they're for the better anyway, so (.) yeah … And the one bad day, you've probably got *a hundred* good days anyway, so it doesn't matter.	'It's not what you imagine. You imagine the big things, which are different, but not all the small ones.' She spoke about how hard it is to do simple things and what a difference it makes to everything in your whole life … it's hard to explain to someone how long things take, even simple things. She also spoke about how tired you get, your whole life is changed. You cannot know how it feels if it hasn't happened to you.

It is obvious which extract derives from which method because of the form of reporting; in the first a transcript of Zelda's direct speech and in the second largely mediated through the observer's notes ('she spoke about…'). In the second extract, Zelda entered into these reflections through a chain of her own associations. The first extract comes from a much longer reply provided in response to a direct question: '11 months on, what's it been like becoming a mother'? Her response starts off 'great stuff. It's just fantastic' and ends, two pages later with 'I'll have as many as I can.'

There are two common themes in the above extracts: tiredness and the importance of small experiences in making the difference. The striking difference in tone to me suggests that in the interview extract, there is an effort to be upbeat: 'it's so rewarding', 'I don't think there's anything better *ever*', 'fantastic', 'great'; four claims at a very general level. Zelda goes on to mention the bad side in a carefully framed way where 'one bad day' is contrasted with a hundred good ones, thus minimising the bad. I am not implying that Zelda distorts her overall feeling about mothering; I believe that she felt hugely positive about being a mother. However, the specific direct question is likely to elicit this kind of positive headline: it is obviously framed as an overarching, concluding question, given the topic of the project and the question's timing near the end of the final interview. In contrast, the observation extract contains a reflection not actively sought but emerging out of the approaching ending of the year-long relationship in which the observer has reliably served as a calm, containing, recognising figure. In this context, Zelda dwells on what cannot have been known in advance. The difference it has made in her life is not calibrated, good overwhelming bad a hundred to one, but attempts to convey the texture of everyday experience, for example how hard it is to do simple things, how long they take (I think of the contrast with her former efficiency). She is able to reflect on the things she did not know in advance, what she has learned from experience.

I found broad confirmation of our expectation that the observation method enabled us to see identities that are less the product of conscious, intentional production through narrative, and more sensitive to affect and practices, to unconscious intersubjectivity and embodied aspects of identity. However, this difference is not simply a product of the respective focus on words or behaviour. It was more apparent from the observations than from the interviews that she was having a hard time managing her anxieties in becoming a mother. There was evidence of this in both methods, but there were also numerous differences in the information she provided, both intentionally and unwittingly. These included differences in the content itself, the tone and atmosphere of what she said and, especially, how she acted in relation to Tom, the baby. Later, I take the example of their relationship during feeding.

In addition to whether the primary methodological medium was talk-based or visual, a fundamental difference in the methods resulted from visit frequency. Zelda met the interviewer three times and the observer 36 times. An obvious effect of this difference in frequency of visits is the inevitably different relationships that Zelda (and Tom) establish with the two researchers. However, their practices are also distinctly different and the way the observers are trained in what to notice and how to use their emotional responses as an instrument of knowing distinguishes the observation method from interviewing, even when the latter is based on principles of eliciting free associations and supplemented with reflective field notes. The containing effects of this observer in relation to Zelda's anxiety will be explored later (Chapter 5) in order to illuminate the consequences for knowing – both in mothering and research.

The different frequency of visits also produces gaps of different lengths: for the interviewer, a gap of five months between the first and second interviews and another six between second and third, whereas the observer's weekly visits (albeit with inevitable gaps) afford access to the ups and downs of Zelda's daily life with a baby. Combine the infrequency of the interview with the expectation of eliciting a narrative of the intervening experience and the ups and downs will necessarily be smoothed out in the generalisation that is required for a narrative of events covering several months. The observation method can capture the mundane practices (and the emotions that are inextricable from these) involved in the going-on-being of mother and baby over time, generally not what is expressed in words.

Despite the FANI protocol prioritising the elicitation of experience-near stories of particular events, the time gap between interviews tended to produce a generalised overview of the intervening period, an organised narrative that achieved a certain emotional distance from some aspects of the experiences of that time as they were lived. For example, in response to the interviewer's question 'so how has every day been since you had Tom?', Zelda launches into a long and detailed account of a typical day, based on routines of sleeping, waking, eating (by this time solids) 'during the day, oh like I say, he's so content', and the parents' patterns as a couple, which have changed to adjust to having a baby, 'we pretty much see friends the whole weekend. We try now to invite people over here.' There were some experience-near stories contained within this, but the emotional tone was governed by these being in the past, done and dusted, like the time she looked after a friend's baby, 'And I'll never do it again' (because they kept upsetting each other and waking each other up, etc.). The story had a conventional structure, ending with 'I eventually phoned my husband from work and I said "you will get here now (laughs) as quick as possible" '. The response to this question is long (about 12 pages of transcript), after which the interviewer tries to elicit some more specific information by asking about what Zelda and Tom did yesterday. We then learn that Tom was quite niggly and wouldn't eat, which is a contrast to the generalised account and therefore appears as a one-off occurrence.

Because both methods are available for triangulation, we can correct and refine the impression that Tom's failure to eat is an exception to the norm. The observations gives us a detailed, regular and frequent record of Zelda's difficulties, particularly in feeding prior to weaning during which, for a long period, Tom squirms and wriggles, is uncomfortable with being held, makes no eye contact and refuses to finish the bottle. For example:

Tom at 3 months and 20 days:

Zelda picked up Tom's bottle and offered it to Tom who became more fidgety, wriggling away from the bottle and arching his back. He wouldn't lie back in her arms and strained to be able to look at the TV. He eventually settled sitting, leaning back against Zelda facing the TV, but he still refused the bottle three or four times, pushing the teat out of his mouth wrinkling his face, turning his head and moaning slightly, and then suddenly he accepted it. He now drank fast, his eyes at first fixed on the TV and then on me. His gaze was rather unfocused and his rapid drinking was unrelaxed. One of his hands held onto his mum's fingers as she held the bottle, his other hand he held near his ear. He squirmed and pulled away from the bottle when it was about two thirds finished.

(Pluckrose, 2007, p.311)

Elspeth Pluckrose, the observer in Zelda's case, then refers to the seminar group's thinking about the feeding experience as it related to Zelda:

thinking in this way, the group wondered about a connection to a continued difficulty for the mother and infant in processing the trauma of the birth experience, a frightening and sudden experience of being separate. The group also continued to notice the way in which the repetition of such difficult feeding experiences served to undermine Zelda's belief in herself as a mother who could get it right for her baby.

(Pluckrose, 2007, p.312)

A seminar note soon after this observation contained many questions (a format which resists closure and is especially appropriate given the changing nature of the mother–baby relationship from week to week). The group's conceptualising (here reflecting a Kleinian understanding of the close correspondence in early life between the processing of food and of emotional experience) are given space but not imposed. For example (from an observation seminar note) 'the repeated attempts to get the bottle into Tom's mouth make Elspeth think he is not hungry, but then he takes it in. Does he have to evacuate something first in order to take it in?' It also records the emotional impact on group members, for example 'the awkwardness of the feed makes it almost too painful to watch/hear'. This example demonstrates the affective flows to which researchers using this method are sensitised, therefore opening up a dimension often unavailable to research methods. The group might draw attention to a particular detail, using the record of observations so far and the memory of the observer, for example 'Elspeth has only seen Tom feed once whilst looking into Zelda's eyes; this is also the case when [the father] feeds him'.

My comments above about the interview data, coupled with its contrast to the above observation note detail on Zelda's feeding experience, suggest that it is quite hard to formulate FANI questions that successfully elicit detail of specific daily events (but that the prompt about yesterday was more successful in avoiding generalisation) and the tendency to generalisation is exacerbated by the length of time since the last visit and the understandable wish of participants to represent the whole period in their accounts. My focus here on differences between the methods should not detract from recognising that they are fundamentally quite similar when compared with the full range of qualitative methods, including standardised questionnaires, use of drawings, focus groups, video recording.

Conclusion

In this chapter I have situated the nuts and bolts of the becoming a mother project design and fieldwork within an overall theme of how important research methods are in shaping what can (and what cannot) be known. I introduced the idea that a psycho-social approach to participants can be guided by a focus on their *relation to* their settings and circumstances and that this can be known more meaningfully if researchers pay attention to our relation to these features as they manifest in the research encounters. 'Relation to' is a holistic syncretistic focus, based on sensitivity to emotional experience (or affect). It also involves reflection – one of the key terms in this book. The capacity to reflect on emotional experience as we encounter participants in the field and later through the data (including with the help of other minds) is central to the psychoanalytically informed account of researchers' knowing that draws on Wilfred Bion's theory of thinking (Chapter 5). Our relation to these encounters provides identificatory access to the mother's relation not only to her baby, but also to all her encounters with 'objects' that make up her experience. The idea affords an accessibly non-clinical route to psychoanalytically informed methodology. Finally I illustrated, via an example, how two methods – even two epistemologically congruent methods – FANI and IO, produce different knowledge about the same mother. These are not in conflict but are useful as a form of triangulation. They demonstrate how much is at stake in choices of method and the principles underlying them.

3
The Reality of Being a Young Mother: Agency, Imagination and Objectivity

This chapter is about the central (but contested) role of reality in knowing, especially in uncognised knowing. In this I am guided by Jill Gentile's Winnicottian treatment of the reality of the material world: 'The material world is critical to our construction of subjectivity...we simultaneously impose our weight upon it and surrender to its unyielding aspects' (Gentile, 2007, p.549).

I take Jenny's relation to reality as an example, analysing her relation to being a young girl, an analysis that makes space for agency through her capacity for imagination and thinking about the difficult prospect of becoming a mother at a young age. This is paralleled by reflections on my relation, as researcher, to knowing Jenny. Using psychoanalysis, I build a psychological dimension into critical realism, the epistemological tradition that 'insists that what is the case places limits upon how we can construe it' (Archer, 1998, p.195). Psychoanalysis problematises subject-object (knower-known, internal-external) distinctions, and, in Winnicott's hands, conceptualises reality and imagination not as binary opposites but as acting together in an intermediate space. I conclude by revisiting the concept of objectivity through a similar, psychoanalytically informed, lens.

Donald Winnicott located an intermediate area of experiencing in his concept of transitional space:

> My claim is that if there is a need for this double statement [individuals with an inside and an outside], there is also need for a triple one: the third part of the life of a human being, a part that we cannot ignore, is an intermediate area of *experiencing*, to which inner reality and external life both contribute. It is an area that is not challenged, because no claim is made on its behalf except that it shall exist as a

resting-place for the individual engaged in the perpetual human task
of keeping inner and outer reality separate yet interrelated.

(Winnicott, 1971[2005], p.3, original emphasis)

Jenny in her milieu: Vignettes from a year, written from observation notes

Jenny is straightening her hair in front of the mirror in the sitting room
when the observer arrives for the first time. The baby is asleep in a swing
cradle, which takes up a large space in an already crowded room. A computer is on the table showing a card game. Several posters of Bob Marley
are pinned on the wall, along with a Rastafari poem. Photos of the family
are on the mantelpiece: Jenny with her next brother; her twin younger
brothers; her parents looking proudly at the newborn baby. Jenny has
a part-time job at a telesales company, selling kitchens on commission,
and she is getting ready to go out. She tells the observer that it is boring, that she feels sorry for the people she phones up, especially if they
are elderly and haven't got the thought of a new kitchen, with all the
upheaval involved. She laughs, 'I want to tell them it's okay and not to
worry.' She explains that it is helpful living at home because of all the
help she gets. A sound of keys in the front door announces her parents,
accompanied by the rustling of shopping bags. Her father comes in and
Jenny explains the observer's presence. He introduces himself and looks
at the baby for a moment. He leaves the room and there is the sound of
cupboards opening and closing as shopping is put away. The baby stirs.
Jenny picks him up gently and explains that she will feed him before
she goes out but that she is part bottle feeding him, so that others can
feed him when she is at work or at college.

The following week, the observer's visit is early in the day and everyone is at home. The observer enters the sitting room to greet Jenny's
father who is sitting on the sofa in his pyjamas holding Davy. He says
something to Jenny and hands over the baby gently, who lies comfort-
ably, as if about to fall asleep, sucking rhythmically on his dummy. A few
minutes later, Julian [the baby's father] comes in and greets the observer
in a friendly way – their first meeting. Jenny says she needs to get ready
and hands over Davy to his father. Davy settles into Julian's arm and
after a while begins to grimace and squirm a little. Julian explains that
he is constipated and it hurts him. He says to him softly 'oh there, it's
alright man' and rocks him, murmuring from time to time. He holds
Davy's hand, letting the baby curl his fingers around one of his own
and caresses his forehead. When he holds him up to his shoulder, Davy

passes wind. When the observer comments on his ease with the baby, Julian says he is the second eldest of seven children. He agrees wryly with the observer that this makes him quite experienced. Davy starts rooting into Julian's chest and he comments that he doesn't know when Jenny last fed him. But he settles Davy again and takes him to their bedroom to put him down.

The week after – later in the day – the observer arrives to see Julian snoozing in the armchair with Davy lying back against his chest, the two looking utterly relaxed and comfortable. Jenny is sitting at the computer, typing. After a while Davy stirs and stretches and Julian follows suit. He talks to Jenny who is helping him with one of his assignments. Davy, having fallen asleep again, now starts to whimper and Julian says to Jenny that he is probably hungry. Jenny looks at the clock and comments that he'll also need his medicine. Julian holds him while Jenny goes to the kitchen and returns with a bottle of milk and a syringe full of medicine. He continues while Jenny gives the medicine and then hands him over to Jenny and they comment on how he likes sweet things. Davy drinks the whole bottle lustily, while Julian takes over the computer. She tells the observer that she has given up the telesales job – it's too far and she hardly saw Julian.

When Davy is 12 weeks old and it is still the summer vacation, Jenny is looking for a job again, combing the local paper, bemoaning the fact that the paper is full of telesales jobs and nothing else and how she hates trying to sell to people things that they do not want. She seems tired. Her father comes in and starts playing with the baby, speaking in a singsong voice. Davy babbles in a lively way. He pulls himself up strongly, holding his grandfather's hands, looking delighted. The two play contentedly for most of the observation, only interrupted when Jenny changes Davy's nappy.

The following week, the observer arrives to find that Jenny is out having a driving lesson. Grandfather is in charge and both twins are in the sitting room, one playing a computer game, and the other playing with Davy, who is in his chair. After a while he begins to whimper. Grandfather is watching a film on TV. He goes out and, as Davy begins to grizzle, returns with Davy's bottle, testing the temperature on his arm. Too hot, wait five minutes. The boy tries to distract Davy and waits. When the five minutes is up, he takes Davy out of his chair and settles himself on the sofa holding Davy gently but confidently on the crook of his arm. Grandfather returns to test the milk and give the go-ahead. Davy feeds heartily, gulping the milk, until it is almost finished. He arches his back, as if feeling wind. The boy tries offering him the last bit and when it is rejected, he puts the bottle down and sits Davy up. Rhythmically he rubs his back until, after about five minutes, Davy gives a satisfying burp. The boy then smells his nappy and takes Davy through to the bedroom. He talks to Davy a little, and Davy's face breaks into a smile as the boy cleans him up.

By the end of November, when Davy is seven months old, Jenny is sitting at the computer again while Davy sleeps on the sofa surrounded by cushions so that he doesn't roll off. She is working on a 2000-word essay due in, along with a project, at the end of the week. She feels a bit stressed. Not only college, she has found a good retail job and works part-time three days a week. After a while, Davy stretches and rubs his eyes, twisting his head around in the direction of Jenny. She immediately smiles and says hello and he begins to make some sounds. She gets up and comes over and Davy tries to turn to reach for her, moving on to his front and getting into a crawling position, but only managing to move backwards. When she holds out her hands, he grabs them and pulls himself up, smiling and happy. He bounces vigorously on the sofa. They repeat the game. After a while, when Davy runs out of steam and is looking expectantly at noises from the kitchen, Jenny looks at the clock. Almost immediately, her father arrives with Davy's lunch – vegetables and rice. Davy looks excitedly at him and waves his arms. Once in his chair, he eagerly accepts each mouthful, only gradually towards the end of the bowl letting it ooze out of his mouth. Jenny leaves what is left and wipes him up quietly, lifting him out when he raises his arms.

On the eve of Davy's first birthday, Jenny and Julian have the evening together and are reminiscing about their year. On the way to the hospital, Julian was meant to go into the shop to get some phone credit and she was waiting in the taxi. He came back with Kentucky Fried chicken instead and then he's asking her if she wants hot wings in the lift inside the hospital and she's like 'no I don't want any hot wings'.

Jenny reflects on her year with interviewer and observer. Julian comes round every day, guaranteed. She doesn't even have to ask him what he'll be doing. They were already spending a lot of time together before she got pregnant; that's not changed, but perhaps it's made them closer if anything. Often, it's just the three of them, in the house, chilling out, quite happy, no major problems or anything. A lot of her friends didn't stick around, which is what she expected, but the important ones are still in touch. Davy recognises them. He's very sociable. He knows Jenny's brothers and Julian's family too, and says mama and dada.

Jenny had to give up college after Davy was ill and in hospital for a while. She didn't want to get bad grades and so will return next year.

Julian continued. She doesn't go out much now, but she celebrated her eighteenth birthday with some friends and got drunk for the first time in ages. But even proper drunk, she was thinking, I've got a baby at home, make sure I go home alright. She can still have fun and look after Davy. Her parents remained strict after Davy was born, but now they have nothing to discipline her about, so it's been alright. They know that if she's out late with Davy she'll only be at Julian's house. She's there loads. She talks to his Mum, also his brothers and sisters. They often go to the park together. Things are better with her Mum, in fact her Mum's happier than she used to be. They don't have anything to argue about any more. Mum will buy the nappies, and Dad buys the milk. It's made everyone closer. It's just been a good experience. She's not ready to move out yet.

She's thought about it a lot and reckons that it's a good time to have a baby when you're a teenager because you get lots of help. If you were a grown up woman, people would think you could just get on with it on your own. There's less time for herself, but she's got used to that. It's made her more patient. One thing she's noticed is how now she can't bear to see a child being hurt or in difficulty.

I discuss later (Chapter 6) the changes to my style of distilling and presenting data for the purposes of sharing information with readers and also how I work to 'know' the data. Here I will just comment that I treat the above information as a form of 'scenic' experiencing accruing into a kind of holistic knowing that may never be articulated through language. Thus the reader gets a different quality of access to Jenny in her setting.

Facing reality

Following reflective principles, after I had listened to each of Jenny's three interviews, I asked myself how I responded to Jenny, whom I never met face to face. (This was a feature of the early data analysis for each participant.) My note starts 'I like Jenny, right from the beginning (...). She FACES REALITY, even though reality is difficult for her'. In the note, I go on to list some of the details that impressed me. They amount to what seems to me an unusual strength of character, or perhaps emotional maturity, for her age and in her situation: her efforts to continue with her studies (but the decision to postpone them when they conflict too much with Davy's care after he is hospitalised), her handling of her boyfriend Julian's initial opposition to her continuing the pregnancy, her approach to the lack of financial resources and the scarcity of reasonable employment, changing her youthful pleasures and concluding she can still have fun, coping with constant tiredness. Her use and development of support from those around her – Julian, her parents and brothers, his mother and siblings and two close friends – helped form her new practices and ways of thinking as she became a mother in the face of these difficulties. The selection in the above scenes is largely guided by my wish to convey this in its sensual, material and intimate relational detail, so that it comes alive to readers. Rereading it, I am struck by how successive scenes illustrate the integration of this new baby and his care into the wider family (and Julian's family too, about which we hear via Jenny). I admired the way Jenny acted on her circumstances rather than succumbing to them and the way she found pleasure in her changed circumstances, despite the losses. As a result, I decided to use Jenny's case here to help my thinking about agency from a psychosocial perspective, outside the intractable binary of agency and structure (with its echoes of individual and social dualism).

Recourse to the concept of reality is fraught with dangers in social science theorising because of the legacy of naïve realism, based on the proposition that a knower's relation to the reality of the external world is veridical, achieved in an unmediated fashion. The 'turn to language' in social sciences in recent decades recognised the power of language in constructing the categories that mediate sensory experience, and much contemporary British social science is characterised by its emphasis on the way that language constructs reality. Psychoanalysis, especially American relational psychoanalysis, has been influenced by the constructionist turn. After pointing out the notable strand in psychoanalytic thought that sustains 'a dialectic between materiality and subjectivity', Jill Gentile comments,

> the status of materiality has suffered somewhat in the turn toward a relational perspective. In part, a post modernist sensibility – which some have taken as correspondent with relational approaches – and which eschews idea of objective reality, universal truths, metanarratives and scientific positivism, has contributed to this 'loss' of materality in our thinking.
>
> (Gentile, 2007, p.552)

The quality of material reality is the starting point for my psychoanalytically informed use, defined by the philosopher Peirce as 'that which is not whatever we happen to think it is, but is unaffected by what we may think of it' (Peirce, 1903, cited in Hanly 2004, p.269).

One implication of this definition is that there is, or needs to be, a limit imposed by matter on imagination. I shall return to a discussion of Jenny's actions in terms of agency when I have laid the groundwork for a psycho-social analysis that goes beyond positioning theory without rejecting its insights. My account below is framed to show how Jenny imaginatively fashioned her life within difficult circumstances.

Facing the reality of pregnancy as a young girl

To animate this theme, I travel back to how Jenny faced the reality of discovering that she was pregnant. Otherwise, from the foregoing vignettes, it would be too easy to build a relation to Jenny based on how it appeared later on (a narrative conclusion of success) when she is benefiting from the early thinking she did that enabled her to arrange her circumstances so well.

> Jenny hasn't plucked up the courage to tell her parents direct and the social worker, about to go on two weeks' leave, has suggested that they are told now, so that there is an adult around who knows. Jenny had missed periods before, checked and found it to be a false alarm. She'd read the leaflets, knew about the dangers but felt it wouldn't happen to her; she wasn't one to be caught out, a girl who always got high grades and planned to be a teacher. She'd got the pregnancy test result by phone and so the woman didn't know **she was just some young girl** as she delivered the news. She is called in to the living room. Her parents are not angry but disappointed, which is almost worse because it makes her feel so bad. They are worried about her studies and she reassures them of her intention to continue. She realises that this means they accept that she keeps the baby.
>
> The social worker was not the first to know: Jenny had straight away told her boyfriend Julian, who had joked 'so I know I'm fertile', and they didn't talk about it for a few days. As she said, 'It was almost like it weren't real.' Then he said she was too young and it would be best for her to have an abortion. She was in two minds until she had a scan and thought 'I can't get rid of it now.' She would feel guilty. She tells him she's keeping it and he'll just have to accept that. So Julian tells his Mum, or that's what he says he's done, but Jenny wonders if he's just said that to scare her and phones his Mum herself. Jenny is asked to come round immediately. They sit around the table, including Julian's older sister. They get a big lecture from

his Mum and a telling-off. She isn't angry at Jenny, doesn't run her down, but she is angry at the situation. She then asks if Jenny is going to keep it and Jenny says yes. Julian isn't happy, still really angry at her and saying some horrible things like 'how do I know it's mine?' His Mum tells him not to be silly, that he knows they've been together all this time. She knows Jenny well enough to know that. So his Mum says basically, 'well I'm not rich or anything and it's not going to be easy, but,' and she makes it clear she isn't going to desert Jenny. It is her grandchild and she'll support her in whatever way she can. Jenny must carry on to college, as she'd planned.

A few days later, when the second early extra scan is due, Jenny asks Julian's Mum to go along with her and they look at the scan together. There is like a little kiddy growing. It is only the size of a pinhead, so tiny, but the heart is beating really fast and you can see it clearly when the camera zooms in. It is really useful to see this. After that she and Julian's Mum talk. Jenny isn't close to her Mum and although they've stopped having loads of arguments now, it's awkward. So, to talk to his Mum, to tell her about her background and the family's situation, the family Julian's Mum has never met, it's good. She says that Jenny can come to talk to her about anything, any time.

For a while, she and Julian have massive arguments about it. She can take it in more easily than he can. She is someone who thinks about things a lot, and is able to accept it. But it's hard for him, a 16-year-old boy, about to start college and going to be a Dad. Not surprising that it's all a bit too much for him, and he is defensive and negative for a while. Even though they are both in the same situation, it is different, like when she could start to feel the baby kicking, and she tries to get him more involved and he says 'No I can't feel nothing.' She notices that it is after he first felt it kicking that he changes a bit. He doesn't want to miss college for doctors' appointments and things, but he comes when she is admitted to hospital for tests, when later in the pregnancy she is getting very breathless. She starts college the same week as the second scan, eight weeks pregnant, trying to miss as few classes as possible. Their peers are excited when Jenny's baby starts to show. Other girls start coming for advice and she says, 'Don't think it can't happen to you, it can.'

Depending on our own beliefs, we – readers of this extract – might be critical of the social worker's suggestion that she help Jenny inform her parents. Or we might be relieved and glad Jenny took it up. Certain discourses (or ideologies) suggest certain discursive positions, providing a way of reading the data that affects a researcher's meaning making. Any such position involves some kind of emotional relation to its subject and objects, and is available to researchers as we include new theory into our repertoires. In this discursive light, the social worker might seem patronising and in danger of positioning Jenny as unable to cope. The strain involved in disinterested data analysis is to notice and suspend our subjective preferences and discover, as best we can and without guessing, what *Jenny's* relationship was to the social worker's intervention. When, as researchers, we make use of a given conceptual repertoire for data analysis, we have to pay attention to counteracting evidence, when the reality of the data bumps into our theoretical and personal commitments. We must notice the discordance in order to avoid imposing unmodified preconceptions.

My thinking about the social worker's intervention worked out as follows. Jenny had not been able to tell her parents on her own, but she evidently did choose to tell the family social worker. The social worker's intervention was helpful: together with her parents they were able to think about Jenny's future, which – as Jenny then came to realise – could include the baby. Jenny's anxieties that made it difficult to think about the coming baby were conveyed to the social worker, who picked up the problem, thought about it at a time when Jenny was unable to because of the enormity of the news, and turned it into a practical suggestion. Consequently the parents were told, who likewise did their thinking about Jenny's pregnancy (painful though this reality must have been), helping her to process her emotional experience, become able to think about, and therefore imagine (a capacity for 'as if' thinking), keeping/having a baby. Several features of Jenny's account provided me with triangulating information about her relation to age and having a baby: Jenny confides in the family social worker about being pregnant and follows her advice; she describes Julian as 'a 16-year-old boy', in the context of how hard it is for him to accept being a father; her parents remain strict about being out late; she feels unready to move out of her parents' home and appreciates the support she receives because she is a teenager. I believe that my construction respects the evidence, but it is of course mediated by language and discourse or theory. Only a naïve realist view of objectivity would suppose anything other.

It was because I noticed with surprise Jenny's seemingly uncomplicated acceptance of the 'young girl' positioning that I chose the above extracts. Once I noticed this surprise and reflected on it, it helped me to eschew one-sided judgements: for example, that Jenny was quite capable of sorting this out herself – adult enough – or that she was too young to cope on her own. Thinking in this way helped me to cultivate a situated process of objectivity to ask what did Jenny do and what is conveyed in the data about how she felt and thought? In this way evidence is used to 'objectify intuition' (Urwin, 2007, p.245). This way of thinking is an example of what Winnicott called 'outside the area of projection' (2005, p.124), by which he meant outside the area of experience upon which we impose our wishes at the expense of reality when the acceptance of an unyielding external reality would be too frustrating, painful or easier and more comfortable to avoid.

Winnicott's accounts of babies' moves from perceiving objects subjectively to 'objects objectively perceived' (1963, p.183) is rigorously developmental, in the sense that he is always careful to specify the conditions that make it possible for babies to change, for example to give up omnipotence, the illusory idea that we control the events that make up our destinies. In his account, the relationship with the mother is bound up with coming to accept the externality of its objects and therefore the limits they impose that cannot be wished away. In good enough circumstances, infantile omnipotence is curbed, gradually, by encountering frustration (in the form of the graduated failure of the mother to adapt to her infant's omnipotent demands), testing the mother to destruction by its rejection of unpalatable reality, experienced as inseparable from her, and finding that she survives. Objects become real, Winnicott concludes, when they are hated as well as loved, but if reality is too painful to bear, disavowal results. Gentile uses some examples from her clinical psychoanalytic practice to explore cases where people experience reality as if it were intractable. In such cases it is a 'struggle to create meaning against the sheer impress of matter' (Gentile, 2007, p.566).

The encounter of reality and imagination is crucial to the development of a creative capacity for meaning making and therefore agency: babies' magical thinking with transitional objects eventually, conditions permitting, becomes adults' creative space. As Jenny faces reality, rather than disavowing or denying it, successive acts of meaning creation occur in between the force of desire or wish and obdurate matter. It is the obduracy of objects when encountered that gives them the quality of externality. Tolerating frustration can be much harder than illusion (it is often unbearable, hence defences such as denial and disavowal), but denial of frustration is not a plausible relief, because reality imposes limits that only become tractable when they can be thought about. Threats to people's capacity to face reality and learn from experience are twofold: denial or disavowal of reality and capitulation to its weight without the imagination to change it. I shall chart Jenny's path between these, the Scylla and Charybdis of facing reality.

Jenny thinks about the reality of her pregnancy

An example of unconscious denial would be if Jenny had failed to allow into conscious thought the knowledge that she was pregnant. But there could have been disavowal once she had received the news explicitly from the GP receptionist; for example, if she had refused to tell her parents, had gone ahead with the pregnancy and covered it up, had fallen out with her boyfriend on the grounds that he thought she was too young, if she had felt she was as capable as any older person to have a child and then been unready when the baby was born because she could not afford to think about the reality that lay ahead. None of these things happened.

At the other end of the continuum, Jenny might have retreated under the impact of material and social limit, seeing herself as faced with an external consensus that said she was too young to have a child – a consensus that initially included her boyfriend and some of her own doubts (she was 'in two minds', definitional of a depressive rather than paranoid-schizoid processing of experience in a Kleinian perspective).

By thinking about it, Jenny could process and be changed by her experience of the living baby in her womb: after the first scan the response 'I can't get rid of it now,' and at the second scan that 'there is a little kiddy growing...so tiny but the heart is beating really fast'. Her desire to have the baby crystallised and she then took a series of actions to alter the tractable, but uncertain, aspects of her setting to make it possible to keep the baby (her parents' permission and willingness to help with the care; Julian's cooperation; negotiations with the college; earning money when possible).

Facing the reality of pregnancy is not the same as passively accepting a given outcome: thinking about it, in all its emotional magnitude, means that Jenny could imaginatively consider various futures. Her parents' response to the news was crucial – a key moment when her imagining various possibilities needed to be linked with the reality of their response so that she could envisage being still at her family home with the baby and what it would be like to continue her studies. After this, she talked about it with her boyfriend in a different way, eventually telling him that she was going to have the baby (not have an abortion) despite his reluctance on the grounds that they were both too young. So he told his mother, Jenny went over and discussed it with his family and came away with his mother's support as well. At the next scan, she took her boyfriend's mother. In other words, the thinking could then be extended, turned into action and further imagining of the future through the support she was able to recruit. Gentile, cited above, summarises Winnicott's treatment of the psychological relation to external realities as follows: 'the material world is critical to our construction of subjectivity... we simultaneously impose our weight upon it and surrender to its unyielding aspects' (Gentile, 2008, p.549).

At first it was hard for Jenny to face the reality: as she tells the interviewer, 'it was almost like it weren't real,' but she started getting pains; her period did not come. This is an example of the intransigence of reality, what Gentile calls 'matter's unyielding in-itselfness' (2007, p.578). It also raises a question of how Jenny moved to a position of experiencing this as a reality – it is not unusual for young unintentionally pregnant women to 'not know' what is happening, even until the baby is born. Jenny does not reject the 'young girl' positioning: she does see herself as a young girl. She makes use of the category in understanding that she gets the support she needs: this is part of the contribution of her imaginative work when confronted with her reality. She puts it into words to the interviewer when, just after her son's first birthday, she reflects that it has been an advantage to be so young because she has had masses of support, whereas if she had been older, people would have expected her to manage on her own. She accepts a reality of being a young girl/young mother without accepting the negative positioning that accompanies it. This is an everyday example of agency.

I started by saying that I admired the way that Jenny faced a difficult reality. There is a connection between this and, as she told the interviewer 'I'm a person who thinks about things a lot.' Evidently this thinking includes admitting the difficulties to thought (not instantaneously, in this case). The connection between these two facets of Jenny lies in the processing of emotional experience. The link between processes involved in thinking and the idea of intermediate or transitional space is expressed in the following quote from a psychoanalyst in the object relations tradition, Christopher Bollas: 'real experience simultaneously slips beyond omnipotent fantasy and beyond a fixed is-what-it-is subjectivity and reality, creating an intermediate space that both enlivens our reality and gives reality to our life' (Bollas, 1992, p.265, cited in Gentile, 2007, p.574).

In these terms, Jenny opened out a transitional space for thinking, between desire and limit, in such a way that her imagination could help her to act on her circumstances and shape the reality of being a mother. Gentile coins the phrase 'transitional subject' for someone

'capable of imagining her/his own life... [who] not only defies the confines of purely material reality, but also is no longer strictly bound
to a purely repetitive psychical reality either' (2007, p.573). For my
purposes, this formulation not only provides a psycho-social basis for
thinking agency, but also helps to conceptualise the relation between
knowing and becoming in subjectivity.

Critical realism and agency

Margaret Archer, a critical realist sociologist, echoes Peirce's and Gentile's attention to reality's intransigence, 'the realist insists that what
is the case places limits upon how we can construe it' (Archer, 1998,
p.195), and goes on to contrast this with the social constructionist tradition that has been so influential in British qualitative social science[1]
(see Wengraf, 2013). I am interested not only in the limits imposed by
what is the case, but in the room they leave for agency. For Jenny, thinking about what was the case – that she was pregnant – was not a simple
matter of a logical thought process leading to an accepted fact. This is
where we need an emotional theory of thinking. For several days after
she got the test result and told her boyfriend, they did not talk about it
at all: he was not able to help her think about it, but rather the reverse.
His immediate reaction (before the avoidance that lasted several days)
was 'now I know I am fertile', as if the other meanings of this knowledge,
the difficult ones, could be banished and replaced by one about which
he could feel proud. It is through processes of thinking and avoiding
thinking (Bion designates these + K and – K), that psychological reality
gradually emerges. It is not about the cognitive analytic process of logical deduction, leading to the conclusion 'I am pregnant'; it is a different
kind of thinking, one that Bion insisted was a process of being changed
by an emotional experience that can be thought about. Being changed
by an emotional experience is central to Bion's distinction between two
kinds of knowing; it characterises 'knowing of', in contrast to 'knowing
about' which uses thinking 'to increase the learner's store of knowledge without producing any change in himself' (Spillius, 1988, p.157).
For example, after an early scan (before any of the adults knew), Jenny
decided, as she told the interviewer, 'I can't get rid of it now', in other
words she was changed by the experience: it was an event in the process
of becoming a mother.

Critical realism builds on the is-what-it-is-ness of reality in making
a distinction between intransitive and transitive objects. Intransitive
objects are 'those things which exist and act independently of our
description of them' (Bhaskar, 1998, p.198), for example, the baby grows

in Jenny's womb and if she did not want it, she would have to abort it. Wishing she had not made a mistake would be no use. I have given a psycho-social dimension to the concept of intransitivity by showing that not all external world facts can be easily thought about: whether they can be depends on the situation and how emotionally neutral or loaded they are, also the containment of other minds. The processing of emotional experience takes time because it changes the thinker. By the time she sees the second scan, at eight weeks (accompanied by her boyfriend's mother), Jenny seems able to think about both these realities and imaginatively perceives 'a little kiddy growing... so tiny but the heart is beating really fast': an encounter with the knowledge of having a baby that, in Winnicott's terms, above, was experienced creatively, imaginatively, in an 'intermediate area of experience to which inner reality and external life both contribute'.

Transitive objects, by contrast, are concept dependent (Bhaskar, 1998, p.198) and these can point in my analysis to the way that social construction and positioning are part of Jenny's challenge in thinking about her pregnancy. An example of a transitive object is Jenny as a 'young mother', where the combined facts of her age and her status as pregnant produce a socially loaded category that affects the way she is seen and to some extent, therefore, the way she feels about that status. The example of the receptionist at the health centre who gave her the test result over the phone, not knowing her age, demonstrates the category of young mother entering Jenny's thinking in the absence of current external positioning: 'I rang and she said oh yeah the test came back positive, and obviously she didn't know I was just some young girl, so she was just normal.' The unyielding materiality of her pregnant condition is shown to be overlaid by a powerful social construct: if the receptionist's reaction was 'just normal', what would it have been like if she had known Jenny's age? This social construction and the positions it affords contribute to the task that Jenny is faced with in coming to terms with a difficult reality: she imagines briefly the potentially judgemental voice of this woman had she known Jenny's status as 'just some young girl'. Here again we see the work of imagination encountering a reality (the phone call with the pregnancy test result) and resulting in thinking that involved the use of cultural understanding.

Positioning and imagination

The concept of positioning does useful work in theorising these examples: Jenny is positioned by her social worker as too young not to have an informed adult around and she positions herself as 'just some young girl' in relation to what the health centre receptionist did not know about her; she positions Julian as young (he is a few months younger than she is); and her parents, in whose home she continues to live, position her through continuing to expect and put into practice a parent–daughter relationship of authority. This does not mean, however, that internalisation of such discourses simply 'positions' Jenny in the sense of constructing her subjectivity, as positioning theory often argues or implies. There is insufficient dynamism or room for the subject's agency, for example, in the following classic statement of positioning theory: 'the constitutive force of each discursive practice lies in its provision of subject positions... once having taken up a particular position as one's own, a person *inevitably* sees the world from the vantage point of that position'? (Davies and Harré, 1990, p.46, my emphasis).

The process of taking up a particular position as one's own is far from simple. Even though this is now widely recognised in the critique of positioning theory and wider cultural inscription theories, it is rare to find the complexities of that take-up explored, except in object relations theory. For Enid Balint, for example, 'external reality can in any case only exist for the individual if it is introjected, identified with *and then imaginatively perceived*' (1993, p.95, my emphasis). Already three powerful concepts, differentiated, are put to use. Peter Redman uses Thomas Ogden's (1983) account of the dynamic 'movement through us' of external objects, which it is important to specify 'can be a person, thing, event or aspect of these' (Redman, 2009, p.58). 'Movement through us' is a phrase congruent with Redman's 'revisiting' of affect theory, with its emphasis on flow, with the intention of demonstrating the value of a psychoanalytically informed account of unconscious communication. The concept of identification is revealed to be complicated: the movement through us 'gives rise to two distinct entities' (ibid, p.59). The first is a component referring to the ego or self's experience of its relation to the object. The second 'refers to an aspect of the ego that has become "profoundly identified with an object representation"' (ibid, citing Ogden, 1983, p.234). 'In short, it is a part of the self that is experienced as if it is the object (or what it is imagined the object is like)' (Redman, 2009, p.59). Jenny's relation to her internal baby's heartbeat is a case in point and she is changed by it. The 'movement through' referred to by Ogden involves taking this externally generated raw experience inside (Balint's introjection), where the agency involved is not to reject, or project back out, and then the two-part identification, both within and outwith. If the emotional experience can be thought, then imaginative perception is achieved. This account does, however, posit an object locatable as external to begin with. Redman (2009) goes on to unfold the complex provenance of the external object in a flux of experience which is always making anew the past as that is constantly available for reworking. The individual is, in a sense, an origin of this made-anew object relation yet, in another sense, is just a nodal point in a larger network of affect flows.

In this way, the process of internalisation can leave room for agency. It is also radically trans-subjective, a theme I shall return to. Over time, Jenny imposes her desires within the limits of external reality. As Hans Loewald, like Winnicott, emphasised, 'the integration of reality is a dynamic process, forever unfinished, which we spend our lives elaborating and organising' (Loewald, 1980[1951], p.32). This focus in on the 'going on being' in changing circumstances and the provisional 'becoming' that these necessitate. Positioning requires a theorisation of how the present, past and future are linked in the act of meaning creation. Constructionism of all kinds misses 'the past's claims on present experience', 'that we are what we have been' and that we 'construct ourselves out of the materials at hand, including our bodies and their attributes' (Mitchell and Aron, 1999, p.xvi). It also misses the imagining of a different future, which is what protects us against passivity in the face of unwelcome realities. Jenny's relation to continuing her studies is a weighty example: it is something she promises her parents to continue, something to give her a passport out of the types of jobs she hates (such as telesales), something she gives up on account of Davy's illnesses, while Julian continues: in Gentile's words, part of reality's 'unyielding aspect'. Yet she cleaves to it as a future intention.

To summarise this argument: whereas material realities are intransitive, impervious to the meanings attached to them, social phenomena are concept dependent and mediated not simply by social beliefs, or positions in available discourses but through an ongoing process of imaginative internalisation. This heuristic distinction, while helpful, is more blurred in practice. Both intransitive and transitive objects can be more or less intractable in the course of actual encounters and both have real effects (perhaps that is why they are sometimes conflated). However, they have different implications for the work of imagination. It should be clear by now that a psycho-social approach to objects and subjects complicates any simple premise of a clear boundary between them. Informed by psychoanalytic object relations theory, it opens out an intermediate space – symbolic, transitional – where imagination and reality meet, where as a result meaning is made and agency is instantiated. The necessity of this encounter is a universal feature of human life, but how people confront the incessant challenges of making meaning out of reality depends on two things: their history of relationship to objects, which settles into patterned modes of organising experience while always making anew, and the character of the current conditions and relations that surround them, notably how tolerable or anxiety provoking these are. The actual conditions, social and material, are more or less tractable through the agency of the human subject, as we saw with Jenny, who applied her imagination not to deny or flout the actuality of her situation, but to act successfully upon it.

Psycho-social objectivity

In Western history, the creation of a clear-cut boundary between knower and known, subject and object, was a defining feature of the 17th century. Descartes' model of knowledge as detached, clear and certain epitomises this development and promised epistemic certainty of a kind that still underwrites scientific knowledge. In Descartes' view, 'subjectivity' proceeds from within the human being and is associated with 'false inner projections on the outer world of things'. It came to mean 'influences proceeding from "within" the human being – not supplied by the world outside the perceiver – which are capable of affecting how the world is perceived' (Bordo, 1987, pp.50 & 51).

Psychoanalysis has been used to identify the reasons for the hegemony of Cartesian objectivity, linking it to a 'flight from the feminine' (Bordo, 1987, p.105) and a conflation of woman and nature (Fox Keller, 1985) in the desire to predict and control which are at the heart of the scientific paradigm. For Bordo (1987, p.4), 'Cartesian anxiety discloses itself as anxiety over separation from the organic female universe, (...) rationalism a defensive response to it' in a desire to exorcise all the messier (bodily, emotional) dimensions of experience from knowledge and to institute certainty and clarity in its place – objectivity banishing subjectivity. Now, both in feminist philosophy and in the recent turn to affect in social science, there is broad agreement that the knower's relationship to emergent knowledge, if it is not to be stripped of life, needs to be characterised by feelings or affect: sympathy (Bordo, 1987) or passion: 'to "depassion" knowledge does not give us a more objective world, it just gives us a world "without us" and therefore without "them" ... a world "we don't care for"' (Despret, 2004, p.131). Of all topics, 'knowing mothers' is bound to take issue with this stand-off between subjectivity and objectivity.

My intention is to include embodied, emotional perturbations as part of a valid basis for knowing: objectivity through subjectivity, transcending both. I do not want to throw out the goal of objectivity, by which I mean a disinterested, trustworthy, fair and valid approach to evidence, with the bathwater of scientific objectivity or objectivism: along that route lies subjectivism where subjectivity is either reviled or uncritically reclaimed. Paul Stenner has drawn attention to the tendency in recent psycho-social theory to champion subjectivity, 'no doubt a reaction against the objectivist biases of mainstream experimental psychology which has long striven to guarantee scientificity by way of the expulsion of subjectivity from the midst of its procedures' (2008, p.91). As long as there is a binary relation between subjectivity and objectivity, the danger of engaging in false certainty remains with either.

   On the other side of the binary, a desirable objectivity becomes objectivism, which 'has totally falsified our conception of truth, by exalting what we can know and prove, while covering up with ambiguous utterances all that we know and cannot prove, even though the latter knowledge underlies, and must ultimately set its seal to, all that we can prove' (Polanyi, cited in Ghent, 1990, p.236). Polanyi called the latter kind of knowledge 'tacit knowledge', but I prefer 'unthought known', or uncognised knowing, because it brings with it a sophisticated and well-evidenced theoretical structure to inform a psycho-social agenda. Either way, this book pursues the possibility that uncognised knowledge – variously construed as the ineffable, embodied affect, emotional experience, scenic understanding, countertransference, enigmatic messages, projective identification, feel-knowing, intuition – although perhaps beyond scientific proof, is not beyond evidence or systematic methodological investigation. Most of these ideas have become thinkable through psychoanalysis, in which the mind is embodied, conscious intention never fully in control, and desires motivate; a paradigm which renders untenable the Enlightenment 'equation of mind and conscious thought or reason' (Henriques et al., 1998 [1984]). As a result, psychoanalysis is relatively free of the troublesome binaries that underpin social sciences: here notably objectivity/subjectivity, external/internal, body/mind, cognition/emotion, imagination/reality. This in my view is what makes psychoanalysis 'first and foremost an epistemology and a methodology' (Devereux, 1967, p.294).

In conclusion

Through the example of Jenny, I have tried to demonstrate the interwoven nature of 'becoming' and the kind of 'knowing' that is embodied, affective and the basis for transitional subjectivity. I showed the connection between Jenny being someone who thought about things a lot and her ability to shape her future and adapt to its intractable elements. I also used the example of Jenny's relation to being a 'young mother' to go beyond what I see as the continuing effects of an agency/determinism binary in theories of positioning. Critical realism draws distinctions between transitive and intransitive objects and I tried to show the value of this distinction in analysing Jenny's relation to the discovery of her pregnancy and the agency with which she acted on her circumstances over the course of her first year as a mother. Throughout this analysis, I kept in mind the question of objectivity, in the sense of how I aimed for a fair, trustworthy, disinterested account of Jenny, illustrated in a data analytic practice that reconceptualises objectivity through subjectivity.

Retaining the terms inside and outside is sometimes seen as an obstacle in our attempts not to privilege either the psychological or the social. Following Paul Hoggett, I associate the intermediate space with the hyphen in psycho-social:

> The hyphen in psycho-social signifies a difference that cannot be dissolved. (...) Individual/social dualism is not overcome by merging them, by making them simply a matter of perspective where, to quote Frosh and Baraitser, 'inside and outside flow together as one, and the choice of how we see them is purely tactical' [2008, p.349]. The hyphen signifies the transitional space, the space of overlap and interpenetration. In Winnicott's (1991, p.103) words, it connotes the link that both joins and separates, the place where things do not fit but should fit.
>
> (Hoggett, 2008, p.383)

I hope that my approach to analysing the experiences of becoming mothers goes beyond the binary in this way without throwing out the distinction between inner and outer.

In this chapter, I have begun a dialogue between object relations and affect theory which continues in the following chapter, where the idea of 'moving through us' is reconceptualised in Ettinger's concept of 'compassion', where in the context of matrixial theory's focus on prenatal relations, it has different implications for becoming and co-becoming.

Part II

Three Psycho-Social Perspectives on Knowing and Becoming: Psychoanalytically Informed Theorising in Mothers' and Researchers' Knowing

4
Weird Beyond Words: The Transgressive Corporeality of Pregnancy and Compassion-Based Ethics

Introduction

This book is in search of a way of knowing that is fitting for a psycho-social insight into the journey women make when they become mothers for the first time. In this chapter I describe a way of thinking about trans-subjective knowing and becoming that starts before birth, characterised by 'transgressive corporeality': the matrixial theory of Bracha Ettinger, artist, feminist and psychoanalyst. Of subjectivity, Ettinger writes, 'we are at the same time both one and several, on different trajectories' (Ettinger, 1996a, pp.152–153) and this feature of identity is embodied in pregnancy.

The central characteristic of birth is seen by psychoanalysis as separation, but Freud did wonder what preceded it and ventured that 'there is much more continuity between intra-uterine life and earliest infancy than the impressive caesura of the act of birth allows us to believe' (1926, p.138, cited in Grotstein, 2007, p.256). When addressed subsequently, this continuity has usually been approached from the point of view of the foetus, separating it off from the maternal experience, in which 'the mother is reduced to being the other of meaning, of individuation, and thus remains only body' (Pollock, 2008, p.11). Wilfred Bion was one of the few psychoanalysts to diverge from separation as a starting point (Meltzer, 1986); Harris Williams, 2010), as we see in his theorisation of normal, or communicative, projective identification (Chapter 5). Donald Winnicott also bucked the trend in his description of 'primary maternal preoccupation' in the perinatal period, emphasising continuity of connection across birth for both members of the 'nursing couple'. With psychoanalytic theorists like these, I had been getting closer to recognising the ineffable aspect of becoming a mother, but I was missing something still. I began to find a way of thinking about this 'missing something' when I came across the matrixial discourse of Bracha Ettinger.

Belatedly in the data analysis I noticed that I had paid very little attention to the prenatal data, all interview-based. I was reading Griselda Pollock's 'Mother Trouble',[1] and was struck by the implications of her argument that most psychoanalysis, including most object relations and relational psychoanalysis (major influences in my approach), start their inquiries at birth (Pollock, 2008, p.16). I realised that this might be the reason I had lacked a way into theorising women's prenatal experience that would illuminate my wider question about becoming. Although matrixial theory is about prenatal/pre-maternal life when distinctions between the foetus and the pregnant woman as separate units are misleading, the continuity of pregnant into postnatal experience is of central significance. Matrixial theory creates a new language that transcends the logic of separation, notably in the idea of trans-subjectivity originating in the language-defying state prior to birth, a state of neither two nor one, in which 'the transgressive corporeality of pregnancy' starts 'a psychic and mental transgression of the boundaries of unicity of being' (Ettinger, 2006b, p.104). In this light, I decided to look specifically at data relevant to the period of late pregnancy, birth and the first few weeks beyond, the period covered by Winnicott's label 'primary maternal preoccupation' (see Hollway, 2012b, for a detailed reading). Was I now going to find traces of extra-discursive matrixial experience in what women told us about their pregnancies?

What is 'weird'?

Rereading the antenatal interviews as a group, I noticed the frequency with which the word 'weird' cropped up. Justine expressed the experience of many in one sentence: 'I can't explain, it's like weird knowing that you've got a life growing inside of you and you can feel the life every day.' 'Weird' references the ineffable here, Ettinger's 'transgressive corporeality'; it points to the extent that pregnancy cannot be expressed adequately in language and consequently it is hard to understand. For my purposes, it is significant that the most common context for its use was to talk about the experience of a life beyond the women's own, inside their bodies. These comments were often, but not always, in response to questions about the first time they felt the baby move and the occasion of seeing their scans. There were other phrases from research participants that conveyed to me something ineffable. For example, pregnant Becky said 'when you feel it moving it's like (long pause) *warms your heart* and you think oh my god it's my, that's my baby sort of thing'. Justine's 'I can't explain' is echoed in Becky's long hesitation as she searches for words with which to communicate her experience.

Let me contextualise Becky's phrase 'it warms your heart'. In response to the first interview question 'Can you tell me the story of your pregnancy so far? How has it been?' Becky replies 'Yeah, it's been (.) nice, been weird [...] like having something inside you, it's just (.) such a weird feeling but (.) really overwhelming.' She then elaborates by contrasting her own feelings about this with imagined others who 'ain't maternal'. 'But when you want a baby, really want a baby, you're really happy about it (.) when you feel it moving it's like (2) *warms your heart* [her emphasis] and you think oh my god that's my baby.' Becky then puts her wanting this baby in the context of a 'devastating' recent miscarriage. Neither pregnancy was planned. Her use of the bodily, sensory metaphor 'warms your heart' to describe the emotional experience connected with feeling maternal comes after many pauses during which she finds the word 'weird' and then, closely linked, 'overwhelming'.

Ettinger transforms the idea of pregnancy. Instead of seeing birth (in French, 'naissance') as the originary event, Ettinger takes the idea of naissance, and in her characteristically playful-creative way with language, uses the word 'co-(n)naissance' (knowledge) to explore the idea that in matrixial (prenatal/pre-maternal) life, mother and child-to-be are in process of being co-born throughout pregnancy, which she defines as 'being alive in creating life' (2006b, p.101). This initiates profound continuities that survive the separation of birth.

According to matrixial theory, pregnancy creates 'openness to fragilizing self-relinquishment' (Ettinger, 2006b, p.105). Browsing in a 1968 newspaper magazine supplement, in a feature headed 'The Psychology of Motherhood', I noted accounts from two mothers recalling experiences from their pregnancies that illustrate the ethical demand of being first and foremost responsible for another: 'I was in a car the other day, going very fast – someone else was driving – and I got extremely angry and told him to slow down. He said "why are you getting like this? You never used to bother." I said, "I wasn't carrying a baby then." ' The second account: 'You have a double responsibility. You must be careful on crossroads, and drive more slowly. And if one day you drive at your normal speed, you feel guilty about it.'

I remember feeling an unfamiliar vulnerability after my daughter was born: perhaps I was driving a car with her inside, or crossing the road (or both). This helps to explain why I notice examples of others citing just such occasions (they are frequent and unsolicited). Theoretically speaking, I was no longer that apparently autonomous subject, free to make unbridled choices with few fears (or perhaps well-managed fears) about a life that felt under my control. In matrixial speak, my trans-subjective stratum, previously foreclosed, was reactivated. The point is not whether this was illusory or real, rather that being responsible for a life that I had created changed me: another life now mattered as much or more than my own. Actually that is to talk in 'phallic' terms; let me rephrase: my life was no longer possible to treat separately from the life of my baby, so the vulnerability of either was the vulnerability of both.

Decades later (following considerable changes in Western gender relations and greater conflicts around autonomy and maternal connectedness, see Chapters 7 and 8, Charlotte recounts having a bleed when a few weeks pregnant and fearing that she would lose her baby.

> I felt very uncomfortable doing anything really very physical. I went back to work, took – I did take a few days off, but went back to work, but up until that point I'd just carried on as normal and then from that point I felt very much as if I had something very precious that I had to protect.

Another's life interfacing one's live body is an experience that falls outside the paradigms of Western discourse. Yet the experience is universal, if we accept that certain forms of experience (what Ettinger calls 'feeling knowing') pre-exist birth: it belongs not just to pregnant women but to everyone, from being in a woman's womb.

Becky distinguished herself as someone who really wanted a baby, implying that other pregnant women would feel different. Sarah might be one such, describing herself and her partner as being 'not the type that goes all gooey after kids'. Nonetheless, Sarah says 'seeing it on the scan and feeling it at the same time, that was really weird'. Part of her puzzlement is that these feelings are uncharacteristic: She tells the interviewer of how earlier that day she was trying to make sense of her experiences of the baby inside her womb, with the midwife telling her how the baby was lying inside her:

> all I can feel is, I know where the legs are, the legs are here. Because I can feel it moving here and I can feel the bum here as well [...] and

the head is there. I still haven't figured it out, I need to sit down and think of it.

Sarah then contextualises the weirdness and excitement by commenting 'I'm usually quite blasé about it, most of the time I forget I'm pregnant.' Sarah's wish to sit down and figure out her baby's position in her belly seemed to me to express her more general wish to master experiences through understanding (this fitted with a consistent pattern visible throughout her data).

Sarah used the word 'weird' after the baby's birth too: 'it's a bit weird the whole fact that I'm, my body's producing food for the baby'. Her body continues to provide the means of life, latterly for infant not foetus. Sarah hesitates in finding a subject for this act, changing from 'I' to 'my body', an example of Julia Kristeva's 'it happens, but I am not there' (1975, p.301, cited in Baraitser, 2009, p.102). This suggests that 'I' didn't feel right, perhaps because it would refer to the conscious intentional agent that feels like her habitual (pre-pregnant) self, the one who is blasé and forgets she is pregnant. Her body is not 'I' in this usage; the provision of food is independent of her conscious agency, which feels weird. Imogen Tyler makes sense of this theoretically:

> the pregnant subject defies the logic of classic ontology (...) it cannot be contained within forms of being constrained by singularity and is at odds with familiar models of self-other relation – there is an impasse between the 'I' that writes/speaks and pregnant subjectivity, which is the exact antithesis of that I's implied individuality.
>
> (Tyler, 2000, p.292)

Sarah's hesitations over the subject of her sentence point to how inadequate classic ontology is, leaving her with a sense of weirdness or ineffability faced with the uncertain location of her self in mind or/and body. We see in this one of the forces of change with which she is faced and needs to think about. For Julia Kristeva, we are 'the first civilization to lack a discourse on the meaning and complexity of motherhood'. She thus proposes a discourse on maternal passion (cited in Pollock, 2008, p.15).

Sarah's first outing with the baby felt 'really weird, really weird because I, your know he's with me, he a small thing protective over him, protective, cold it was cold, is he going to be OK'. Her language breaks down, as if she is directly re-experiencing how she felt at the time, scarcely able to impose a symbolic structure on the raw, albeit remembered, emotional experience. Her overwhelming experience of responsibility for this dependent new life meant, for example, watching every step, because 'what happens if I fall over' [carrying the baby]. When Sarah looked back at the 'baby blues', in an interview when her baby was about five months old, she remembers crying because the shower went cold when a tap was turned on elsewhere in the flat. She links this to her relief to 'get back to normal' (identified as when she stopped breastfeeding) when 'everything's much more in control', making it clear how unhappy she was in a state where she felt her emotions were unreasonable and overwhelming. This state is an example of Ettinger's concept of fragilisation and suggests why such states of mind threaten the self.

Phallic logic and the matrixial feminine

' "I" am not "I", I AM not, I am not ONE'
(Irigaray, cited in Tyler, 2000, p.288)

Thinking about the weirdness of such experiences, I initially found it impossible to find the right word for this relation of transgressive corporeality: 'connected' still assumes two, like Raphael-Leff's (1991, p.397) formulation 'two persons under one skin', which I do not find quite accurate in respect of the status of the unborn foetus. The situation is asymmetrical and neither two nor one. Lisa Baraitser calls it 'a new subjective category, the condition of being both singular and plural simultaneously' (2009, p.45). What Ettinger accomplishes in the statement 'at the same time both one and several on different trajectories' goes further in two ways: first, 'severality' does particular theoretical work and goes beyond the notion of two separate unitary entities, a notion that still finds echoes in the concepts of intersubjectivity and relationality; second the idea of different trajectories contains both the principle of continuing movement and the non-substitutability of oneness and severality. It also suggests that dynamic conflict will be the ordinary basis of living. It is worth quoting Pollock at length here:

> The very logic of the prematernal/prenatal as a co-affecting, asymmetrical, repeating, and poietic severality appears bizarre, mystical and unthinkable within systems of language that are premised on the thetic rupture that creates the subject only through a dramatic break dividing the monadic subject from confusion with the archaic mother. Here the journey into subjectivity is achieved only by means

of separations (birth, weaning from the breast, the voice, the gaze, the body of the mother) and then the symbolic cut (castration) which retrospectively catches up and redefines all preceding separations into its dominating logics of on/off, presence/absence. The modelling of subjectivity and sexual difference in many psychoanalytical traditions has been intricately linked by a shared phallic logic: to become a sexed subject is to be severed from the maternal in the real (birth), in the imaginary, and by the signifier. The maternal is reduced to being the other of meaning, of individuation, and thus remains only body.

(Pollock, 2008, p.1)

So what alternative to phallic logic does matrixial theory provide, given my interest in finding a language that can express that condition beyond one and two? 'Matrix' refers to 'a primordial encounter of the mutual but different, co-affecting but pre-maternal/prenatal severality' (Pollock, 2008, p.4). It is also 'a zone of encounter between the most intimate and the most distanced unknown' (Ettinger, 1993a, p.12). The idea of 'trans-subjective' goes beyond 'intersubjective' and 'relational', which still posit two entities and as such remain inside a phallic, binary logic that is a logic of substitution, based on on/off, +/−, present/absent, subject/other, masculine/feminine.

Phallic logic is no accident: men are likely to find it difficult to think openly about the procreative power of women that spells their own lack. Freud's 'penis envy' is plausibly seen as a defence against what Karen Horney (1967) saw as 'womb envy'. By this she meant a more general envy by men of women's reproductive capacity: 'the intensity of this envy [in her male analysands] of pregnancy, childbirth and motherhood, as well as of breasts and of the act of suckling' (Horney, 1967, pp.60–61). For Ettinger, however, any feminist tendency to substitute a female organ for a male one (womb envy for penis envy) does not escape the stranglehold of phallic logic nor the way that the biology of sexual difference has been imprisoned in that logic. I return to these themes in Chapter 7. For now, I can summarise by saying that if and when women procreate, their experiences push at the boundaries of available language, as we saw in the resort to a word like 'weird'. Like Sarah, their bodies become particularly salient extra-discursive holders of raw emotional experiences that are likely to be denied recognition through symbolisation. Some women, depending on their prior identity formation, are more thrown by this than others: Becky was joyful about it.

As we have seen, the characterisation of matrixiality puts pressure on available language 'as Bracha Ettinger bends and realigns words to capture concepts, processes, in-between conditions and returns' (Pollock, 2004, p.48). As regards the intrauterine condition – and importantly the potential that it lays down for later – matrixial phrases capture the dynamic severality of relations: 'joint eventing', the meeting between 'the co-emerging-I and unknown-I' (p.25), 'jointness in separateness' (p.9), borderspaces that are subject to 'a perpetual retuning and rehoning... never stabilized as a cut, split or division' (p.33). Subjectivity in this stratum is an ongoing encounter. Ettinger uses the term metramorphosis for this

> process of change in borderlines and thresholds between being and absence, memory and oblivion, I and non-I, a process of transgression and fading away. Through this process the limits, borderlines, and thresholds conceived are constantly transgressed or dissolved, thus allowing the creation of new ones.
>
> (Ettinger, 1992, p.201)

Metramorphosis is characterised by transmissibility and relating without relations (Pollock, 2004, p.32). The concept of com-passion – feeling with – is grounded in Ettinger's imagined physics of matrixial space: 'forget wombs insides and organs. Think instead of traces, vibrations and resonances, registered sonic and tactile intimations of othernesses, sharing spaces but never fusing, encountering but never dissolving their boundaries, jointly eventing without ever knowing fully the other's event' (Pollock, 2008, p.14). This trans-subjectivity is the original territory of maternal co-becoming. It is also ground for an originary ethics based in com-passion.

Matrixial ethics

Ettinger's ethics is encapsulated in her claim that 'becoming responsible for traces of the other as if they were mine is a matrixial ethical move' (Ettinger, 2006a, p.221). Her approach benefits from a tradition of feminist thinking in which a fundamental critique of masculinist and rationalistic approaches has been coupled with inquiry into the relationships among ethics, care and the maternal (see Hollway, 2006, Chapter 1). By the end of the 1980s, a decade of writing on the ethics of care ground to a halt, stuck in a seemingly insoluble cluster of problems concerning its feminine gendering: whether women's or mothers' care was enhanced by their connectedness to others or whether it led to a failure to recognise and therefore respect the other's difference; whether autonomy and separateness (figured in binary relation to connectedness and relatedness) are a necessary basis for care ethics and emphasis on women's connectedness a concession to the idea of women's passivity. Jessica Benjamin's (1995) feminist use of relational psychoanalysis furnished an account of maternal care not as symbiotic and unseparated, nor as passive and exploitable, but rather, based on subject–subject relations that recognised the other's difference. Mothers could subsequently be celebrated as 'subjects in their own right'.

However, Ettinger's matrixial idea, 'contravenes the long held psychoanalytic tenet that holds that the realm of the psychic is only initiated by birth, by separation of the child from the mother's body, and that the prenatal or intrauterine is therefore, by definition the field of biology, outside and beyond psychoanalysis' (Pollock, 2008, p.16). So for matrixial thinking, the infant is already com-passionate, literally 'feels-with', starting in the matrixial intrauterine space characterised by metramorphosis, a 'co-(n)naissance – a transformational knowledge of being born together with the other whereby each individual becomes sub-subject in subjectivity that surpasses her personal limits and whereby another might become (...) an occasion for transformation' (Ettinger, 2006a, pp.221–222). This is the sort of co-becoming that I have in mind, which re-emerges with motherhood, but also exceeds the bounds of the mother–child relationship. It is to adult ethical subjectivity that I now turn, with the eventual goal of considering how its matrixial theorisation relates to researcher ethics.

In the realm of ethical philosophy, Emmanuel Levinas cut through assumptions about the learning of ethical conduct by 'my attempt to situate the unicity of being, the power to say "I", in the responsibility for the other – that is the heart of my philosophy' (Levinas with Ettinger, 1993/2006). In other words 'subjectivity is not for itself; it is (...) initially for another' (Levinas, 1985, p.97). The call of the other presents itself as a demand which is an absolute responsibility, so that 'we are for the Other before we are even a self who can be for ourselves' (Baraitser, 2009, p.31). Levinas' idea of the 'Face' represents this infinite responsibility for the other and the 'order of the face' is part of being human (Levinas with Ettinger, 1993/2006, p.139). In the phrase 'Otherwise than being', Levinas situates this demand of and response to the other 'before and beyond meaning, consciousness or any notion we could term "I" ' (Baraitser, 2009, pp.36–37).

Despite her critique of Levinasian ethics, Ettinger starts with this tenet of primary ethical responsibility in her matrixial ethics (which is a proto ethics in the sense that it describes what is prior to selfhood and symbolisation). She tells Levinas 'you restore to woman that which was taken away from her: a certain symbolic principle of creation, an ethical space' (Levinas with Ettinger, 1993/2006, p.143). She is referring to Levinas's use of 'woman' to represent the subject who puts the other first, woman being 'that human possibility which consists in saying that the life of another human being is more important than my own, (...) that the other counts before I do' (op cit. p.142).

Although it appears to approach a matrixial account of maternal 'feeling with', Levinas's notion of alterity denotes an absolute kind of otherness, a radically separate other. In contrast to the relational approaches favoured by much feminist thinking, for him relations are characterised by a set of negative characteristics based on the assumption of an autonomous subject to whom the other's demand is a burden.[2] This emphasis makes salient the ancient meaning of care as burden – highly relevant, of course, to maternal becoming.

In the Levinasian view, subjects are not primarily connected in passion or love, nor pleasure, nor mutuality. Kristeva comments of Levinas that there is no concept of mingling as communion, no understanding of the joys of fluidity (cited in Alford, 2002, p.71). Levinas explicitly uses the figure of the mother to describe the infinite burdensome responsibility of care for the other, but because of the absolute alterity of the other, the absence of trans-subjective feeling, the burden is not mitigated by the pleasure. It is this version of alterity that Ettinger transforms by depicting the feminine ethical space as a radically trans-subjective one in which primary compassion precedes the emergence of subjectivity. 'The not-yet subject-I that is yet to appear is not in absolute alterity to the m/other-I'; far from being Other, the infant is as yet 'presubject, partial subject and non-I in transgressive shareability', it is 'an almost-other, borderlinked in encounter with an I' (Ettinger, 2006b, p.104). This provides 'the psychic unconscious basis of what for Levinas is a conscious obligation' (Ettinger, 2006b, p.124). Whereas Levinasian ethics refers to a conscious subject in face-to-face relating, in matrixial theory this relation is preceded and undergirded, but not replaced, by

a psychic and mental transgression of the boundaries of the unicity of being starting from the *transgressive corporeality of pregnancy*...in-formed by the feminine maternal presubjective compassion. This matrixial sphere is *supplementary* to the phallic arena both in the psychic domain of the unconscious and in the ethical domain inasmuch as trans-subjectivity traverses each subject and permeates it, and presubjectivity doesn't disappear when the subject appears'.

(Ettinger, 2006b, pp.104–105, original emphasis)

My dual focus – on researchers' and mothers' knowing – means that I need to trace what happens after birth, when the phallic trajectory develops. Ettinger emphasises two principles in this regard; first that neither trajectory ever substitutes for the other (they coexist, on different registers) and, second, that there is variability in the extent to which one or other is to the fore. As the above quotation makes clear, compassion ('feeling with') is central because trans-subjectivity traverses and permeates every subject. A phallic gaze (based on separation) produces the other as object. A 'matrixial gaze does not "replace" the phallic gaze but aids in its moving aside from its destructive aspects...a life long unending process' (Ettinger, 2006b, p.111).

In the I's compassionate position toward a non-I on the sub-subjective level, there is no self sacrifice, no masochism, no understanding of the non-I, not justification for the non-I, not even forgiveness or thankfulness and no blame, since the primary compassion is before and beyond them all.

(Ettinger, 2006b, p.123)

This helps me put into language what many mothers struggle to verbalise about the quality of their relationship with their child(ren). The way matrixial language enables us to transcend all that emanates from elevating the principle of separation into an exclusive worldview is, in my view, its great value. This is the radical legacy of the concept of com-passion, used as an ethical principle. Because of its rejection of the logic of substitution, the idea of an originary trans-subjective stratum does not replace a separate (phallic) stratum after birth, just as separation does not erase trans-subjective experience. They remain separate trajectories, where life's experiences can powerfully foreclose – and also powerfully reopen – trans-subjectivity and its correlate fragilisation. This is where the implications on situated adult subjectivities can be taken up, for both maternal and researcher subjectivity.

If compassion is foreclosed, for all, as a result of 'the risk of vulnerability' it carries (Ettinger, 2006b, p.115), nonetheless, opening the matrixial stratum is different for men and women: 'the matrixial cluster that can't normally be entirely lost for women, but from which adult masculinity is more radically split' (1997, p.388). And again, 'from the angle of male sexuality, the matrixial stratum must be foreclosed (...) from the side of female sexuality (...) it should remain accessible to her as a *potential* mother-to-be' (Ettinger, 1997, p.387). Self-fragilisation is entailed in ethical relations beyond the maternal: 'as long as the subject fragilizes itself to allow an encounter of the feminine matrixial kind... [in which] the I contacts the vulnerability in the other, neighbour and stranger' (Ettinger, 2010, p.2).

Jenny's com-passion

To help make these rather verbose theoretical claims come alive, I shall consider an example from Jenny. When her son was nine months old, after several weeks break over Christmas, the observer, Ferelyth Watt, records the following sequence in her notes:

> I asked Jenny how she felt now, nine months on. She told me that she felt 'good really'. She described feeling a bit tired sometimes 'but you get used to it.' She described finding it really hard now to hear or see anything about children who were being hurt or in difficulty. 'I used to feel sorry for them but not in a way that was difficult. It didn't really mean so much to me. Now, even if I'm watching a programme about animals and something happens to a baby animal; I feel like crying.' Jenny continues by telling about a recent event with a close friend of hers who had just had her baby. Jenny had visited her in hospital and when the baby had begun to cry and wasn't soothed by the mum. Jenny had felt a tremendous urge to take the baby and hold him. She said that she 'knew she couldn't because I wasn't his mum, but I really wanted to'. It was situations like this that now touched her in a way that they hadn't before. She said, 'That was unexpected, you don't know that before you have children.' She says whenever she sees a child in distress of any kind, she just thinks of Davy and can't bear it.

There are several ethically significant features of this account, which starts with a reflection on an ethical state easy to recognise as compassion ('finding it really hard' to encounter 'children being hurt or in difficulty'). This feeling-with, which makes her want to cry, extends beyond human babies. She is quite clear about this being new and describes her prior, less compassionate, state as one in which an other's hurt or difficulty did not *mean* so much to her. I stress her use of mean, because it illustrates the way that a new access to an emotional state enhances or amplifies the prior, more separated, meaning, but it is now more difficult. An example comes to Jenny's mind, her being with a young baby who is not being consoled by his mother. The 'tremendous urge' she feels to give help resembles Levinas' insistence on Face: faced with the call of the other (the distressed baby). Jenny experiences it as a demand that presents as an absolute responsibility in the face of the Other's distress. If this makes sense of the tremendous urge, it does not address Jenny's reason for not picking up and trying to console the baby: she is not his Mum. At this point an ethical conflict appears, because she must not override the baby's mother's responsibility for the baby. The tremendous urge suggests com-passion for, feeling with, the baby. Holding back involves some identification with the new mother (a position she was in nine months before). After telling the observer about that encounter, she draws the conclusion, reiterating that this has changed since she had her baby and that any child in distress reminds her of her own son and sets off the same feelings; feelings that I am calling compassion.

Jenny's account of her ethical transformation seems to me a good example of Ettinger placing maternal compassion at the centre of ethics. It also fits with her definition of wit(h)nessing as 'witnessing while resonating with an Other in a trans-subjective encounter-event' (Ettinger, 2006a, p.220): Jenny is moved by – transformed by – the crying baby's affective communication. What about Ettinger's claim that compassion is accompanied by fragilisation, occasioned by the reassertion of the trans-subjective stratum over individualised boundaries? Jenny used to feel sorry for others, but 'not in a way that was difficult', so there is something difficult about the experience of compassion now. It extends to other vulnerable people too: in her telesales job over the summer break, 'Jenny feels sorry for the people she phones up, especially if they are elderly and have not got the thought of a new kitchen, with all the upheaval involved. "I want to tell them it's OK and not to worry" ' (observation note). The observer later notes Jenny repeating how she hates selling people things they don't want. She quits the job before long.

For Ettinger, it is the vulnerability of compassion that prompts foreclosure of the trans-subjective stratum available to all prior to birth and still alive in infancy. This is where Ettinger's concept of 'fragilisation' does important work in her ethical perspective. Matrixial coemergence and the transgressive nature of compassion (the fact that it transgresses the boundaries of the individual) require 'self relinquishment and fragilization' which makes it 'potentially traumatising' (Ettinger, 2006a, p.219).

Earlier in the chapter, I quoted Sarah saying that she was relieved to be 'back in control', after the fragilisation she experienced during the early weeks after her baby's birth, and to some extent during pregnancy (when she implied that she had gone 'gooey'). Winnicott observed that, after the first few weeks, most women experienced a recovery from the 'almost illness' of primary maternal preoccupation. The mother recovers 'as the infant releases her' (Winnicott, 1956, p.302). However it seems, for example from Jenny's account, that aspects of fragilisation continued, if not in such an overwhelming form. A theme that matrixial theory offers for analysing the project data is therefore how women experience the ongoing conflictual dynamics between the matrixial trans-subjective and the phallic separate strata of subjectivity.

Research ethics

Selma Sevenhuijsen (1998) argued that research practices need to be rethought based on an ethic of care. Ettinger bases 'herethics'[3] on the indeterminacy of subject and object in pregnancy that I have detailed above (Baraitser, 2008, p.102); here, I want to follow matrixial theory into research methodology, coupling com-passion with Bion's principle of abstaining from certainty and from the kind of knowing that is driven by satisfying the knower's need for closure and order. These together form the basis of an alternative, or supplementary, research ethics. They can be applied to every aspect of the research but are never completed, nor are the inherent contradictions ever fully resolved. Most particularly, of course, it applies to relations of researchers to their participants, both face to face and also through data analysis and writing, but it is relevant to the whole research field: the conflicts of interest, considerations for colleagues, how the research topic is represented in public arenas. In the following example I examine in detail successive encounters with a research participant, Rabiya, starting with a potential conflict of interest in gaining consent.

A participant's consent to participate is only a clear-cut, closed matter if it is construed as a tick-box procedure culminating in a signature. A psychoanalytically informed ontology, based on the idea that dynamic unconscious conflict is an ordinary part of psychic life, enables us to recognise participants' and researchers' ambivalence. My field note in relation to Rabiya began as follows:

Rabiya is our last interviewee recruit and it feels important to hang on to her. However, when I phoned, she knew little about the project and said that she didn't think she wanted to take part if the interview was to be audio recorded. I continued to talk and we arranged to meet to give her information about the research.

The defining characteristic of *reflective* field notes is to record the meaning of the encounter, replete with its emotional significance, as experienced by the researcher. Note here a key principle of my approach to both meaning and ethics: that they are to be found through recognising and using the emotional experience that accompanies all relationships, carrying in it the significance of the reality of the situation, for example here the fact that Rabiya is our last recruit and it feels important not to lose her from the sample. This entails what I call ordinary conflict, in this case the conflict between wanting her in the sample and accepting the reality that she might decide not to participate. Meanwhile I lived in uncertainty.

According to Bion (1962a), if the frustration of uncertainty cannot be tolerated – for example if I had not tolerated thinking about the possibility of her withdrawing from the sample – then further thinking cannot happen. This would have communicated itself in the conversation, probably conveying to Rabiya that there was no space between us to think about how she could participate in a way that felt right for her. Actually, I was attracted by a different solution: by this time I was familiar with observers' exemplary detail and fidelity in their observation note-taking and was interested to try working without an audio record:

> There is no guarantee that she will agree to being recorded. If not, I will interview her and make notes immediately after. On the phone, when she'd agreed to meet me, I asked if I could bring the recorder or if I should come without, use the meeting to tell her more about the research, and return another time if she agreed. This was near the end of the call and she was decisive by then that I should bring it. There had already been a change in her feelings about the research during the call.

In what sense was the decision 'ethical' and how might we understand this claim as a dynamic feature of the phone encounter and what followed? Partly because I was interested in the idea of not using a recorder, I provided a genuine option which appeared to open out a space for

Rabiya to (re)consider its use. I also did this to protect her from pressure she might feel to change her mind if, by bringing it, it would seem as if I was still intending to persuade her to use it. I picked up the change in her feelings about this, as well as the change in emphasis of the outcome. The word 'decisive' conveys the settled quality of her interim decision that I could bring the recorder. At the end of the field note, covering three phone conversations, the theme of trust reappeared:

> Rabiya has a strong, quite low voice (...). There's something very open and trustworthy about her and I think that the negotiation of trust has been a strong theme in our phone conversations.

The recruitment took a further turn when, on the train to go and meet her for this further discussion, I received a text to say that she was in hospital and had just given birth: 'sorry for the incom...' the text trailed off and I felt a surge of guilt at the idea that she had taken the trouble to text me in the midst of such an important and demanding event. But what would it mean for our arrangements? Whatever the importance of ensuring she was joining the sample, I held off contacting her for two weeks, although she was often in my mind. When I phoned, to my dismay she was in the middle of getting the baby to sleep and sounded drowsy herself. I asked her when would be convenient to phone again. When I did 'I was relieved she'd picked up'. During this conversation I noticed that her earlier preference for not meeting in her home no longer figured. When she said that she wasn't going out yet, I asked her if this was a problem for arranging the meeting and she said it was not. I started to tell her about the research on the phone and she appeared increasingly interested. On hearing that there were only three interviews in all, she seemed relieved.

From doubts that manifest themselves in several considerations (venue, frequency and recording) towards the end of that conversation, I concluded (field note) that

> her ambivalence seemed in the end to be located in the tape recorder: yes to the interview, no to the tape-recorder. I guess I could have got over her hesitancy but [I said] I would like to interview her anyway [and that] I'd want to take notes afterwards. She said I could take them during and I said I'd probably prefer not to because taking notes made it difficult to focus on listening. That seemed fine with her – she understood that.

Once we had reached a clear agreement, she introduced a new note into the phone conversation:

> she told me about the two nights the baby had not slept and said she supposed that wasn't bad, out of two weeks. She also told me that she was breastfeeding and that, like that morning trying to get him to sleep, all he wanted to do was feed. It sounded as if he was constantly at the breast. I think I must have felt positioned as an expert on infant care because I remember casting around for what to reply. I said something which felt lame like 'at least she had the breast there to give him' – I then wondered if that mis-recognised her experience – evidence of his demands.

Here again I was documenting my feelings in response to our conversation. Her spontaneously telling me about the sleepless nights and the constant breastfeeding suggests that she wanted to tell someone, to share what was a difficult experience, and that once enough trust had been established, she could use me – and her participation in the research – in this way, even in advance of our first interview meeting. The uncertainty I felt in response is expressed in the above note: did I behave as an expert? Did my response rise to the requirement (lame)? In my comment, did I underestimate the demands on her?

Making the ineffable empirical? An experiment lacking an outcome

'daring to allow the unbidden'

(Oeser, 2010, p.9)

Given my commitments to empirical research, I have faced something of a contradiction: documenting and analysing what partially evades discourse.[4] By this time, the fieldwork was finished, so the challenge was in the data analysis. Paying attention to what felt weird in the prenatal interview data was fruitful but – given my critique of the limits of interview talk and my interest in a psychoanalytic epistemology, where should I take my data analytic methodology to address the ineffable features of becoming a mother? According to psychoanalysis, dream material goes beyond what is consciously known. In interviews we sometimes asked about participants' dreams, but I am uncomfortable with interpreting dreams outside the clinical setting, given how idiosyncratic their meanings are.

Thanks to its emergence within psychosocial studies, I encountered the method of social dreaming, based on the same Bionian principles that prioritise uncognised knowing (Chapter 5). Bion saw dreaming and reverie (sleeping and waking dreaming) as the precursors of thought (departing from a Freudian view of the repressed unconscious). Social dreaming, different from individual dreaming, is produced through the organisation of what Gordon Lawrence (the inventor of social dreaming) calls the social dreaming matrix (SDM), a gathering of people who come together to recount their dreams and share their associations to them. The choice of the term 'matrix' (not directly connected with matrixial theory) is 'being used in its basic sense – a place out of which something grows – and refers to the emotions and feelings, both conscious and unconscious, that are present below the surface in any social gathering' (Lawrence, 2010, p.2). In this context, individual meanings of dreams tend to get filtered out. Lawrence and Biran describe the difference between social and individual dreaming as follows:

> Whereas Individual, Therapeutic Dreaming has the Dreamer as the focus of attention, follows an egocentric path by concentrating on issues of self knowledge, by dramatizing the personal biography and occurs *within* the clinical situation, Social Dreaming follows a different orientation. It focuses on the dream by holding a socio-centric view-point. It is knowledge of the environment that is important, as individuals face the tragedy, and comedy, of being. This is *outside* the clinical situation.
>
> (Lawrence and Biran, 2002, p.224, cited in Lawrence, 2010, p.3)

Having attended four SDMs, with different configurations of participants, I was amazed by the relevance of what emerged in dream metaphors about the 'temporary system' that participants experience in common through the matrix. I became interested to explore its potential as a method for analysing my project data and organised a social dreaming weekend workshop of 15 participants, led by Gordon Lawrence, consisting largely of psycho-social researchers with experience of, or at least an interest in, social dreaming.

Initially I expected to use a single-case extract, chosen from interview data concerning the perinatal period, but realised that the social focus of the method suggested a use of data that went beyond individual cases. Eventually I compiled a 20-minute audio recording consisting of 11 of the women's voices. The extract from Becky, featured early in this chapter ('it warms your heart...'), was the inspiration for my compilation and the first voice, affectful and commonplace at the same time.

When playing the recording to social dreaming participants, I provided no information about the participants, who were not given names: this helped move away from individual experience (the voices were digitally anonymised to add a level of confidentiality). Additionally the time gap between one woman's voice and another was only two seconds, so the sequence had a dream-like quality, hard to follow for a listener seeking a coherent narrative that can be organised and made knowable through conceptual categories. Julian Manley (one of the participants) describes this terrain as 'on the edge' and in this way the mothers' voices were consistent with social dreaming:

> Because the language of communication in the social dreaming matrix is that of dream, the participants do not experience understanding in 'normal language' mode, as they would during a debate or discussion, for example. Instead, meaning in social dreaming seems to be embedded in a collage of images that seem, in turn, to be laden with feelings and emotions.

> (Manley, 2010, p.1)

After Friday evening arrival and dinner, workshop members convened for a short introduction to the aims of the workshop and then listened to the audio recording, afterwards dispersing for the night. The following morning the first session was conducted in the standard way for a SDM, led by Gordon Lawrence, with no reference made to the data from the previous evening. The opening question is always the same: 'what is the first dream'? This formulation, and the arrangement of seats in a snowflake pattern (not all facing each other as if in a group), is intended to be 'a physical statement of the different container structured for Social Dreaming (...) One dream is offered, perhaps another, and then another. Then free associations begin to follow' (Lawrence, 2010, p.3). A note-taker was appointed for each session.

My intention was to produce a psycho-social form of data analysis, based on this psychoanalytically informed method of eliciting uncognised knowing, accessible for further analysis. Unfortunately I do not have a product to offer here. To date, the kinds of analysis that exist within this method seem to me to be too far outside my expertise and research formation to find a place in this account, or possibly too far outside social science research method. My own dream that Friday night might cast light on my difficulty:

> There's a woman manager at a demonstration. She has a huge scab on her chin, about to fall off. It's crusty and thick. I was impressed she hadn't picked it off. The skin was cured underneath. T. said that I should be told, people should know that I had crossed a line. I said: 'You can call me a scab but your whole way of looking at this is out of date'. I was really cross.

The SDM probably represents the furthest I have taken my explorations of psychoanalytically informed method. It has psycho-social potential, but the step required of me is here revealed to be full of conflict.

Conclusions

In search of the ineffable aspects of participants' experience as they become mothers, I returned to the data, starting with the prenatal interviews, prepared through matrixial theory and its critique of phallic logic to notice features that exceeded the usual discourses and concepts available to mothers and researchers into mothering. If pregnancy is thought of as a profound experience in which the category 'I' is transgressed, with all the layers of identity investment involved, and if the experience initiates profound continuities that survive the separation of birth, the resulting necessary rearrangement of theoretical understanding is profound, for example notions of intersubjectivity need to be rethought.

The consequence of using matrixial theory is that 'the beginning', of the child and therefore also of mothering, is moved from birth backwards in time to the transgressive corporeality of pregnancy that undermines the unicity of being for those women becoming mothers. The communication – the joint eventing – that precedes birth provides the basis for a new mother's connection to her infant after birth. This connection defies language, but it is nonetheless the basis for maternal knowing, through 'feeling with', across a border (internal to the pregnant woman's body) that both links and distinguishes. For this, Ettinger introduces a vocabulary from physics (waves, rhythms, resonances, strings) that is far more dynamic than the biology to which most treatments of pregnancy have been confined. Com-passion entails fragilisation and therefore the wish to foreclose those feelings, precipitating responses whose range I illustrated through differences between

Becky and Sarah. Through the example of Jenny I illustrated how the resultant identifications with others applied to others beyond her son and precipitated heightened ethical sensibility. This is laced with ordinary conflict that, in Ettinger's model, results from the co-existence of a trans-subjective and a phallic or individuated track, the latter emerging gradually after the separation of birth. The phallic stratum or track,[5] structured around separation and the elevation of individual autonomy, is not only hegemonic in contemporary post-Enlightenment cultures, but also has been successfully embraced by many women in the name of gender equality. The lack of a discourse on maternal passion is symptomatic.

Using field note data, I examined the mundane encounters that occur in the process of negotiating consent and following up. In matrixial terms, the extracts from my field notes describe the start of 'wit(h)nessing' as Rabiya experiences the upheavals of early mothering and I begin to know a stranger. Wit(h)nessing in a research encounter seems to be the opposite of Othering, what matrixial theory describes as 'becoming responsible for the traces of the other as if they were mine' (Ettinger, 2006a, p.221). To the extent that it is accompanied by fragilisation (all the small ways in which I was thinking 'did I do/say the right thing?'), it requires the toleration of difficulty, frustration or pain. I had to imagine the possibility of losing our last recruit to the project.

As I revisited my relation to Rabiya during writing, I remembered a powerful feeling – on the occasion of the second visit – of wanting to give Rabiya the silk scarf I was wearing, after she commented on how much she liked it. I discarded this wish on grounds of role boundary. At this moment I regret that decision! – one legacy of my fragilisation as a researcher, an example of becoming through exploring different ways of knowing. On a pre-publication read of this chapter, Yasmin Gunaratnam picked up a significant question of difference around the scarf, namely would Rabiya not wear the scarf in a different way? (Methodologically, Yasmin's contribution illustrates the value of other minds in analysing data, to compensate for the blindspots in an individual's insights.) Rabiya was a woman who covered when she left the house, so indeed she would have used her scarf differently. As Yasmin pointed out, my relation to the materiality and symbolism of the scarf, a response to Rabiya's gesture of something shared, also constituted a co-becoming. During the research and subsequently, I have become aware of many instances of changes in my subjectivity, a succession of micro-becomings occasioned by com-passionate encounters and in this sense more like co-becoming. The detailed, specific changes in the ways I can let in the participants have largely been occasioned by the methods that are increasingly available to me – ones I have characterised as tuning in to emotional impact, the time and occasions for reflection and the value of other minds.

5
How Does Zelda Know and How Is Zelda Known? Psychoanalytically Informed Data Analysis

The theorisation of knowledge in Wilfred Bion's Kleinian-inflected psychoanalysis has been my central resource, influential in the emergence of the book's key themes of mothers' and researchers' knowing and how they are linked together. In this chapter, I illustrate the value of Bion's key concepts – anxiety and splitting, the processing of raw, always emotional/affective, experience, containment, reverie, communicative projective identification and learning from experience – through applying them to a single case, Zelda's. At the same time I examine their use in my psycho-social approach to data analysis, especially in the contentious area of psychoanalytically informed interpretation.

The underlying paradox of mothers' knowing and knowing mothers was introduced earlier in the idea of the ineffable: how can a new mother – how can I as researcher – find and speak out about what is inexpressible and not to be uttered, suppressed in discourse? This is where Bion's account of uncognised knowing ('knowing of', as opposed to 'knowing about') is valuable. However, I have already made a case for matrixial language helping to unearth the weird embodied experience of pregnant metramorphosis (transgression of borderlines and transmissibility between I and non-I). According to matrixial theory, moving from a prenatal focus to a postnatal one requires both that I keep in mind the trans-subjective stratum after birth (never erased but inevitably foreclosed to a varying extent) and that I recognise the changes occurring from birth on. The data help to remind me of the dramatic change as well as the continuities. For example, Juhana's experience changed from the 'perfect feeling' of her baby 'there inside' to the demanding otherness of a baby whose feeding and sleeping she felt she had little control over. Postnatally, the baby is no longer automatically taken care of by an insouciant maternal body. Lisa Baraitser emphasises the centrality of the child's alterity in postnatal maternal becoming:

> An account of maternal subjectivity, as opposed to a description of mothering, would in part entail imagining what it is like to be in close proximity to the 'open structure' [Sarah Ruddick's term] that is a child. This would mean thinking more deeply about women's childrearing experiences from the perspective of being responsible for a child who is not just initially experienced as other, but remains irregular, unpredictable and essentially unknowable, and the pressures and strains as well as the generative potential that this may have on the maternal psyche.
>
> (Baraitser, 2009, p.26)

In the context of a history of psychoanalytic debate often unhelpfully stuck in a binary between merger or fusion and separation, the introduction of alterity is productive. However, I want to qualify the idea of 'essentially unknowable' and modify, through Bion and Ettinger, Baraitser's claim of 'inassimilable otherness' (ibid). I have found that Bion's concepts of containment and reverie, detailed by his account of the processes involved in communicative projective identification, enable us to grasp how new mothers can – partially and uncertainly – know 'what is the matter' with their babies. I then ask how these accounts of postnatal relations may be congruent with the claims of matrixial theory outlined in the previous chapter of a trans-subjective stratum that survives birth, albeit inevitably somewhat foreclosed; a stratum that coexists alongside an emergent individuated stratum. In Chapter 4 I demonstrated the value of Ettinger's 'com-passion' to research ethics; in this chapter I make a similar case for Bion's 'containment'.

Zelda's anxiety

The following data analysis is framed by my aim to illustrate the use of retooled psychoanalytic theory, specifically the foundational concept of anxiety and related concepts in the post-Kleinian tradition, which both inform the project's methodology and its approach to maternal subjectivity at a time when new mothers process the awesome responsibilities involved in caring for a new life that they have created. Many mothers were explicit about being anxious or, in Marie's case, anguished. As an addition to the project, I conducted two informal interviews with Marie, a recent first time French mother, taking notes in a mixture of French and English). She dwelt on the word '*angoisse*' (literally anguish), which overlaps with '*anxiété*' but has a more existential connotation. She talked of two parts ('lots of happiness and lots of anguish') and of this anguish being new since the birth of her son. It accompanied the increasing love she felt for him as they got to know each other. She didn't realise it could be that strong, for example the smile of your child, all the happiness in your heart, a moment of complicity; the only attachment that can't be untied, nothing else can be so strong, but this is tied to the anguish. The difficult part was imagining the worst; it was a mistake to read expert advice and look on the internet rather than trust your feelings. At six weeks old, the baby lost consciousness while breast feeding, a condition never diagnosed, but for months she lived in fear of it happening again. Neither she nor her husband could sleep, although she said her anguish was definitely stronger than his and didn't know whether this was because she was the mother or it was just her personality. Eventually they went to a support centre and she felt that there she learned that you can't control everything, you can't know everything, you will always find something to worry about. I start with this because it is characteristic of many, but not all, of the participants.

Zelda's 'anxiety' (the shift of vocabulary feels appropriate) was salient from the start: the first observation seminar group noted 'there is a sense of being very anxious'. As well as its role in Zelda's becoming a mother, I am interested in how the researchers pick up this anxiety, and how reliable and valid is this knowledge. Zelda's story situates her anxiety, the conditions that warranted worry and the resources that helped her to cope with it. Zelda became a mother while she and Braam, her boyfriend (later husband), lived in London, having come to the UK to earn more money as teachers than was possible at home. This young white South African Christian couple tried for a baby and six months later Zelda was thrilled to become pregnant. The start to their parenthood was horribly disturbed when Zelda nearly lost the baby shortly after the pregnancy was confirmed. The research followed their experiences for a year, starting before Tom was born, until they returned to live in South Africa.

Zelda was a self-confessed worrier, as she discusses at length in the first (prenatal) interview with Ann Phoenix. For example: 'Oh my husband says I'm just ridiculous, because I – I can – although I'm seemingly quite relaxed, I worry about little, little things bother me.' I treat this at its face value as a verbal claim based on what she accepts as accurate from her husband's opinion about a pattern that she displays, but I also notice what is less transparent. The emotional loading of this statement is evidenced in her signs of difficulty; first hesitation ('I – I can'), then partial qualification ('although. seemingly quite relaxed'), then retraction (changing her claim from the term worry to something she is more comfortable with, namely that little things bother her). The wider pattern of her talk illustrates a 'rush of talk' with hardly a pause, as she responds to the interviewer's question 'so what sort of difference do you think having the baby actually... will make to you?' The observer noted this on her first visit (and on many subsequent occasions). I was even aware of it in my embodied response when listening to the audio recording: I felt a bit breathless, as the word 'rush' conveys. I noticed from the audio recording how, one time when she had Tom on her lap, her volley of talk was accompanied by her unselfconsciously patting him on the back hard enough that it sounded like a dull thump. (This was not, however, the experience of the interviewer.)

In the prenatal interview, Zelda's anticipation of the imminent changes show her being bothered about 'details': how you find the time to bathe, clean the house ('I'm really nervous... [what if] I don't hear him'); 'I'm just nervous for things like (.) when he starts to cry then (.) do you [meaning, would I] know why.' Zelda links the worrying with the need for organisation (prenatal interview again): 'With me, you can solve the problem by yourself. With a baby it's a completely different story. And I'm just (.) *unsure* of, will I get – will I get it right really? So (.) so but I won't be as organised obviously.' And again, 'I always know what's pretty much going to be happening, and I can plan for everything.' This is highly effective but it may have a negative side. For example, the observation seminar group notes that 'Zelda is constantly looking forward, making plans, talking of cutting Tom's hair in December [this was in August]. Leaping ahead allows her not to be so thrown by being left behind. Tom is quickly moving forward.' (The note reads 'She said that she had planned to get his hair cut in December before the trip home but might need to do it sooner as it was growing so fast now.') According to Bion, tolerance of doubt and a sense of infinite possibility enable knowledge (1962a, p.94). Bion cited the poet Keats describing 'negative capability', the capacity to be in 'uncertainties, mysteries, doubts without any irritable reaching after fact and reason' (Bion, 1970, p.125).

After worrying about the future, Zelda associated to a reassuring idea (a kind of irritable reaching?): 'That's one thing that's good to have somebody close by at the beginning, just to be there to say, "Relax, everything's OK".' Again soon after, she repeats the pattern of articulating her nervousness and then the solution: 'It's just that when he [the baby] comes I'm just nervous that I don't (.) I don't come up to the expectations that you should really. So (.) but my husband is fantastic, so he'll be there to help anyway so that's not too bad.' A little later, she adds, 'He's more relaxed, take it as it comes, whereas, like I say, I'm more organised, get everything sorted out. But I think he'll calm us both down [meaning her and the baby], so – which should be good anyway.'

Zelda unselfconsciously demonstrates a different effect of her anxiety, an attempt to paint her experiences in an unrealistically good light, presumably to reassure herself. For example, having given an account of the traumatic problem during the pregnancy, she continued, 'But since then, everything's been really, really good, I've had a wonderful pregnancy, besides – besides morning sickness…I was just ill pretty much until about 17 weeks.' Melanie Klein understood such forms of thinking through the idea of splitting, based on the observation that the bad and the good in experiences are often split off from each other in an attempt to protect the good and reassuring feelings from the negative ones of anxiety and frustration that can feel unbearable. It is not hard to understand how undermined Zelda's positive feelings about pregnancy had become with the traumatic early experience and therefore how this splitting might be needed to preserve her good feelings about expecting a baby. The casualty of this kind of splitting can be a realistic recognition of reality, in Zelda's case illustrated by her depiction of the rest of her pregnancy as wonderful, even though she had constant morning sickness for weeks to come. This tendency to emphasise the bright side to the point of distortion of reality becomes evident as a pattern, it appears to be part of Zelda's 'idiom' (Bollas, 1989).

Zelda's excitement on becoming pregnant was rapidly superseded by the trauma that threatened the baby's life and the consequent fear that the baby would be damaged as a result. This fear is not expressed as part of the account of the pregnancy threat; the emphasis of the narrative there is rather to rejoice in the baby's strength in surviving the toxic threat. The fear surfaces during the second interview because Zelda is telling an experience-near specific story, a good example of how productive this principle is in devising interview questions. Zelda graphically describes a moment during a scan at 22 weeks (one of the many that were now added by the hospital):

they found a little cyst on his brain, which obviously (sigh) it upset me completely. Because, he was doing the scan, and you know when the doctor just starts going slower, and he like stops, and he does this and he does this by the brain the whole time which, oh, was really nerve wracking [...] and I didn't know why...but you could sort of see in someone's face if something wasn't right.

After some detail that tells us that it was 12 weeks later when the danger was resolved, Zelda makes the connection that I want to pick up:

> I think it was such a *shock* because of what happened right at the beginning. Because you just think that all the medicine that was pumped into my body when I was in hospital could have had some kind of effect on the baby. But like I say, when we went back for the 34 week [scan], it was *gone*, and he's perfect, and everything's fine now.

The dread and relief are vividly conveyed through the experience-near quality of the doctor's hand on the scanner, slowing down as the screen image shows the baby's brain. Later, when she has a 'perfect' baby, she allows herself to express the frightening connection – the potentially damaging effect of all the medicine pumped into her body when the foetus was still only six or seven weeks old – and so it is not surprising that this idea is quickly followed by the 'happy ending' at the next scan, so that the threatening idea is barely presented before it is cancelled out by the emphatic 'gone', 'perfect' and 'fine'. As researcher, it is necessary to contain the troubling idea for longer than a split second in order to realise that Zelda and Braam had to live with the fear for 12 weeks in between the scans.

It is in this historical context that Zelda's tendency to deploy words like 'perfect' and 'fine' should be understood. For example, 'since then [the threat to the baby's survival] everything's been really, really good, I've had a wonderful pregnancy, besides, besides morning sickness. Because I had 24/7 sickness [from the day I got out of hospital], I was just ill pretty much until 17 weeks, I think.' Again, following straight after the account of those long weeks of morning sickness, 'And then, yeah [faster] like I say, since then everything's been perfect and every-thing.' The couple's Christian faith helped when anticipating the birth: 'we're both Christians and stuff, so we believe everything will be fine anyway...I'm praying for everything to go good anyway.'

Anxiety as a theoretical concept enables thinking about a range of relevant data, partially accessible to consciousness, and make concep-tual links within a wider theoretical whole. The examples of Zelda's anxiety are not all of the same 'thing', because they emerge through several layers of data analysis, and derived from all four of our data types (recorded interviews, field notes, observations and observation seminar notes) and triangulation of these. Specifically, examples of evidence of anxiety can be found in: conscious claims; defences against anxiety in interview talk; extrapolation from fear-provoking events and situations; the non-semantic characteristics of talk such as hesitation, tone, pitch and pace; Zelda's 'idiom' as revealed through patterns claimed by her and directly observed over time; splitting in her relations to objects, and experiences by researchers of anxiety that does not feel to belong to them. In a psychoanalytic framework, aspects of the anxiety are understood to be inaccessible to conscious thought where the evidence is symptomatic. In such cases, they could be inferred, for example through the theoretical idea of splitting good and bad, as above.

Kleinian theory is sometimes criticised for treating intra-psychic dynamics, such as splitting, as if they determined mental life, but Klein had this to say about the internal and external in infant–mother relations, which is especially pertinent given Zelda's difficulties with Tom's feeding:

> However, it is not only that the infant's feelings about the external world are coloured by his projections, but the mother's actual relation with her child is in direct and subtle ways, influenced by the infant's response to her. A contented baby who sucks with enjoyment, allays his mother's anxiety; and her happiness expresses itself in her way of handling and feeding him, thus diminishing his persecutory anxiety and affecting his ability to internalise the good breast. In contrast, a child who has difficulties over feeding may arouse the mother's anxiety and guilt and thus unfavourably influence her relation to him. *In these varying ways there is a constant interaction between the internal and external world persisting throughout life.*
>
> (Klein, 1963, p.312, my emphasis)

When Zelda first tried to breastfeed, Tom could not latch on to the nipple and despite her determined efforts to breastfeed and express breast milk, her milk supply was insufficient and she had to give up and bottle feed. This must have felt like a harsh example of her inability to control important events once she had a baby. The following example is taken from an observation note when Tom was two months old, chosen for its typicality:

> Zelda said perhaps he'd like to try the milk again now and laid him back and offered him the bottle, he took it eagerly in his mouth

and sucked hard but then quickly rejected it and spat the teat out, wriggling his legs and squirming as if uncomfortable. 'You see' Zelda said to me, as she comforted Tom, holding him up to her shoulder and patting his back and making sympathetic noises. He quietened and Zelda said that perhaps he had wind. She continued to hold him at her shoulder rocking him gently and patting his back. He gazed towards the window, and Zelda commented on him being interested in the light and in looking at things. [A little later during the same feed] Zelda wondered whether he wanted a bit more milk before he slept. She offered him the bottle and again he took it eagerly, he lay back and seemed to relax for a moment, but then closed his mouth and pushed the teat away. He pulled his knees up and wriggled. Zelda frowned and said to Tom 'why don't you like it. what's the matter? What is the matter?' Tom cried, a moaning, quiet cry.

Unlike the 'contented baby who sucks with enjoyment [and] allays his mother's anxiety' (Klein, ibid), we can see how Zelda's anxiety is fuelled by Tom's discomfort. Tom's feeding only improved once he could control the bottle for himself and when he was eating solid food. Theoretically speaking, Zelda's anxiety potentially makes it hard or impossible to contain and process Tom's painful state and leaves her in need of containment. Where this dynamic starts is a matter of conjecture, but there are some clues: Zelda was a worrier before she got pregnant; she had a traumatic start to the pregnancy which must have set in train huge tensions that she was not able to process because the idea of damaging her unborn baby was too unbearable to think about (we have seen some of the ways in which she managed these thoughts through splitting). A further crisis immediately after the birth left her drained and dazed, recovering from dangerous blood loss after the birth and getting little sleep. At that point the observation seminar group commented on the 'flat manner' in which Zelda described the birth experience and the observer noted the new baby's unusual stillness and how he lay with his hands open flat (babies' hands are normally curled and the openness suggests muscular tension). Tom was constantly ill with rashes, eye infections and constipation. This suggests the embodiment of difficult states that could not be processed, 'psychosomatic dysfunction' (see Britton, below). For a month, Zelda's mother had been there to support her: the observation group, thinking about the observation at which she was still present, commented on a feeling that she was directing her care to her daughter primarily, presumably in recognition of Zelda's fragile state.

All this points to salient external events that amplified Zelda's anxieties, which proved hard to manage. When Zelda, as a new mother, is placed in this psychologically demanding situation – and all new mothers are to some extent – how does she bear her baby's distress? In interpreting the patterns in Zelda's data, although informed by psychoanalytic concepts, it is sometimes hard to separate these from common sense. For example, by labelling the above a traumatic experience I am designating it, in the everyday sense, as serious and anxiety provoking. What psychoanalytic theory adds (based on a wealth of clinical evidence) is that this experience will have psychological consequences unavailable to consciousness. The severity of these will depend on a complex range of factors, not only external events like Zelda's subsequent experiences of pregnancy, childbirth and early mothering, but how these are 'processed' internally.

Processing emotional experience: Bion's theory of thinking

The seminar group, reflecting together on Zelda and her baby's experience of feeding ask 'what is it that can't be processed and who can't process it and what contributes to this'? It is a big multiple question, appropriately framed in a relational grammar that does not place within a single individual whatever it is that can't be processed, and therefore thought. The seminar group's use of the Klein- and Bion-based concept of 'processing' extends its potential in data analysis beyond the common sense understanding of the idea of mental processing, which is assumed to be intra-psychic. Klein based her model of thinking on digestion, so central a process in every infant's experience. Digestion necessarily involves stuff that is taken in, processed and used, with the residue eventually evacuated, got rid of from the body, 'projected'.

In his theory of thinking, Bion's starting point is the idea that 'an emotional experience occurs, and if it is not processed into symbolic representations... then the ' "accretions of stimuli" (to use Freud's term which is particularly applicable here) must be evacuated from the mind in some way' (Meltzer, 1986, p.23). Angela Sowa conveys vividly the emotional responsibility – burden even – of thinking: 'To sustain a thought is to continue to allow it to exert pressure upon us, to allow it access into other chambers of the mind, to lay no claim to the limits of its expandability in spite of having to take responsibility for its outcome' (Sowa, 2002–2003, p.33).

Taking as his starting point Klein's 'epistemophilic drive' (*Wissentrieb*, meaning literally the urge for knowledge), Bion extended the analogy of digestion to mental nourishment, positing two basic 'hungers', the first physical and the second the need to understand experience. He designated the latter K (for knowledge). Klein had already partially departed from Freud's emphasis on pleasure and pain; to her notions of love and hate, she added the need to know. Designating these L, H and K, Bion introduced two radically new propositions. First he treated L, H and K as autonomous (that is, love and hate were no longer related to each other as opposite poles); each had negative as well as positive poles (-L, -H, -K). Second, these were no longer conceptualised as drives but as key links in human relationships (Meltzer, 1986, p.26) or intrinsic links to objects, *relations to*. In the words of Ron Britton: 'Taking Melanie Klein's formulation that "there is no instinctual urge, no anxiety situation, no mental process which does not involve objects, external or internal" (Klein, 1952, p.53), I think it is better to say that we love things, hate things and want to know things than to speak of abstract drives' (Britton, 1998, p.3). So K refers to the link between one who needs to know an object and that object. Zelda's need to know Tom is expressed painfully in her repeated 'what is the matter?' It is through wanting to know that the alterity of the baby ('object') is not entirely inassimilable. Bion explains how this kind of uncognised knowing works and fails to work.

In the extract detailing Zelda and Tom's difficulty in the feeding relationship (a pattern of difficulties absent from the interview data, see Chapter 2), the observer is included as a witness (' "You see" Zelda said to me, as she comforted Tom, holding him up to her shoulder and patting his back and making sympathetic noises'). The observer needed to contain these painful experiences, both ethically and to enable her to process the experience, a crucial element in understanding Zelda's experience of becoming a mother. At a distance both in time and space, I too found that I needed to pause and reflect on my emotional experience of reading this in order to grasp how hard it was for Zelda to go through this, day in, day out. Bion's concept of containment links these two issues: Zelda's containment of Tom's distress and researchers' containment of the scenes of the feeding couple (as well as other occasions when anxiety was salient).

Ethics of interpretation

I have already illustrated the deployment of two psychoanalytic concepts, anxiety and containment, in data analysis. We need cautiously to adapt this paradigm for research, finding a 'psychoanalytic "sensibility", a way of working with human participants that instigates a constant reworking of the knowledge bases that we come with' (Baraitser, 2008, p.426). Infant observation, coming from psychoanalysis and being an integral part of psychoanalytic training, has already developed outside of clinical psychoanalysis for 50 years. The FANI method is still an upstart of course, grounded in a research tradition with a set of principles and practices required by empirical, qualitative, field-based research, which grounding must frame questions of interpretation.

Interpretation has wider meanings than psychoanalytic interpretation, for example in hermeneutic and phenomenological traditions where interpretation functions as an essential part of human meaning making. Frosh and Emerson are emphatic that 'without a doubt, *all* interpretive research, whether derived from psychoanalysis or from other strategies of reading such as conversation analysis or discourse analysis, involves the application of some pre-set theoretical concepts to the material at hand' (Frosh and Emerson, 2005, p.309). They point out that there are variations amongst qualitative procedures (I would add amongst psychoanalytic practices too) between those that are relatively 'bottom up' and those that are 'top down'. The latter are 'dominated by theoretically-derived categories imposing an interpretive "grid" on data in order to interrogate it according to the assumptions or perceptions derived from those categories'; those that are 'relatively "bottom up", eschew theory as far as possible at least until the data has been examined performatively in terms of its own emergent properties' (Frosh and Emerson, 2005, p.310). In what follows, I hope to show that the practice of interpretation can be more nuanced, retaining the strengths of both principles. To constrain so-called 'wild analysis' is an obvious challenge for research knowing. The cultivation of a research stance based on openness is complex and psychologically challenging, both at the level of theory and research practice. Our data analytic practice was based on sensitivity to researcher's affective response accompanied by opportunities for reflection, aided by the support of others through group data analysis and supervision (see Chapter 2). The FANI method is premised on the theoretical proposition that anxiety requires defences and that everyone is susceptible to these to a greater or lesser degree, and in different situations.[1] The concept itself derives its explanatory value from the whole psychoanalytic framework in which anxiety is consequential precisely because, when it leads to defences, it gives rise to actions and talk that are not transparent, that require interpretation. Zelda's 'wonderful', 'perfect' later pregnancy was a case in point.

Containment and projective identification

Bion distinguished elements in need of containment from those transformed by containment by the symbols β and α (beta and alpha), a distinction that has wide ramifications for his theory of thinking. Alpha elements are able to be symbolised and therefore available for further thinking; beta elements are precursors of thought, 'not so much memories as undigested facts' (Bion, 1962a, p.7). There are three ways in which beta elements can be removed from the mind: 'first into the body; second into the perceptual sphere and, third, into the realm of action – in other words, into psychosomatic dysfunction, perceptual hallucination or symptomatic action' (Britton, 1998, p.22). Alpha function is Bion's term for processing raw elements of emotional experience. According to Donald Meltzer, 'the process of alpha-function is always attempting to find representations for our emotional experiences, if we can tolerate them' (2009/1986, p.11).

Infants cannot transform their own beta elements into symbolisations; in other words, they cannot 'think', so what happens to their emotional experiences, especially painful or frustrating ones, as in Tom's feed, above? Bion's answer was that the mother (or carer) performs this (alpha) function. To describe this, he introduced the terms container and contained (denoted by the ancient symbols for female ♀ and male ♂) as a way of understanding how experience is transformed by containment. In *Learning from Experience*, he describes how containment is crucial for the development of thinking and the capacity to learn from experience:

> Melanie Klein has described an aspect of projective identification concerned with the modification of infantile fears; the infant projects a part of its psyche, namely its bad feelings, into the good breast. Thence in due course they are removed and reintrojected. During their sojourn in the good breast they are felt to have been modified in such a way that the object that is re-introjected has become tolerable to the infant's psyche.

> From the above theory I shall abstract for us as a model the idea of a container into which an object is projected and the object that can be projected into the container; the latter I shall designate by the contained.

> (Bion, 1962a, p.90)

This explains the way containment works through projective identification. The underlying principle is that emotional experiences, dynamically attaching to objects, move back and forth across the psychologically porous boundaries of individuals, as unconscious inter-subjective dynamics. This mostly happens in fleeting ways that are experienced as changes in affective, bodily states not registered consciously. Freud had introduced the term identification for these, 'the earliest expression of an emotional tie with another person' (1922, p.105) and had already used the concept of projection to convey the idea that something psychological can be got rid of by being expelled from a person's inner world. Klein used this term but in 1946 introduced the concept of projective identification, which has subsequently been central to Kleinian thought. A state of mind or experience is, in phantasy, projected out and identified as residing in another object. The concomitant action of the other person – also not engaged in consciously – is called introjection, which does not necessarily follow. Projective identification 'entails a belief in certain aspects of the self being elsewhere, with a consequent depletion and weakened sense of self and identity' (Hinshelwood, 1991, p.179).

This version of projective identification emphasises pathological processes, but in 1959 Bion proposed a normal form of unconscious communication that originates in the mother–infant relationship and continues to underpin communication after the acquisition of language. Bion's communicative projective identification is a necessary precursor of thinking: the infant, lacking understanding of painful sensory experiences, communicates the associated state of mind and the mother can receive it, if it is bearable. If she is able to transform it into alpha function, digested and detoxified, the baby can take back the now contained state of mind. In his clinical practice, Bion identified the same processes in transference–countertransference and gradually they came to be understood by psychoanalysts as characteristic of communication beyond the clinic. The baby's alterity is not necessarily, in this view, wholly inassimilable.

The mother's containing state of mind has a further quality, described by Bion through his concept of 'reverie', 'a concept referring to the analyst's state of receptivity to the patient's unconscious experience and the mother's receptivity to her infant's symbolic and asymbolic [or presymbolic] experience' (Ogden, 1989, p.45).

Zelda's receptivity to Tom's state is exemplified when she wakes him up from a morning sleep, as captured in an observation note. Tom is ten weeks old.

She watched him as he woke, and talked gently to him. She asked him if he was waking now . . . his eyes had now returned to shut although he continued to wriggle and moan. He opened his eyes and Zelda put her hand on his tummy and said to him: 'You're not quite sure are you?' She stroked him and spoke to him again, he stilled and opened his eyes, she moved the sheet from his face, and asked: 'Are you ready now... Are you ready now?' She released his arms from the sheet and touched his chin and lip, speaking to him brightly and smiling at him. 'Are you ready to wake up Tom? Are you Tom? Are you?' She stroked his chin and he smiled at her: 'Ah that's better, perhaps you are ready?' She stroked his chin again and he smiled again. 'What a lovely smile: you are nearly ready?' She smiled and kissed him lightly on the nose. Zelda then moved away telling him she was just going to open the blind. He lay in his cot gazing towards Zelda and then following her voice with his eyes as she moved to the window. When she returned she stroked his face and tummy again, and again he smiled, she said: 'You are ready... ' She picked him up and held him against her shoulder.

In this extract, Zelda is receiving her baby's communications, so encouraging him without rushing him, 'holding' him with her voice even when she walks out of his sight and introduces light into the room by opening the blind. Long before he knows the meaning of her words, her emotional tone will contain the potential fright of a rupture in his state of being, such as when the darkness suddenly changes to brightness. In various languages of psychoanalysis it is plausible to claim that she is able to identify with the fragile state he is in, that she is exercising 'com-passion', that in a state of reverie, through projective identification, she can receive Tom's communications, contain them and offer them back in a bearable form. This requires changes in her own pace, which is an embodied aspect of who she is (someone who is often in a rush).

Zelda's capacity to act as a container to her baby was in turn affected by the containment she found for her own unprocessed experience. Zelda was keen on welcoming both interviewer and observer into her life and was strikingly uninterested in the research, as if she was intent solely on having these additional supports as she became a mother. It is useful to add the containing function of talk to the more obvious containment provided by people's support, although these are never separable. Zelda seemed to find comfort in articulating her experiences and as we have seen, the way that she storied her experiences typically ensured reassuring endings. Sometimes there was no such resolution, however; sometimes uncertainty had to be tolerated. For example, suddenly faced with the possibility of returning to South Africa, when the observer arrived (by now a much valued weekly resource) she first continued to talk and act as if nothing had changed. She talked of preparing to carry on with upgrading her teaching qualifications for the English educational requirements. According to the observation seminar note, at this stage there had been 'a quality of how much more settled things are'. Then, once both were sitting down with cups of tea, she broke the news: 'things are really complicated because Braam has a job offer...she said that she feels very unsettled; it feels very up in the air' (observation note). The group also noted 'a discrepancy between the huge news of moving and the delivery of this [to the observer]'. Gradually Zelda began to unload her worries to the observer:

> She speaks about her upset when a possible buyer for the house fell through. At the end of last week she had been very excited and then felt terribly disappointed. She told me that she has had to give up her plans for having another baby....She said that she felt sad about it, and that it is hard at the moment with such a lot of uncertainty to manage....She can't get excited or organised for moving as she will get too disappointed if it doesn't work out. She can't tell her Mum as she would be too disappointed if it didn't work out. Zelda said that it has been really very hard in the last week, she and Braam have been arguing a lot in the last couple of days as she just can't bear not having a clear plan. Braam keeps telling her 'I don't know yet, we don't know yet', when she asks him what they should do or what is happening. She knows he's right but finds it very hard.

It seems as if Zelda needs to process with the observer the shocking news of what to her is a premature, unexpected return to South Africa, gradually enabling the new reality to impinge upon her earlier plans, based on remaining in the UK, now probably but not definitely redundant. We see her in the middle of this process of psychic change, using the resources of other minds (Braam and here the observer) to help her accommodate these out-of-control external changes in her thinking. Especially hard is the uncertainty – how can she plan? Her usual strategy for coping with anxiety has to be put on hold. Braam's counsel that they don't know requires living in uncertainty, which is what she finds so hard. In such an example, we can see the micro-processes of psychic change, for which Bion's account of alpha function is useful.

Learning from experience, given time

Being open to Tom's communications is not always easy. Ordinary events can be highly invested and difficult to think about, as illustrated during a swimming lesson attended by the observer when Tom was about six months old. Tom was miserable from the moment he touched the water to the time (almost at the end of the class) when Zelda got him out of the pool. Bion's concept of 'learning from experience' is based on the principle that thought and learning require emotional openness in the face of the risk of being frustrated by or disliking the unknown outcome involved in every act of learning. This is profoundly true of first time mothering and underlines how inevitably anxiety-provoking these change processes are.

On the way to the pool, Zelda tells the observer 'Tom doesn't usually like it and cries a lot [last visit he cried the whole time]. She's not sure whether to continue with it.' The swimming teacher tells the observer how the babies relax and enjoy it. Later when Tom was crying, the teacher said that Tom wasn't really upset just cross and that Zelda should not give in. The observer comments 'I had the impression she found the teacher hard to stand up to.' At one point, Zelda said to Tom 'you'd better stop crying or we won't be allowed to get out'. Zelda gets Tom out of the water a little before the other mothers and babies: 'Immediately we were away from the pool, Tom stopped crying and seemed to relax.' Afterwards when Zelda comments to the observer, she repeats that she is unsure what to do next, says that Braam would 'just say stop bringing him' and comments that 'it seems such a shame as she so loves swimming'. She points out how happy Tom is 'now we have left' and repeats about her indecision.

We know from elsewhere in the data that Zelda taught swimming to children when she was in South Africa. We know that Braam is a keen sportsman, and that swimming is Zelda's sport. Perhaps these two factors, added to the insistence of the swimming teacher in relation to whom Zelda appears to feel like a pupil herself ('we won't be allowed...'), explains her uncharacteristic insensitivity to Tom's dislike of the swimming pool and her preparedness to continue his unhappiness for the half hour lesson. She was faced with the power of an expert discourse, expressed via the instructor who said that Tom should not be taken out of the water while he was crying (the observer comments that it looked unlikely that Tom would stop crying). Zelda was reluctant to 'learn from experience', the repeated experience of Tom's misery in the pool. She faced an expert discourse, which might have been exacerbated by her identification with the teacher, and as someone for whom swimming is a pleasure. It was not that she did not notice his unhappiness, but that at the time, she did not think about it with the com-passion that would have enabled the simple conclusion to stop (a position that evidently was not difficult for Braam to adopt, even while not present for the experience). She would have had to tolerate the frustration caused to her own wishes for him to enjoy swimming in order to learn from this experience. In the event, Zelda did not return for further classes. Perhaps the observer's presence helped her subsequent reflection; perhaps Braam repeated his advice; perhaps the physical distance from the instructor helped her to include an understanding of Tom's emotional experience in her thinking. Presumably she had to suffer disappointment and frustration to reach this conclusion, emotions that according to Bion are essential to thinking and learning from experience.

In his emphasis on suffering, or frustration, and its avoidance, Bion elaborates the Freudian ideas that secondary process thinking comes from the postponement of gratification, and that symbol formation evolves to deal with the absence of things. Suffering accompanies thinking. Instead of the search for pleasure, 'the crucial determinant of mental growth is whether the individual "decides" to evade frustration or to tolerate it' (Symington, 1996, p.6). The shift is from a motivational category to an emphasis on the emergence of truth, or the facing of painful realities. Sowa's formulation, cited earlier ('to lay no claim to the limits' of a thought's 'expandability') implies the concept of mental space, much used in object relations psychoanalysis, following Klein and Bion. Space for thinking is not automatic. It involves containment, creating a space – and time – to bear experience, ruminate it, metabolise it and reflect upon it. Crucially, the development of a mind – the capacity to think and learn from experience – depends on ones relationship to others and the key quality of that relationship is the emotional link. According to Bléandonu, 'the linking of preconceptions and realizations, be they negative or positive, engenders a process which leads to "learning from experience"' (1994, p.147). Zelda's preconception (we love swimming) was linked after some difficulty with the negative realization that Tom hated it: she learned from experience, but not in one instant.

Zelda had learned over the year that she could use the observer's capacity for containment. At their final meeting, for example, Zelda talked of her main worry being how to manage her mother-in-law. Laughing she added that 'perhaps she will send the observer SOS emails for advice, or perhaps turn up asking for a bed for the night'. She also shared with the observer a disturbing detail about her childhood that she had never mentioned before. Perhaps more striking evidence of the observer's containment can be inferred from the following note:

> As we walked back to the tube, Zelda spoke about how important it had been to come and say goodbye. She said that she had been speaking to Braam about it and telling him that she [Elspeth, the observer] is the one adult who *really knows* Tom and has seen him grow up. She added that I [Elspeth] knew him much better than either of his grandmas or anyone in South Africa. She spoke about how much she had changed in the year that she had known me and how much she valued my support. I spoke about how many difficulties she had had to manage, she'd had such a difficult start and Tom had not always been easy. Zelda agreed and said again how sad she felt to say goodbye and how much she wanted to keep in touch. (...) This conversation felt very heartfelt and sad and it was hard for us both as we made our way to the tube and onto the platform. (my italics, see below)

In this passage, containment as an ethical feature of the research relationship is demonstrated. Beyond the support she valued during the big changes in her life, what struck me was Zelda's thoughtful agreement with the observer's comments about the difficulties she had faced and how Tom had not always been easy. The tone of this whole exchange conveys quiet reflection in the midst of the chaos of moving, so that Zelda's agreement is not passive but demonstrates the ability, through the observer's containing mind, to bear the knowledge of the difficulties that she has been through and that her experiences with her baby have not been all good. She is helped by her experience of the observer as one who 'really knows'. Perhaps this phrase provides the kind of containment that Britton refers to, when he describes how one function of the experience of containment is to provide meaning and how this makes it possible to draw on the whole symbolic system of language:

> If a name enshrines a psychic quality – like love, for example – the word provides a container for the emotional experience, putting a semantic boundary around it. It also places it in a ready-made context of significance provided by the place in human affairs of love and the place of the word in an existing language. At the same time,

the experience of the emotion gives meaning to the word for that individual.

(Britton, 1998, p.21)

Despite the demands and uncertainties that Zelda is facing about the return home, Tom is in good shape: 'Tom studied me for a moment and then smiled. He put his hands flat on the table and banged them down, enjoying the sound, and he chattered to me, he was lively and smiley.'

Zelda's knowing

Zelda's 'what is the matter' when confronted, once again, with Tom's feeding discomfort took us into the emotional turmoil surrounding knowing and not knowing, being able or unable to control events. Zelda had to live with the anguish of not being able to make it right for her baby but continuing to do her best in an open, unknowable situation. The anxiety-provoking quality of the reality was exacerbated by her tendencies to worry and we saw her drawing on a range of resources, including the serviceable defence of splitting, as she struggled to learn from experience in the face of the child's alterity. She suffered the rather new, for her, situation of not knowing what will happen next. Even Tom's hair grows faster than she plans!

Extrapolating from matrixial theory, the baby's alterity is not entirely 'unassimilable' because of the continuing trans-subjective existence of com-passion, the 'feeling with' established prenatally through continued joint eventing, through 'traces, vibrations and resonances, registered sonic and tactile intimations of othernesses, sharing spaces but never fusing, encountering but never dissolving their boundaries, jointly eventing without ever knowing fully the other's event' (Pollock, 2008, p.14). Ettinger is critical of the idea that 'the fetus presents a "primary total undifferentiatedness" and the mother's womb a passive receptivity' (Ettinger, 1997, p.369, citing Little, 1986, p.136). She provides instead the idea of jointness in differentiation, prior to birth. Ettinger contrasts the accounts of fusion with a hypothesis that there exists a 'certain awareness of difference' as a result of the prenatal baby's 'borderlinks to the mother-to-be's experience and fantasy during pregnancy'. She specifies that she is referring to the 'last part of the prenatal life when the infant is post-mature' (Ettinger, 1997, p.379). This is 'metramorphosis', a 'co-naissance – a transformational knowledge of being born together with the other' (Ettinger, 2006a, pp.221–222).

However, although this account decisively leaves behind the model of fusion/ merger followed by necessary separation, it needs to consider what happens to this potential with the emergence of a new 'phallic' stratum occasioned by postnatal development. In Pollock's words, the earliest stratum of human subjectivity emerges as trans-subjective, in the space of the intrauterine 'waiting to be imaginatively, ethically and aesthetically elaborated'. It is a

> potentiality for transsubjective co-emerging and co-affecting compassion, which avoids from the start notions of monadic narcissism and violent separations, symbolic fusion versus individuation (...) even while allowing all these processes their place in the larger drama of subjectivity post-natally.
>
> (Pollock, 2008, p.16)

Ettinger also touches upon what happens after birth, insisting that 'matrixial potentiality does not replace the phallus, it operates along a different unconscious track' (Ettinger, 2006a, p.220). The meeting of tracks is more available (or less avoidable, depending on your perspective) because

> the woman doubly experiences the matrixial borderspace: first in the last period of prenatal life in the maternal womb and through appropriate sensorial development (here *she* could be of either sex), and second, as someone who has a womb, at various levels of development and awareness, whether she is a mother or not.
>
> (Ettinger, 1997, p.391)

Alpha-function, possible within the container-contained relation of mother and pre-mental infant, starts in prenatal experience, according to Bion. There is congruity between metramorphic communication and the embodied experience of communicative projective identification. Both Bion and Ettinger treat the communication as asymmetric and two-way. Together these approaches to maternal subjectivity and maternal becoming provide insights into an intuition-based kind of knowing which, while it is accessible to all, originates in early maternal experience, reprising the earliest trans-subjective relations. Zelda illustrates that access to this uncognised knowing is neither easy nor guaranteed, but she also demonstrates how the profound connections with her baby made the attempt – with the psychic changes that it entailed – impossible to shirk.

Conclusions

Bion's theorisation of thinking and knowing occasioned the theme of this book, especially the connection he made between mothers' knowing and the origins of thought in unconconscious transjective communications. I was interested in reflecting on my uses of Bionian and other object relational concepts to explore their relation to my newer discovery of matrixial theory and to think through the ethics of deploying these theoretical frameworks to analyse data. I have tried to make this process transparent as I introduce theoretical concepts in the service of data analysis.

Alongside examples of Zelda's use of the observer to express and contain her anxiety, I provided three example of Zelda's relation to Tom: feeding, waking and at the swimming pool. These demonstrate the vicissitudes of maternal com-passion in the face of the baby's alterity. In Tom's fragile state transitioning from sleep to waking, it seemed that Zelda can, for example on the occasion of waking him, 'assimilate' his alterity, if this means take it in, process and transform it and give back what he needs through her actions to make his experience more tolerable. Ogden's account of the two-part quality of the object relation helps to explain this: in the swimming example, she was herself (wanting them to enjoy the pool) and also identified with Tom. On this occasion the second part was partially foreclosed; she was unavailable to his communications, his otherness was temporarily inassimilable. The heightened anguish of motherhood appears to reside in the tension of matrixial com-passion on one hand and the child's alterity on the other.

6
Scenic Writing and Scenic Understanding

Introduction

This chapter introduces the concepts of scene and scenic understanding from Alfred Lorenzer, German cultural analyst and psychoanalyst in the Frankfurt tradition[1]; concepts that are explicitly psycho-social and congruent with the psychoanalytically informed epistemology and methodology that has inspired my research practice. In this tradition, 'Imagination is scenic in its format: it inter-relates all informative, sensual and situated impressions in holistic images' (Salling Olesen, 2012, para 3).

I illustrate the value of the concept of scene in two interconnected research areas, namely, writing and analysing data. By 'scene', Lorenzer means 'an affective and embodied register of meaning' (Bereswill et al., 2010, p.225), so 'scenic understanding' refers to 'a process by which researchers reflect on their affective and embodied experience of their data' (Redman, Bereswill and Morgenroth, 2010, p.217). Lorenzer suggested that it was possible, through scenic understanding, to access a form of unsymbolised socio-cultural knowledge, a kind of societal-collective unconscious (Hollway, 2013a). I borrow his concept of 'scenic understanding' to inform the way I introduce a case as a 'scenic composition' (Froggett and Hollway, 2010), introducing readers to 'Jenny' and discussing the principles involved.

In Lorenzer's work I found two of my central ambitions shared. First he aims to understand the complexity of subjectivity, seen not as an individual attribute but as an 'embodied experience of interaction which has conscious and unconscious levels' and 'a relational and dynamic aspect of social interaction' (Salling Olesen, 2012, para 1). Second, Lorenzer takes this view of subjectivity into 'empirical studies of social interaction in everyday life' (ibid.). He used a 'depth hermeneutic' methodology (avoiding the label 'psychoanalytic' for applications outside the clinic) for the cultural analysis of texts. In this tradition the term culture serves to open up a perspective on 'a social level of reality which is present both as an environment and *as an embodied meaning* of the individual' (Salling Olesen, 2012, para 10, my emphasis). His concept of scenic understanding enables both the imaginative interpretation of personal meaning and – these are not separate – how the whole of a socio-cultural milieu is represented in the scene that is the subject of interpretation. At the beginning of this chapter, the summary of Lorenzer is about imagination as scenic, sensory, situated and holistic. His emphasis on imagination enabled me to link his approach to Winnicott's theorisation of imagination (Hollway, 2011) and thus to build on and extend my familiarity with British object relations psychoanalytic treatment of an intermediate area of experience that is the basis for uncognised knowing (Hollway and Froggett, 2012).

As we shall see, writing scenically requires the emergence of what is known holistically. I contrast this with the use of social identity categories and discuss what might guide their ethical use. Likewise I discuss how to use and theorise language in a way that preserves the emotion therein. Scenic understanding, syncretistic perception and reverie are all viewed as drawing on a holistic, undifferentiated kind of knowing that does not split off intellectual understanding from feel-knowing or intuitive knowing. Connections with matrixial theory and with Bion's treatment of knowing are easy to draw.

I have experimented with different writing styles (Hollway, 2011b), taking inspiration from diverse traditions. For example, Ted Hughes, English poet, discovered a form, 'rough verse', that best preserved 'the fresh simple presence of the experience'. When, in his journal, he 'happened' to write in rough verse:

> I discovered something that surprised me. In verse, not only did I seem to move at once deeper and more steadily into reliving the experience, but every detail became much more important.
>
> (Hughes, 2008)

In my rough verse in Chapter 1, I wanted to preserve the 'fresh simple presence' of Juhana's experience, not smooth it over with an expert researcher voice that risked losing its aliveness. I wanted to use her case data so that readers' imaginations could conjure changing scenes throughout the year. In a different tradition, Laurel Richardson explained why, as a social science researcher, she switched to poetry in writing about her participants to address her former experience that 'even when the topic was ostensibly riveting, the writing style and reporting conventions were deadening' (1992, p.131).

Writing scenically

> *Twenty minutes have passed and Jenny still waits in her bedroom. Clothes on hangers bulge from the top rail of the bunk beds; around the room are various soft toys and on the wall a couple of Bob Marley posters. In the sitting room, her family's social worker, who she has known all her life, tells her parents the news: Jenny is pregnant.*

(This scenic account continued with the vignettes in Chapter 3, p. x–xx.)

I had several false starts in applying Lorenzer's concept of the scenic to the practice of case writing. I was helped eventually by using the theatrical metaphor, specifically the idea of a scene in a play that presents the audience with a matrix of setting, characters, actions, talk and relational encounters within a short period of time. The visual sense is in play through imagination. More broadly, however, my aim in re/presenting Jenny in this scenic way is to enable her to come alive in the minds of readers, to keep close to her experience so that it is easier to identify with her, to traverse imaginatively the distance between you and her, a place 'in between' (see below). For this purpose I used the present tense. Moreover I was interested in going beyond social categories in how I portray her. The conceptual tools and methodological conventions that researchers use to represent data in our analyses have, not surprisingly, reflected the central trope of difference in social theory and social research. When several years ago I first summarised Jenny's case in 'pen portrait' form, I started as follows:

> *Jenny is black British, of African Caribbean heritage, and lives with her parents and three younger brothers in a council flat. When she discovered that she was pregnant, she was 17 and about to start studying social sciences at college.*[2]

Identity categories

I must have felt it necessary to start off with some facts, but of course these facts are heavily mediated by their selection and by the use of a set of social identity categories with particular connotations. These categories occupy a powerful position partly because they are both ordinary language and social science categories. In the latter, social categorisation has been a key analytic tool in sampling and generalisation. Contemporary social science (both quantitative and qualitative) is dominated by a set of overarching social identity categories: sex, race and class; also sexuality, ethnicity, dis/ability and faith, whose importance is in rendering visible a set of inequalities, exclusions and power relations. In psycho-social research, social identity categories also contribute to researcher reflexivity.

In my two original introductory sentences, italicised above, I provide readers with information about Jenny's class, race, ethnicity and age. They afford, without being explicit, a label 'young black single mother', a label loaded with negative stereotypes. Not only are these in danger of blinding the reader to Jenny's actuality (for example, how salient is the experience of being black for Jenny and in the setting of what relationships?); not only will they narrow and distort the reader's (and researcher's) emotional experience of Jenny, but these social identity categories are liable to reduce the analysis of subjectivity to a sociological one, where they are used to explain subjectivity. At the same time, however, if these categories are avoided by researchers while being used by participants, this would constitute a distortion. Consequently, I look out for their use by participants (recognising that use is not the only indicator of their presence) and let that guide me.

In writing a scenic portrayal, it was not easy to abstain from using social identity categories: only at a later draft, for example, did I delete the starting phrase 'seventeen year old Jenny', reasoning that it is obvious right away that she is young (this fact defines her dilemma in telling her parents). I also wondered whether it was necessary to tell the reader that Jenny is black. After all, the purpose of a diverse research sample is to ensure that research findings do not get assimilated to a model of new motherhood that for decades was based on white middle-class norms. I decided to resist the wish to pin something down, to let uncertainty survive for longer while readers encounter Jenny through the fine details of her setting and the events that she confronts.

I tell a story by conjuring scenes, as a theatrical play does. The narrative element remains necessary because my major theme is identity *transition* and also because narrative was used by participants to represent their experience. The information on which scenes are based derived largely from Ferelyth Watt's observations (Watt, 2007). Without this, or some equivalent ethnographic style of writing detailed (but, of course, not exhaustive) field notes, a scenic representation would have been almost impossible. The scene requires an act of imagination through which it tells each reader something about Jenny. For example, we get information about Jenny's age without being told it or knowing it exactly: it comes across multi-dimensionally from the objects in her bedroom and the fact that she is so worried about telling her parents, with whom she still lives, that she enlists the help of the social worker to tell them that she is pregnant. The scene should leave us wondering about some features: the existence of the social worker, the significance of the Bob Marley posters. These provide openings for future learning about Jenny, fuelled by imagination. (Winnicott talked of reality – here the data – providing the brakes on imagination.) Some of what we imagine will only later be tested by further evidence, until which time we try to remain open to what these details mean.

In the above snippet and the longer vignettes in Chapter 3, I have tried to supply details that are a veridical part of Jenny's setting and activities, which give accurate information without drawing attention to social identity categories, thereby risking reification. For example, I echo Jenny's words about receiving the news of her positive pregnancy test on the phone; words in which she positions herself as 'just some young girl', by commenting about the medical receptionist's ignorance of her age. Implied in the phrase is a load of cultural baggage concerning young mothers (Phoenix, 1990), a phrase which is nonetheless addressing her. The way her young age emerges is then not as a social or chronological fact so much as a lived experience, an embodied relation to culture.

The status of words

As with the use of factual categories in case writing, participants' own words have often been used as a demonstration of the researcher's objective treatment of data. I have experimented with how I use Jenny's words, because of the danger of reifying participants' words by treating them as if they constitute a guarantee of truth. Their meaning depends on context, ordering and selection, as well as what the writer and reader brings to sense-making. In the vignettes, I used a great many of Jenny's words, but my purpose in doing so is better explained as trying to capture Jenny's 'voice' or 'idiom' ('the unique presence of being that each of us is', Bollas, 1989, p.9). At first I relied heavily on data from interview transcripts because I could cite participants' words as evidence, but observation notes afford a greater emphasis on the scenic and helped to release me from treating words as the representatives of facts.

The rigorous use of speech marks to distinguish participants' words from researchers' has also been a basic principle in social scientific writing, for obvious reasons. However, I have mostly left them out in this scenic writing. I read a literary writer claiming that speech marks were redundant if the voice within them was true to the character's idiom, because that would make it clear who was speaking. Although I am not writing fiction, I think that the same principle applies here: I hope Jenny's voice is faithfully represented in the above scenes, through my attention to her idiom, as well as to the actual content of the case data and the links that she makes between ideas.

In departing from entrenched conventions of qualitative social science in this way, it is necessary to ask if and how my representation is still fit for the purposes of an in-depth analysis of Jenny's identity changes as she becomes a mother for the first time. Although I can refer to the details as they appeared in all four of the usual data sources (interviews and reflective field notes, observation notes and observation seminar discussion notes), I am engaged in an act of meaning creation based on a complexly mediated encounter with Jenny, an encounter with someone I have never met face to face (but I have listened to her voice).

Scenic understanding, imagination and the 'in-between'

Lorenzer understood the 'scenic' to exist *in between* the action and the reader's experience of what was taking place and it is this idea of the in-between – what Winnicott (2005[1971],) called an intermediate area or transitional space – that for me makes the concept so fruitful for a psycho-social analysis. Lorenzer claims that 'if we want to understand the analysand's life practice, including his concrete social reality, we must follow the path laid down by his subjective ideas and fantasies about relations [imagination, in my usage]'. Along this path, 'we must become attuned to his scenic interaction forms as these unfold before us' (1977, p.125). Scenic interaction forms are built up through a lifetime of routinised interactions (with people and non-human objects), and are therefore inherently relational and societal. They 'lie between the "inside" and the "outside" ' and 'their interplay accounts for everything' (1986, p.41–44). According to Lorenzer, 'interaction experiences become embodied during the embryonic phase and the first few months of life' (Salling Olesen and Weber, 2012, para 35). Although Lorenzer's account differs from Ettinger's, the principles are consistent with matrixial theory in stipulating their embodied effect on later experience: 'Such interaction patterns which become ingrained in the body stand for an entire lifetime in a constant dialectic with the discursive demands of the social environment' (ibid.).

This is a radical place from which to start textual interpretation because the scenic must be approached through the (research) analyst's uncognised knowing, through a state of reverie, in Bion's terms. We are challenged to redefine the relationship between what Lorenzer calls concrete social reality and subjective ideas and fantasies. In British and American methodological traditions, these are usually understood to be in a binary relationship, mutually exclusive. As a result, what the research analyst understands through her personal, necessarily biographical, ideas and fantasies is cast as dangerously subjective, idiosyncratic and in contrast to what is social. Lorenzer thinks differently; he does not operate this binary between the individual and the social. For him, the ideas and fantasies available in an individual's unconscious as well as conscious life are 'societal-cultural'. Because of this quality they constitute 'a collective unconscious... not in Jung's sense[3] ... possibly spread over many epochs' (1986, p.28–29). It follows for Lorenzer that, although meanings are configured in biographically specific ways, they also afford access to a societal collective fund of knowledge (Hollway, 2013a). Given my methodological interests, I am led once more to ask how researchers can approach these meanings in order to produce valid knowledge.

Countertransference and reverie

In Chapter 5, I described the origin of Bion's 'reverie' in early mother–infant communication. In matrixial theory, it is seen as part of the transgressive corporeality of an originary stratum of trans-subjective knowing, and (as above) Lorenzer treats the origins of scenic understanding in the earliest stages of life. It is worth remembering that Lorenzer too was trained in a psychoanalytic methodology that uses the principle of free-floating attention, relies on abstaining from the pursuit of certainty and from pinning down ideas cognitively, but rather on opening oneself out as an instrument to how the patient is affecting one. This psychoanalytic epistemology originated alongside the concept of countertransference.

The terms transference and countertransference refer to a fairly basic idea about the flow ('transfer') of unconscious dynamics between people and within groups. Deriving from the clinical context, it tends to connote a dynamic only accessible within the highly defined clinical relationship[4] in which the analyst receives unsymbolised communi-cations from the patient, makes sense of them and can then use his or her understanding to bring them to symbolisation in interaction with the patient. Countertransference has come to be understood, in British psychoanalysis following Bion as communicative projective identification, enhanced by containment. Bion was part of a 'remarkable metamorphosis' of the concept of countertransference in 1950s Britain (Hinshelwood, 1991, p.255). Paula Heimann's influential article on the subject (1950) argued that it was 'an important "instrument of research" into the patient's unconscious' (cited in Jervis, 2009, p.146). At the same time, the analyst's own feelings (distinguished from those deriving from the patient) came to be recognised as part of the dynamic, giving rise to a broad acknowledgement that these might get in the way of the analyst's understanding. Now a relational emphasis in psychoanalysis has produced wide agreement that in general there is 'no transference without countertransference' (Clarke and Hoggett, 2009, p.13). The cul-tivation of an open-minded stance helps to protect against the intrusion of the analyst's/researcher's distortions, for example, Bion's injunction to approach observation and interpretation in the psychoanalytic ses-sion 'without memory or desire', which involves engaging in a kind of 'reverie', akin to Lorenzer's 'scenic understanding' in which ideas and subjective fantasies emerge.

As we have seen, the psychoanalytic observation tradition has fol-lowed a similar approach, a 'kind of mental functioning [which] requires a capacity to tolerate anxiety, uncertainty, discomfort, helplessness, a sense of bombardment' (Rustin, 1989, pp.20–21). Similarly, Enid Balint, describing the use of observation in medical practitioner groups, talks of 'amassing facts and feelings about the facts at the same time' (1993, p.3). It requires 'tolerating the absence of a consistent story', 'using muddle', 'using imagination', but in the safety of structure and training (1993, pp.4, 5). She addresses the role of inference in observation and counsels that the analyst must not infer too much from initial obser-vations. Rather 'they will stay in her mind latent, arousing curiosity and a kind of readiness to hear more, but must not obscure anything else' (Balint, 1993, p.11). To achieve this, the observer or analyst 'must not guess'. These descriptions derive from a non-clinical practice and use non-clinical language, but draw from the same source, namely a psychoanalytic epistemology.

These were the principles that guided the infant observation side of the research method, and informed my practice through the way that Cathy Urwin led the observation seminars. The injunction to tolerate the uncertainty of not knowing is particularly relevant for academics (a class of people who are supposed to know). An example for readers from this chapter's scenic composition emerges when, early in the scene, you find out that Jenny's family has had a social worker throughout Jenny's life. In what sense are they a family that needs this social services support? It was because of parental disability and not 'problem family' status. The above principles ask you to suspend judgement, not to guess for example that they are a 'problem' family, with its implications for how you imagine Jenny.

An associated principle in the psychoanalytic methodological repertoire is that of emergence. In our joint work using Lorenzer, Lynn Froggett described her approach to analysing data extracts, consistent with Lorenzer's scenic understanding, as follows:

> I have to leave aside the work of analysis and take distance from the object – usually by waiting a period of time and allowing an unconscious processing of the material to take place. I write the account 'as it comes', when I feel ready, after a period of something like 'reverie', and without re-visiting the analytic material. I find that a scenic structure *emerges* and although I may later compare and craft the details, the principles of selection and organisation are affectively and aesthetically driven and are unlikely to change. The resulting composition conveys the 'feel' of the interaction as I experience it. It is partly a product of my own association and unconscious phantasy.
>
> (Froggett and Hollway, 2010, p.288, my emphasis)

Provocation

Lorenzer advocates following the provocations in a text as a way of accessing scenic understanding (Bereswill et al., 2010). His method of following the provocation is very similar to that in psychoanalytic infant observation, a practical way of noticing one's affective (that is, embodied) responses. For example, Cathy Urwin, leading infant observation seminars in the research context, demonstrates the use in data analysis of feelings of shock (Urwin, 2007), surprise (Urwin, 2012) and confusion (Urwin et al., 2013). Historically the earliest, Devereux (1967) recommended noticing 'disturbances' in his discussion of the role of anxiety in research method. Once registered, the emotional response of the (data) analyst brings together the subjective fantasy and the concrete social reality: 'texts are not...empty formulae to be filled, their provocation lies in a quality present in the text itself' (Lorenzer, 1986, p.28). Here, the implication is that, the provocation's significance does not just reside in the receiver; what provokes is collective in the sense of shared socio-cultural meanings drawing on the necessarily social quality of collective experience embedded in interaction forms.

In the following section, I take the observer's 'feeling like an intruder' as a key 'provocation' via which it is possible to trace not only the individually specific but the collective aspects of experience that emerge in the intermediate area. The method requires that analysts note the provocations in our own experience and reflect upon them.[5] When the observer notes, below, how Jenny's brother's appearance provoked in her a feeling that she was intruding, she was following a central principle in psychoanalytic observation, noting her emotional responses in a register carefully separated from a detailed and descriptive observation of the setting and scene.

Scenic understanding: A data analytic example

The following scenic composition is closely based on the observation note made by Ferelyth Watt, the observer, at her fourth visit to Jenny, who lived with her parents and brothers. I rejected my original plan of using the observation notes directly because this scenic composition provides a synthesis that used the relevant detail for my methodological purposes here (omitting detail about the baby). Guided by Lorenzer's concept of the scene, I wanted to preserve as much holistic information as possible. In addition, by taking a bird's eye view that places the observer within the scene, my purpose is to encompass the socio-cultural meanings that enter by virtue of her presence.

Imagine the following scene:

In the living room of a cramped East London council flat, three people and a baby are gathered. Jenny and Anthony sit sifting through the jobs pages of a London newspaper. Jenny is holding a young baby, 11-weeks old, who faces out, dribbling. Anthony is in high spirits, celebrating his exam success. A white woman in her forties sits alertly, looking at the baby and asking Jenny how she and the baby are. She asks if the young man is an uncle. Jenny laughs and replies 'no man, huh some uncle. He's a good friend, aren't you Anthony.' Jenny and Anthony engage in youthful repartee and the older woman continues to observe the baby, not being drawn in to laughing along with Anthony's good humour. The TV is tuned low volume to an MTV station playing reggae and hip-hop. Loud music is playing in a bedroom from which another young man emerges, briefly looks in and moves off down the corridor. The woman observing the baby feels a ripple of unease, which she notices and registers through a feeling of 'what is this person doing here?'

Jenny puts the baby in his baby chair and she and Anthony discuss telephone techniques for making job enquiries. Anthony play-acts speaking to a potential employer: 'Yes, em, good afternoon. My name is David Harding and I wonder if you have any vacancies. Oh you want people of a very high standard, more than one GCSE, better than a D grade? Yes, well I think I can meet that, I've got eight'. (Pause) 'Yes, well there's twenty of us and we're all hoodies,[6] *that okay?' Anthony then calls to Jenny's brother to 'turn down that black music, yar. How can you have that stuff on so loud? Turn it down!'*[7]

I would like here to ask readers to reflect on your own emotional responses to the scene.

This scenic composition was written originally as part of a paper jointly authored with Lynn Froggett in which we set about using Lorenzer's method and theory to inform our data analysis (Hollway and Froggett, 2012). We 'followed the provocations' in the text, paying particular attention to those signalled by the observer herself, who physically belonged to the scene. Our attention was first drawn to the part where the brother *emerges, briefly looks in and moves off down the corridor.* The observer *feels a ripple of unease, which she notices and registers through a feeling of 'what is this person doing here?'.* In classical psychoanalytic terminology, the ripple of unease is felt by the observer in transference-countertransference mode. Lynn and I reflected together, at various points, on our emotional responses to the above scene. I wrote:

> Like the observer, I can readily imagine Jenny's brother wordlessly conveying a question about what this woman was doing sitting in the living room, because it seems to fit what I imagine to be the likely reality of the situation. Identifying with her, I wonder how she managed to transcend the experience of feeling like an intruder sufficiently to continue with her task. I also receive, via her notes, a lively feeling of the good relationship between Jenny and Anthony and of Anthony's quick-witted humour. I find myself liking these two teenagers, but feel unsure about the brother.

Intrusion

I wondered why the feeling of intrusion (the observer's and mine) applies in particular with the brother. I found relevant evidence earlier in the observation note about the observer's arrival, where she records her unease about going inside when she discovers that Jenny has forgotten the appointment: *'I say "You don't look as if you are expecting me" and Jenny shakes her head. I think of asking if it's okay but don't. I pick up my bag and enter, following Jenny and the young man down the corridor. Jenny doesn't seem to mind.'*

The theme of intrusion continued. For example, later in the visit the observer is left on her own in the sitting room as Jenny, followed by Anthony, takes the baby to her bedroom for a nappy change and is soon joined by the baby's father, just arrived, after he has greeted the observer. The observer comments *'I remain in the living room, feeling that to go into the bedroom would be too much.'* [8] We followed various trains of thought about this, including the social differences (of ethnicity, class and age) and the potentially intrusive role inherent in infant observation.

At this point, another unwelcome intrusion occurred, for Lynn, via association with an uncomfortable memory that surfaced from her professional experience many years previously when she worked as a social worker in a child protection team. Lynn wrote:

> The bedroom scene bothered me and although I initially thought this was because I had taken on the observer's feeling that going into such an intimate space with a couple of teenagers would be 'too much', this didn't really explain why it made me so uncomfortable. A scene formed in my own mind of a social work visit I had reluctantly had to make to the flat of a sixteen year old with a one month-old baby. The flat was full of young (white) people who I experienced as hostile at the time and who retreated to the bedroom leaving me with the feeling that they were laughing at me and planning some form of humiliation.

This unwanted scenic memory did not emerge the first few times that Lynn read the text. Instead the observer's discomfort produced an inchoate sense of dread in her, unavailable for symbolisation. She continued to wonder about the intrusion in conversation with me and through this process the earlier scene emerged in her mind.[9] When not-yet-conscious material is activated – in this case because Lynn was reluctantly impelled to associate the feeling of intrusion with another scene of personal significance – it is because the figures have a 'demanding or yearning quality that pushes them to enter consciousness' (Lorenzer, 1986, pp.28–29). In a Bionian perspective, it seems to exemplify the tenet that 'it requires two minds to think a person's most disturbing thoughts' (Ogden, 2009, p.91).[10]

Societal-collective unconscious contents

For Lorenzer, unconscious dimensions of a scene contain a 'configuration of memory traces' – interaction forms that hold 'life experiences' and form 'praxis-figures' (configurations of action). These figures are embedded in a cultural (and therefore collectively held) unconscious, experienced from infancy and built up through concrete patterns of relating with significant others and the wider environment (see Bereswill, Morgenroth and Redman, 2010; Leithäuser, 2012). An example will help put some flesh on the skeleton idea of a 'societal-cultural' unconscious.

The scenic composition directed me to the content of what emerged into symbolisation, in Anthony's play-acting, in the observer's notes and for both Lynn and me in different ways. A slice of urban British early 21st century socio-cultural reality emerged in shared unconscious significance. Pervading the scene hovers a social history in the UK of employment of black people in low paid, unskilled jobs (of which tele-sales is a contemporary example) and also black male school students' underachievement, against which Anthony is contrasting his own success. Yet probably racialised and class-based job discrimination were colliding with Anthony's pleasure at his success, an undercurrent pressing into language to threaten the idea that his exam results would be enough to earn him an interesting summer job.

Provocations in the last part of the scene

One of the criticisms of both Jung's and Lorenzer's social unconscious is that it assumes a shared experience of social reality whereas there is considerable cultural heterogeneity and social difference, as is represented amongst the participants in this scene. Anthony's playful identification with a gang of hoodies ('we') makes clear that the social realities associated with his identity status are inside as well as outside. Yet shared affective meanings emerge despite – in a way because of – the discomfort generated by differences of age, class, 'race' and professional status. Shared means different things depending on what level of conceptual generality we are interested in.[11] The observer is not black or 16 or unemployed or liable to be labelled as a hoodie. Using Bion's distinction, she knows *about* these things. Anthony knows *of* them.

Nonetheless, through com-passion – literally feeling with – it is possible partially to bridge such a divide (only partially because it involves recognising her own difference). It seems to me that all concepts of supra-individual unconscious processes are premised on the idea that meaning-full affective flows impinge, in their situated particularity, on everyone's emotional experience and the question then is what do we do (individually, collectively and societally) with frustrating, threatening and painful, as well as pleasurable, experience. Do we – this is not just the job of the fieldworker – allow it space and find out where it leads, or close it off? Can the observer note her feelings of intrusion? Can Lynn resurrect her social work memory? Can we, as later analysts of this scene, attune to its meanings through our emotional responses? This is the territory both of Bion and Lorenzer, as well as Ettinger. The individual and social as binary terms are a travesty. We are looking instead within the hyphen of the term psycho-social, 'the link that both joins and separates'[12] (Hoggett, 2008, p.383, citing Winnicott's *Playing and Reality*).

How appropriate is Lorenzer's label 'societal-collective' for the content that emerges? Let me focus, to end with, on 'race'/racialisation as an example. In Anthony's final remark (of the play-acting episode), he segues into the repeated demand to 'turn down that black music'. He is not referring to the music playing low volume on the MTV channel, that he has chosen, but the music of Jenny's brother, the other young black male present in the scene. Via this double displacement (not him, not his music), Anthony brings the idea of black into speech for the first time, at the same time encompassing the observer's whiteness, because the music would not attract this label if the three black young people were in the flat without her presence. An age difference is brought in simultaneously: it is the young who play music too loud for older people. In this way, the white observer has in common with the privileged employer most of the social identity categories in play (and signifying the power to confer employment). The play-acting also confers a relation to Anthony's own position, starting a job search weighted against him despite his exam success, because – as Anthony dramatises in the employer's imagination – behind the well-spoken inquiry lurks a gang of hoodies. In a process of emergence into symbolisation, of allowing the unbidden to emerge (not unlike the process of social dreaming), Anthony creatively draws on his societal-collective experience to communicate something profound and complex to the observer. As researchers we need to notice and reflect upon it: that is where a psychoanalytically informed methodology comes in.

Conclusions

After introducing Lorenzer at the beginning of this chapter, I used his idea of the scenic to inform the principles of an imaginative style of writing participant vignettes that is more holistic, visual and affect-laden, and to contrast this with a more typically social scientific style based on social identity categories, hoping to use the strengths of both. I have illustrated some data analytic styles that draw on psychoanalytic epistemology and foregrounded an example to illustrate the availability of 'societal-collective' imaginings that emerge unbidden (in Anthony's play-acting) because of the interactional context of the encounter and what it contains of past, present (and anticipated future) societal-cultural realities, embodied over a lifetime and becoming interaction forms.

The analysis of the scene of Anthony's play-acting, constructed from the observer's notes, is meant to provide a clear example of the location of 'the social' (or socio-cultural, or societal-collective) both outside and inside and in between (that is, in the interaction that is played out during these featured moments of the observation). I am not just talking about an interpersonal 'in between' (the interaction between the observer and Anthony), but rather about that transitional space, or reverie, in which scenic knowledge can emerge, personal and social simultaneously, which is registered by those present, by those engaged in subsequent data analysis, and – it is to be hoped – by readers. The style in which the data are written for subsequent perusal is an important factor in making scenic understanding possible.

Part III

Analysing the Politics of the Maternal Psycho-Socially

7
'I'm Not the Mother Type': Gender Identity Upheaval

In Chapter 4 I posed questions about gender difference through three of Ettinger's matrixial claims:

- that because the foetal experience of trans-subjectivity is available to all, people of whatever gender (and women whether they mother or not) have access to feeling ethical com-passion;
- that trans-subjectivity is more likely to be foreclosed among men;
- that metramorphic experiences of pregnancy precipitate the kind of transgression of the boundaries of unicity that last beyond pregnancy and can provide the basis for maternal care.

I hinted at a new non-binary conceptualisation of gender in matrixial theory that is relevant to how becoming a mother is understood, precisely because it is based in the 'transgressive corporeality' of pregnancy. In this chapter, I take further Ettinger's theorisation of the matrixial feminine and non-binary gender difference. I do this in the context of Arianna who experienced profound ambivalence about becoming a mother and whose conflict, I surmise, is bound up with her relation to her career and to her gender equal right to pursue it as a priority.

Who will want to look after babies?

In 1990, Didier Anzieu, French psychoanalyst, delved into the conflicting ethical and political implications of the climate of gender equality, which poses 'a danger for humanity' because looking after babies is devalued. His analysis, provided in an interview with Gilbert Tarrab, is worth quoting at length:

> I think that the fundamental question that arises in an acute way nowadays, with the development of methods of contraception, with

the fact that girls and women have acquired great sexual freedom and are no longer handicapped by the threat of unwanted pregnancy, and with the growing equality that they are achieving in the social, professional, and conjugal domains, and as lovers – the important question then becomes the following: there is a fundamental biological difference between males and females in so far as, in mammals, it is the female who bears inside her and gives birth to young and who has in the first days, weeks and months of life a decisive influence upon the psycho-biological development of the young. I understand completely that women are trying to escape from a position of inferiority in which they have been kept for too long on the intellectual, social and political levels, I feel I am with them in their claims. But analytic experience shows us that the psychological fate of a personality is sealed very early: a bodily and psychic relationship with a mother and an environment well adapted to his needs is an essential element in the baby's future development; which so far as the mother is concerned, presupposes that she devotes herself to her baby during the first months and that she suspends her social, professional and intellectual appetites until she can resume them at an opportune moment. The danger that people will no longer want to look after babies seems to me as grave a danger for humanity as the demographic explosion.

(Anzieu, 1990, pp.107–108)

I noticed tensions in my response to Anzieu's analysis of the conflict of interest between women's autonomous freedom and the requirements of motherhood. I was provoked, disturbed. I both agreed and wanted to disagree. Some of his analysis is supported from within feminism. For example, Daphne De Marneffe (2004) concludes that in the contemporary West, women's desire to mother does not get strong social approbation and criticises the binary of career and motherhood as a 'scheme that pits individual and maternal aspirations against one another'. Lynne Layton includes in her argument changes in formations of subjectivity. She observed what she thought was a different psychic structure among young high-achieving American women students. When teaching classes referring to feminist writing on mothering in the relational psychoanalytic tradition,[1] Layton concluded (2004, p.34) that, almost a generation later, these students 'did not find Chodorow's and Benjamin's submissive nonautonomous, relational woman familiar'. She argues that one trajectory taken by this career-orientated group of women involves a changed psychic structure away from the traditional relationship-based femininity, based on the maternal, towards a defensive autonomy that formerly characterised mainly men. A well-established feminist critique deconstructs the post-Enlightenment, Western idea of subjects as autonomous 'individuals', showing how this is historically based on an ideal type of masculine, monadic, separate, Cartesian subject (Henriques et al., 1998; Flax, 1993, chapter 4; Blackman et al., 2008; Roseneil, 2009). Nonetheless, dominant gender equality models are based on this 'autonomous individual' ontology, implicitly drawing on models of masculinity. Defensive autonomy is involved when autonomy is split off from relational needs and capacities, thus denying its embeddedness in relationships. For Layton, feminism began to change 'the proper way to live a white middle-class female heterosexual identity', the liberated woman was now 'expected to have a career, not a job, a career' and that 'to fit into a man's world, women had to be able to inhabit the male version of autonomy, the psychic requirements of which conflict dramatically with those of the so-called "relational female" ' (2004, p.34). The middle-classness of this pattern was apparent in our Tower Hamlets sample of new mothers, with implications that can be traced through to the transition to maternal identity, as we see in what follows.

Nonetheless, the starkness of the conflict Anzieu outlines was uncomfortable for me, partly because, perhaps, it encompasses the terrain of women's reproductive biology so problematic for feminism. Objections started to course through my mind. For example, I noticed a move in vocabulary from 'she' (the birth mother) to 'people' (not wanting to look after babies any more) that seemed to contain the remnants of a contentious feminist issue: where do other people, notably fathers, come into the picture of care when these constructions of sexual difference are based on a logic of mammalian sexual difference meaning that females bear new life? Yet females do.

I decided that Arianna's case example could provide a way of exploring further Anzieu's fears. My argument is that Ettinger's thinking on the subject of the matrixial feminine can help transcend the way that sexual difference is thought within phallic logic and is so tormentingly experienced in Arianna's own subjectivity as she becomes a mother. Her example illustrates and explores the ensuing psychological conflicts when a woman has passion for, and commitment to, her career and her autonomy in pursuing it; who, in Anzieu's terms, is unwilling – perhaps unable because of her identity investments – to 'suspend her [...] professional appetites'. Arianna, whom I interviewed, was also notable for the courage with which she defied the conventional discourses of mother love to articulate and face her negative feelings about being a mother.

Chronological portrait of Arianna

(Arianna was not part of the observation sub-sample.)

First interview, in her workplace office: Eight months pregnant

The field notes remarked how small her bump seemed, 'a very small amount of space allowed in her body and in her life'. She did not touch the bump throughout the interview. She was very open about her fears and used vivid language, for example that her body shape was 'torment'. The field note format included noting, at the end, what feelings the interviewer was left with. My note reads, 'I felt quite anxious for her; I wanted to tell her to let the work go.'[2]

The story of Arianna becoming pregnant reveals her profound doubts about becoming a mother. She and her husband, Vincent, had agreed to talk about 'whether or not we wanted any children' when she 'hit thirty five'. When they first met, Arianna 'was adamant I didn't want any children . . . and um, he was very fond of babies . . . he's very nice and kind hearted so he really wanted a baby and I didn't'. Not long before the birthday deadline, she missed a period. She pushed it to the back of her mind. Since they 'took precautions against it', it did not occur to her that she could be pregnant and she imagined that hers was an early case of menopause (she had recently read about this possibility). She therefore arranged to see a gynaecologist. A friend prevailed upon her to do the common sense thing first – to buy a pregnancy test kit just to check. 'I said OK, I will have the test but I was so positive it was going to be negative, um, it was a complete surprise. I – I – I didn't believe it. I couldn't believe it [laughs].' Her reaction to the test result was confusion and 'the first thing that popped into my mind was "what's going to happen to my project?" [. . .] that was my main concern, also the other pieces of work that I was trying to finish . . . .'

Arianna arranged to have an abortion. The night after she told Vincent she might want an abortion, she 'dreamt of a little baby and it was a girl'. She remained deeply conflicted until the planned abortion was imminent, at which point she phoned up to cancel. The weekend before the Monday abortion appointment,

> We just sat down and we, we thought about everything that had been going through my mind. I managed to sort of pull everything

together and make a list in my head . . . and we just decided that – we just – well *I* decided, that I wanted to keep the baby, and it was just certainly something that Vincent wanted anyway.

They had held off telling their parents because after that an abortion decision would have been impossible ('the long awaited first grand-child'). An influential factor in this decision was that she had arranged a specific meeting with her project manager where it was agreed that she could continue working informally on the project during her maternity leave.

Her unhappiness ('I do not remember it as a happy time') was com-pounded by the extreme sickness she went through for at least three months. 'I don't know why they call it morning sickness because it went through the whole day [laughs] and became really bad in the evening, er I could barely stand on my feet after about five o'clock . . . I couldn't do work, I couldn't do anything. I couldn't function properly.' But that was not all: 'the other thing . . . of course the changes in my body . . . and I felt uncomfortable'.

I hated that, I still do, the body which I feel that it's not mine and I have no control over it [. . .] it doesn't matter what I eat or not eat [. . .] it's out of my control at the moment [. . .] Plus the thought of after the birth I will still be trapped in that body. [. . .] I mean my hips, my breasts, my everything, I feel that this is not *me*.

The first scan left her unmoved but when the midwife 'first located its heartbeat' tears came to her eyes.

It was the heartbeat that made it real, it is really something living inside me that made it very, very real, I really have fond memories of that. And I still today every time I hear the heartbeat, I always feel very excited. It's the one thing I like listening to.

Nonetheless at the time of the interview (four weeks before the birth was due), Arianna finds it hard to picture the baby, 'I also feel like it's never going to happen. I find it very strange that both me and Vincent feel familiar [with] a person who really – [we] don't even know what it looks like. I find it very strange.' Arianna comes from a South-ern European country but speaks English when she talks to the baby inside her: 'I haven't really managed to talk to it in [mother tongue]

[...] that has always perplexed me [...] strange that I have no wish to communicate in my own language with the baby.'

Arianna is scared of the birth and 'I don't know how depressed I'll be afterwards.' She is adamant that she will not breastfeed. At the end of the interview, she raises the 'big worry with my Mum being around in the house for five weeks' [after the birth]. 'I'm worried that she's going to take over the household – for my mother I'm still a five year old.' She repeats how this bothers her ('very scary'): 'she's my Mum, and she has the authority, but will she grant me that I am the mother of that baby?' She imagines the totality of worries that she will have, 'so many things to deal with, least of all my – my body, I imagine, which probably will drive me insane'.

Second interview: At Arianna's home: Baby girl, nearly five months old

Arianna had a Caesarean birth because the baby was breech. She preferred this because it was organised in advance. She quickly passes over the details of the birth, saying the time in hospital (four days because she lost huge amounts of blood after the delivery) was good when Vincent was there but afterwards 'it was just too much change'. She wanted the injection that would dry up her milk but it was not available so she had to bear the milk production even though she never wavered in her decision not to breastfeed. After this she repeats how much she misses her work and how the baby would not let her do any work. Her mother 'took over completely', which was helpful because she needed to sleep, but diminished her confidence, 'I mean I'm not even the baby's mother any more, ... for my Mum it was just really two children in the house but one older.'

Arianna was told that she 'had post natal depression'. She felt 'desperately alone'. [In the following extracts, numbers represent seconds' length of pauses]

> For five weeks I think I avoided her, (1) avoided my parents, I avoided my husband, I was (1) just trying to (2) I think I even avoided *myself*, I was just trying to (.) find out who I am (1) it was very (1) *s-strange* erm (4) to to to know that I had a baby you know I – I (3) I'm not the person who can have a baby, I'm not the mother type.

Arianna then goes on to talk about herself as a professional woman with a career. She didn't like to go out because if the baby cried, she worried that people would think she was a bad mother. In fact 'I was really petri-fied that people might think I'm a bad mother (.) probably because I *felt* like I was a bad mother because I didn't love her. So I stayed pretty much at home and it drove me insane (baby making sounds).' She remem-bered how, when she was short of iron during pregnancy, the midwife had referred to babies as parasites, and after the birth, Arianna 'kept thinking of her really as a parasite', 'sucking away my life'. Her com-munication with her husband broke down: 'I really thought that some (1) point there was a point that we're not going to make it (inaudible).' By this time, however (nearly five months after the birth), things were changing. 'I think now finally I can say that I love her, I think, yes, after all this time, we have finally come to an understanding, haven't we sweetie' (Arianna is addressing the baby in a soft, affectionate voice). Now she thinks her baby is beautiful.

She liked the fact that she still mattered more than the baby to her father but

> with my Mum (2) it's still very hard I mean a (.) I mean I – I even I even confronted my mum I told her that you really love the baby more than me and she cannot even deny that (.) I mean to her credit she is not a liar...she really loves the baby more (1) than she loves me now.

As for her husband 'he loved her from the start (.) unlike me (.) but he *really* loves her and she loves him back. You can see the way they inter-act and they play together.' When Arianna is trying to work at home, she keeps her close by in the pram 'she can look at my screen or we talk'. She couldn't be left upstairs except for a nap because 'she just doesn't like being alone' and therefore it would be impossible for Arianna to work.

She hated the fact that the house was messy with boxes still unpacked:

> I have very (1) strict (1) order. I mean my office and everything is just for me perfectly or everything has a place (.) everything (...) this (the house) is just not me (1) I can't work like that (...) it was just really everything I felt because my life was completely out of control.

Things improved when Arianna could go back to her work office: 'really my sanctuary (.) I go there and I'm alone and it's my place...and every-thing's so perfect in my office (.) When I went into my office I – I – I – (.) I don't know (2) it felt (2) I don't know I just, like I have conquered the

(.) tallest mountain or something (.) in the 13 foot in my office again (2) so beautiful (sighs) erm I've missed it so much.

When she went to stay with her parents, she completed an enormous amount of work while her mother, a professional self-employed woman who took the entire time off to be with her granddaughter, looked after the baby, 'I did a lot, yes (.) it was the only way for me to remain sane.' Now the baby attends more days at nursery and Vincent looks after her at home one day each week. Arianna says 'sometimes [I] really (1) can't wait to see her (1) but I don't miss her during the day because I know that this is my time for work (...) she seems so happy with the other children... I don't think she *cares* that I leave her.' She thinks the baby is pleased to see her (she always breaks into a big smile) 'but *honestly* (1) if she didn't see me (2) ever again... I don't think she would have any recollections of me.' She worries how much more she will have to adapt when the baby is crawling: 'It's such hard work', she doesn't understand how people have more than one child... 'I think it's one of the hardest things I've ever had to do.'

I have selected many extracts to communicate to readers the quality of Arianna's upheaval and conflict in the first months of her baby's life and in the process run the risk of opening up the powerful 'bad mother' discourse that is available to us all. The field notes provided a useful anti-dote to such dominant tracks of meaning-making because the embodied interaction between Arianna and her baby was more affectionate than the transcript of her account implied. Although the audio record bet-ter conveyed her soft-voiced communications, it could not record, for example, that 'baby spends almost the whole interview on Arianna's lap', ... Arianna seems 'relaxed with her, strokes her hair and plants fre-quent kisses on her forehead'. Later when the baby pulls her hair, she 'grimaces and quietly extricates it without complaint'. When the baby drops a toy twice, Arianna tells her 'in a very firm voice' that she 'will not pick it up next time if baby drops it again'. 'Baby does not drop it.'

Third interview, Arianna's place of work: Baby 14½ months

Arianna starts by saying how happy she is to be back at work, which means that 'things have got better' but continues that she finds moth-erhood 'extremely stressful'.

> My feelings towards my child are completely different from my feelings about being a mother... I worry about many, many things and I'm not really enjoying being a mother to her, not because I don't love her... but because of all the things that come with

being a Mum... I'm worried about when she's older and she goes to school... I'm just really worried about so many things, all this, about her future... it's a constant worry.

According to Arianna, 'she is an extremely temperamental child'. She eats well and is sociable, but she still wakes them up in the night. When she has picked up the baby from nursery and gets home, before Vincent gets home:

> I have an hour and a half to try, as I said I have to do the washing, have to wash the bottles, you know, make sure her bag is ready, we talk, whatever I do she follows me... but all she wants is to be held... I have to tidy up, clean the kitchen, clean the bathroom... make her dinner.

When Vincent gets back he cooks dinner. He also plays with the baby, who wants to be picked up by him too, 'but' explains Arianna 'she knows that er, she's not going to get picked up by me, not while I'm doing something'. Arianna likes spending time with her daughter but 'I wish I were more relaxed to spend more time with her without worrying about what's going to happen, without worrying that the house looks untidy or whatever.' She doesn't see this as a possibility because 'there will always be something in the back of my head, bugging me, whether it will be work... I'm afraid that's my nature'. However, the baby 'adds a huge amount on to it. I mean I do not like things I cannot control (...) I don't like this uncertainty.' She knows many mothers are content 'but for me, it's not a fun thing, or, it's just responsibility, something you have to perform at your best, because the tiny mistake can back fire... I mean the performance has to be so immaculate in order for the results to be perfect.' 'I feel ten years older and I just feel that the life is being sucked away from me with all these worries.' When the interviewer asks 'what gives you the most pleasure?' Arianna's response is to repeat the question as if it is not clear and then, surrounded by two very long pauses, say that she cannot think of anything. Her untypical loss for words makes her reflect further, 'strange, it's a very good question'. At the time of the first interview, in Arianna's office, a postcard of a dog was displayed which read 'If you're happy and you know it, you're unusual.'

Despite her earlier fears, Arianna had soon lost all the weight she gained during pregnancy, but then lost even more weight. When asked if she was pleased with the result, she replies 'Er don't know, I think

I have too many issues with food and er body image to be pleased with any result.' She clarifies that although she is temporarily satisfied when she loses weight 'then I start feeling unhappy and it has to be even less, and that has to stop'. She is 'concerned I might pass on to her my own problems with food', but happily the baby is 'a great eater'.

When Arianna's daughter was three years and three months old, I received an email reply to a follow up contact. Arianna starts, 'It actually feels a lot better to have a (female) three-year-old. There is verbal communications now, which I very much enjoy. We go shopping together and it is like having a "miniature" girlfriend with me.'

Autonomous gender equality and phallic logic

Speaking of women who do not work outside the home, Arianna says 'I have nothing against them but I'm not the type (.) I can't (1) plus I can't see why women work so hard all these years to (.) to to to have equal rights so we can be stuck at home for days with a baby.' This self-positioning reiterates what Ettinger calls the 'phallic logic' of feminine sexual difference and suggests that Arianna places herself within a discourse of gender equality through assimilation to a masculine autonomous world, where 'being stuck at home for days with a baby' feels like a prison sentence. In what sense is this an expression of the 'phallic logic' central to matrixial theory and its critique of Western language and thinking?

'Phallic logic' derives from the French psychoanalytic tradition, starting with Lacan and involving critiques by many, including Laplanche (who coined this critical term for Lacan's psychoanalytic turn in 1970) and a feminist tradition including Irigaray, Kristeva and latterly Ettinger. Pollock explains, 'the early Lacanian model in which Woman/Other/Thing are joined in their shared relegation to the unsignifiable zone of the Real' (2008, p.6), so that language and the Symbolic realm, the paternal principle, defines subjectivity ('the phallic and its universe of meaning encoded in language', 2008, p.10). In this model, subjectivity is 'achieved only by means of separations [...] and the symbolic cut (castration) which retrospectively catches up and redefines all preceding separations into its dominating logics of on/off, presence/absence' (2008, p.11). 'The maternal is reduced to being the other of meaning, of individuation.' (ibid)[3]

How, if at all, does the critique of phallic logic apply here? Ettinger (1997) addresses the question, focusing on the post-Kleinian thinking of Bion and Winnicott in particular, with an emphasis on the prenatal/prem. period and its sequelae. She lists a set of psychoanalytic concepts, including Bion's alpha- and proto-mental processes, Winnicott's subjective objects and Bollas' unthought known, that have emerged to deal with 'affect-laden time-space-body experiences that induce archaic (...) psychic traces' (...). Though it is the postnatal phase that is referred to by all these concepts, they also fit the prenatal/feminine encounter' (Ettinger, 1997, p.379). This combination of concepts (matrixial for a prenatal track and object relations for postnatal including adult individuation) helps me to illuminate Arianna's ambivalent relationship to becoming a mother and to contribute a psycho-social analysis of her conflicts. I hope I demonstrate that they express Arianna's situation, her relationship to it and her agency (conscious and unconscious) in relation to the turbulence she is experiencing in becoming a mother.

The feminine-matrixial

Above we saw Arianna take up a position which I have located within phallic logic. It is necessary to pose the question of how discourses of autonomous gender equality are actually reflected in mothers' subjectivities. Matrixial theory makes very specific claims about femininity within the structures of phallic logic. Ettinger distinguishes feminine[p] (feminine to the power of the phallus), which is premised on gender and sexual difference, from feminine[m] (feminine to the power of the matrixial). Pollock (2008, p.13) describes the latter as 'a supplementary, shifting stratum of human subjectivity and meaning (...) delivered to us all'. We shall see how the unstable collision of these two strata of Arianna's subjectivity pervade and plague her becoming a mother. Perhaps, in Layton's terms, she has been living out a masculine-identified 'defensive autonomous' subjectivity. It looks as if the possibility of becoming a mother threw open a conflict of sexual difference that had been settled in her adult life with Vincent and her career up to the point when the question of becoming a mother could no longer be set aside. My interest is in how Arianna's settlement becomes unsettled, as a co-affecting matrixial trans-subjectivity presses into awareness, previously under erasure by phallic logic (see below for her response to this analysis). There is a conflict between the fragilising effect of Arianna's matrixial potentiality, largely foreclosed, and the way that she lives under the 'subjectivizing features generated postnatally [in Arianna's postnatal life] under the logic of castration', which together imply a 'necessary separation from and abjection of the maternal' (Pollock, 2008, p.5). Following the logic that 'matrixial potentiality does not replace the phallus; it operates along a different unconscious track' (Ettinger, 2006a, p.220), I explore this track.

For years Arianna's gender settlement worked: I mean by this the way she arranged her adult life within the contradictory terms of binary sexual difference. She had a good equal partnership relationship, based on symmetry (similar career trajectories in the same employment sector), reciprocity and the capacity to articulate experience through language in rationality-based exchange between them as autonomous individuals. For example, 'We just sat down and we, we thought about everything that has been going through my mind. I managed to sort of pull everything together and make a list in my head' [then] 'we decided (. . .) well *I* decided'). Reliable contraception means that heterosexual sex can, at a conscious level, be shorn of the meanings of procreation. This had been the character of their partnership for many years. Perhaps – we will never know – Arianna's gender settlement would have remained stable if Vincent had been as opposed to parenthood as Arianna. Not only did it not pose the same threats to his identity (no time bomb under his gender settlement), but he was always 'very fond of babies', 'he's very nice and kind hearted so he really wanted a baby and I didn't'. So is she not nice and kind hearted? It seems that these 'feminine' characteristics were outside Arianna's self-definition, subject as it was to the binary phallic logic of autonomy and relatedness.

Becoming pregnant, becoming feminine?

The story of Arianna's becoming pregnant demonstrates the intensity of Arianna's conflict, faced with the advancing 35th birthday deadline.[4] Arianna made clear when she met Vincent that she didn't want children, yet despite her antipathy to motherhood, a decision loomed about having a baby. Arianna represents contemporary Western women who have sought and largely achieved equal status with men, aided by contraception, and then face the choice of motherhood, confronted by their advancing age. What ensured that she became pregnant before it was too late? Their plan was to make a (conscious) decision and follow it through (continue, or stop, taking contraceptive measures) but unbeknown to her conscious awareness, Arianna conceived. Faced with a missed period, she (almost) settled for an unlikely alternative explanation, that she was going through a very early menopause. (It took a friend who thought the obvious to persuade her to do a simple pregnancy test.) What kind of agent made this happen? Choice, in Arianna's situation, presumes a unitary, as well as a rational subject, putting modern women in charge of their maternal destinies. Arianna seems to recognise that she was not in charge as she tells the story and the laughter is shared: 'counting back, I was already pregnant by the time [of her 35th birthday deadline], which is really very bizarre if you think about it [both laugh]'. Her 'choice' can be seen, psychoanalytically, as acting out, 'a shift into action that abruptly short-circuits speech and realizes an unconscious desire without the subject noticing' (Anzieu, 1990, pp.88–89). This account involves unconscious dynamics – an 'unconscious track' in Ettinger's phrase (above) – consistent with 'matrixial potentiality' (Ettinger, 2006a, p.220).

Arianna's account here appears consistent also with a classic psychoanalytic idea of the repressed unconscious. Anzieu's definition foregrounds the role of speech in bringing such a desire to consciousness. A matrixial account finds a further dimension operating in the 'really very bizarre' way that Arianna became pregnant: an originary transsubjective stratum foreclosed (not 'repressed' in this paradigm, because not previously part of conscious awareness) and then ignited by her current dilemma. If the yearning to become a mother has timeless qualities, it is also populated by contents clearly located in contemporary time and post-feminist Western space that define Arianna's conflict between career and motherhood.

Using this concept of a foreclosed matrixial stratum, inaccessible to conscious thought because it is based in archaic encounters, raises questions about its exclusive link to women. Matrixial theory is explicit: 'the woman *doubly* experiences the matrixial borderspace: first, in the last period of prenatal life in the maternal womb [. . .], and second, as someone who has a womb [. . .] whether she is a mother or not' (Ettinger, 1997, p.391). From this perspective,

> wanting a child may be a matter of wishing for a reencounter with the kind of otherness-in-proximity that is the gift of our mothers to us as woman-subjects, a gift to all subjects that may also be reactivated in a variety of other ways as well, notably in relations with others.
>
> (Pollock, 2008, p.15)

Matrixial theory is not in opposition to the more classic psychoanalytic idea of acting out, which also pertains to aspects of subjectivity excommunicated from language, but it adds an earlier stratum of subjectivisation, as I introduced above, in which, 'bodies which have the potential to generate . . . are already border linked to the sexual-feminine, maternal at the level of unremembered memory and imaginative projection that may be foreclosed under phallocentrism' (Pollock, 2008, p.15).

This potential to generate is definitional of the feminine in a matrixial logic, but it looks very much as if it has been foreclosed under phallocentrism for Arianna. Now it stirs a part of her that is unassimilable to masculine autonomy, hence her extreme foreboding as the decision deadline loomed (shall I ever become a mother?) and beyond into pregnancy and the first few months of motherhood. This foreboding manifests in Arianna's feelings about her changing body shape, tormenting her as she looked in the mirror at 'my breasts, my hips, my everything' and framed the desperate reply, 'this is *not me*'. Her body – breasts, hips – was changing in ways that signified fecund womanhood. The gender-equal 'me' was not based on a female (which is also a maternal) body; it was feminine[p], based in her relation to an embodied feminine difference as other from a man and abjected. She had long since been controlling the feminine shape of this body through dieting and now it was out of her control.

Assertion of the feminine[m]

Arianna arranged to have an abortion. Having articulated her preference for an abortion to Vincent, she dreams about a baby girl. The multiple meanings of the dream can only be guessed at. Dreams (Freud's 'royal road to the unconscious') involve a processing of emotional experience in which the inadmissible can arise. In a different modality from conscious language, Arianna imagines a baby girl. Perhaps this is Arianna's first encounter with the possibility of motherhood that is not captured by the terror associated with phallic logic, the loss of her autonomous individuality. Imagining a daughter (she did not 'know' the sex) would tap into an aspect of the feminine as elaborated in matrixial theory, namely ' "she" repeating at a new register what once she co-evented at the register of her own becoming', 'severality on two temporal registers' (Pollock, 2004, p.26). Two further occasions provide evidence of this ongoing encounter involving affectionate connection with the prenatal other whose existence transforms Arianna into the becoming-mother; first when she hears the heart beat (tears indicate a feeling that manifests directly in the body) and second when she felt the first movement, 'a slight sort of "hello" '.

In both cases Arianna is able to transcend phallic logic, to which she normally cleaves, and is receptive to the matrixial register of communication where '[A]ffects are transferred across the entire psychic borderspace of severality; traces are emitted, transmitted and redistributed, opening new affective passageways for reception and transmission, shareable by resonance' (Ettinger, 2006a, p.222). The heartbeat, Arianna says, makes 'very, very real' 'something living inside me'. This idea is central to matrixial theory, with its recognition of 'pregnancy as a state of being alive in giving life' (Pollock, 2008, p.6). The consequence is that 'the maternal subject wants to live beside that given life' (ibid).

Most of the time, however, Arianna fails to sustain the pleasurable feeling of giving life to another life; rather having a baby 'feels like it's not going to happen'. But here again there is a new experience, conflicting with the phallic logic of the gaze, 'I find it very strange that both me and Vincent feel familiar [with] a person who really – [we] don't even know what it looks like. I find it very strange.' While in phallic logic this is almost a contradiction in terms, in matrixial logic, the prenatal non-I of the trans-subjective encounter is familiar, despite being unknown. The baby-to-come is familiar in two temporal registers (ibid), 'diachronous as well as synchronous'. The diachrony is particular to Arianna as the becoming mother because 'at the same time memories of the primordial condition of her own becoming [...] are newly reactivated from another position: the transsubjective matrixial encounter in a trans-subjectivising archaic environment [...] asymmetrical, regressive, remembering and at the same time anticipatory and projective into living futures to come' (Pollock, 2008, p.9). The primordial condition is available also to Vincent, synchronously, deriving from 'what once *he* co-evented at the register of *his* own becoming' (emphasis added) (ibid). Vincent 'loved the baby, really loved her, from the start', unlike her, Arianna suggests. It is in this sense that femininity to the power of the matrixial (feminine[m]) is 'open to all', if they are available to fragilisation.

Arianna cannot bring herself to talk to her baby inside the womb in her mother tongue (which she finds strange). Perhaps it would be too fragilising, in which case she keeps certain archaic feelings at bay which would be resurrected by the language of her mother, the language whose rhythms would have co-affected her in the joint encounter of her beginnings: 'the resonating voice of the m/Other is a primary affective feel-knowing transmission tool (...) trembling in different ways' (Ettinger, 2006b, p.120). Instead Arianna uses English (not Vincent's mother tongue either), the language she learned as an adult subject. Such is Arianna's fear of the changes to this subjecthood that the baby-to-come is imagined as a parasite draining her of (her autonomous) life, when it depletes her of the iron she needs. At the time of the third interview, she expresses a similar idea: that now she is a mother 'life is being sucked away from me with all these worries'. Arianna fears being devoured: 'In matrixial encounter-events we are extremely fragilised, the fear of being abused, devoured and abandoned is therefore at heights' (Ettinger, 2006b, p.125).

Being responsible for another life

It is worry that sucks away at Arianna, the worry of not being in control of life, which now includes her daughter's life. Domestic disorder ('I wish I were more relaxed to spend more time with her without worrying [...] that the house looks untidy or whatever') contrasts with pleasure at the perfect order of her office space, over which she feels in complete control ('everything's so perfect in my office [...] so beautiful (sighs) erm I've missed it so much'). The need for perfection is closely tied in with the imposition of order and is a powerful theme in the last interview when Arianna reveals how it poisons her enjoyment of her daughter: 'I worry about many, many things and I'm not really enjoying being a mother to her, not because I don't love her... but because of all the things that come with being a Mum.'

Before pregnancy, Arianna could exercise a great deal of control over her life (witness her appetite control and the order of her office). What she experiences as a mother ('all the things that come with being a Mum') is her daughter's alterity: she cannot fully control her daughter's life although she feels utterly responsible for it. This sucks the life out of her and makes her feel ten years older. Regarding worrying, she says,

> I'm afraid that's my nature' [and the baby] adds a huge amount on to it. I mean I do not like things I cannot control (...) I don't like this uncertainty (...) for me, it's not a fun thing, or, it's just responsibility, something you have to perform at your best, because the tiny mistake can back fire... I mean the performance has to be so immaculate in order for the results to be perfect.

Arianna is insightful about all of this, but she cannot control her worrying. The connection she feels to her daughter, evident in the worry, defies her autonomous subjectivity: she cannot control her daughter's life. She mentions in this connection that her own mother was overprotective.

It could be seen as paradoxical that Arianna's separate subjectivity did not lend itself to an easily detached relationship with her daughter: in practice the trans-subjective connection means that she is never free of worry (like Marie's '*angoisse*', Chapter 5); that her passion means that only perfection is good enough. The jointness facet of matrixial 'jointness in differentiation' is consistent with Arianna's extension of existential anxiety to her daughter's wellbeing. She succeeds in articulating this new disjuncture, which I conceptualise as the product of ongoing encounters (often collisions) between matrixial and phallic strata of subjectivity: 'My feelings towards my child are completely different from my feelings about being a mother.' She dislikes being a mother because it is so stressful, 'a constant worry'. She loves her daughter with a maternal passion characterised by Kristeva in the claim 'as long as she is alive, the mother is there to guarantee life to the best of her ability' (2005, p.1).

Fragilisation and sanity

Maternal passion in itself would be fragilising. Indeed Kristeva, like Winnicott, suggests that it resembles borderline states,[5] and that then 'a certain detachment-depassioning takes place in most cases' (2005, p.3). More prosaically, there is a great deal of evidence that Arianna experienced threats to the self she had constructed prior to becoming a mother. Matrixial theory is clear that fragilisation, the reassertion of a foreclosed transsubjective stratum of subjectivity, goes with the territory of becoming a mother: 'matrixial coemergence has a healing power, but because of the transgression of individual boundaries that it initiates and entails, and because of the self-relinquishment and fragilisation it appeals to, it is also potentially traumatizing' (Ettinger, 2006a, p.219). Describing the way she threw herself into work after the baby was born, Arianna said, 'yes I did a lot . . . it was the only way for me to remain sane' and this did not seem like a loose use of language. Winnicott noticed the 'flight to sanity' in some new mothers who could not take the risk of suspending their usual boundaried subjectivity in order, as he saw it, to identify more fully with the state of their new infants (Winnicott, 1956; Hollway, 2011a).

Arianna's so-called postnatal depression seems to be based on a terrified inability to 'feel with' her baby's vulnerability, the antithesis of her implicit notion of subjecthood. In matrixial theory, such 'feeling with' ('com-passion') is definitional of what continues from pre- to post-maternal life: 'Becoming responsible for traces of the other as if they were mine is a matrixial ethical move' (Ettinger, 2006a, p.221).

For example, when the baby is four months old, Arianna tells me[6]:

> I mean now she's interacting with me and she can smile back and talk to me with her own way but then (1) it's just a really blank

face (3) Whatever you do she never smiled (.) she never I mean it's just somebody who demands from you (.) and doesn't give anything back (.) anything not even a smile let alone (2) and I was just furious because I wanted to do things and (1) she just wouldn't let me most of the time (1) [...] (.) uh sometimes it just drove me up the wall she would just wouldn't let me concentrate I really didn't feel (2) I didn't (.) understand why erm (.) women say that all this (.) fall in love with the child (1) erm when it's born (.) I just (2) I really thought it was all a load of rubbish (banging noise in the background) I just didn't feel anything for her for weeks (baby making sounds) (.) (Int: mm) (.) anything I mean whether she was mine or somebody else's (.) uh (.) and I think whoever was looking after her it was the same (1) I didn't have any sympathy (baby making sounds) (.) I didn't feel anything (2) I mean I didn't (.) I – I also thought I was losing myself as well (Int: mm) and I found that very hard (.) to cope (.) 'cus she didn't let me be myself any more.

In this extract we see evidence of three of Winnicott's (1956, p.302) claims about new mothers with 'big alternative concerns' (in Arianna's case, her career) that mean they take 'flight to sanity'. First, she feared losing her former identity; that is, the baby put unbearable strains on her to change her former self when she needed to preserve it intact. Second, she was incapable of identifying closely with (in Ettinger's sense of com-passion as 'feeling with') the state and capacities of her infant (such a state was too distant from the rational subjecthood in which she was invested). Third, Arianna could not embrace the asymmetrical, non-reciprocal relationship that was all her new baby was capable of (the demands without giving anything back).

In this third point, we see the way Arianna unwittingly imposes an image of relationship that works between two autonomous subjects in symmetrical relationship, a relationship that is impossible with a new born ('just demands', 'giving nothing back'). The same model underpins how she understands her baby's feelings about being left at nursery: 'I don't think she *cares* that I leave her.' She thinks the baby is pleased to see her again (she always breaks into a big smile) 'but *honestly* (1) if she didn't see me (2) ever again [...] I don't think she would have any recollections of me.' The idea behind this startling (to me) claim, central to phallic logic, is that before the aware subjecthood that comes with language, a child will have no memories, no connections, only needs that any caring adult could meet. This is also the dominant logic of contemporary Western European childcare policies when, as often is the case, distinctions are not made regarding the child's age. Perhaps Arianna's assumption of a separate subjectivity in her daughter is linked to her need to separate herself from the baby's demands, an example of projection. At any rate, when she is cleaning and tidying, she does not pick up her daughter, who has come to learn not to expect it (of her mother). Winnicott's account of primary maternal preoccupation as 'an organized state (that would be an illness were it not for the fact of the pregnancy)' (1956, p.302) is strikingly consistent with Ettinger's concept of fragilisation. Winnicott resists the conventional phallic logic of Freudian psychoanalysis in his account of new mothers' states of mind in the perinatal period.

Co-becoming and alterity beyond biology

When Griselda Pollock introduces Ettinger's understanding of the feminine and its connection to the maternal, she is explicit about the sensitivities she expects to arouse amongst feminists. For example (Pollock, 2008, p.11): 'Ettinger invites us to recognise, to re-cognise, a subjectivizing partnership that is primordially *feminine* [. . .] Let me be careful here,' and Pollock goes on to differentiate Ettinger's use of 'feminine' from feminists like De Beauvoir, historically influential in the 'gender equality on male terms' strategy (Hekman, 1999; see this Chapter 8). For De Beauvoir, the feminine was 'understood to be the stereotype of woman from which feminism was in revolt' (Pollock, 2008, p.11). Matrixial theory provides 'an understanding of a certain deforming imposition of negativised otherness onto the feminine as the cipher through which the masculine is positivised and rendered both dominant and universal' (Pollock, 2008, p.12). This is the 'feminine' that Arianna is rejecting. The matrixial feminine reconceptualises the feminine body so that it is no longer about deriving a gendered/sexed identity from a bodily organ, the womb; rather the body is 'imaginatively understood as cycles, pleasures, sexualities, surfaces, contacts, even traumas' (ibid.) Because it is available to any being that emerges from intrauterine life, this matrixial version of the feminine (feminine[m] as opposed to feminine[p]) does not reduce to the maternal, although it is intimately bound up with the maternal as guarantor of life and founder of a proto-ethics based on com-passion. Ettinger addresses a feminist political objection when she clarifies that her matrixial approach

> doesn't indicate any limitation on a woman's rights over her body, quite the contrary! As a concept, the matrix supports women's full

response-ability for any event occurring with-in their own not-One
corpo-reality and accounts for the difference of such response-ability
from the phallic order

(Ettinger, 1997, p.370, footnote)

Quite where womanhood is to be found in here ('the difficulty of pars-
ing "woman" from "femininity"', Baraitser, personal communication)
remains a question. It is probably what Arianna is struggling for in
amongst the spectres of abjection raised by her becoming mother.

Ettinger's becoming mother is always a co-becoming and Arianna's
is no less so for the defences she uses against the fragilising threats
of her transjective[7] connections with her baby, defences that continue to find refuge in her work identity. Co-becoming does, however, raise the figure of the child and its capacity to be other to
the mother (the child's alterity). Arianna's daughter does not bend to
her will ('extremely temperamental'). What the child brings into the
co-becoming is its difference. This does not arise originally from the
separation of birth out of a prior fusion. Rather it is a 'metramorphosis':
matrixial 'relations without relating' are differentiated in jointness, resonances across a border (a dual interface) that always affords both
linking and spacing. The use of physics concepts, such as waves and
resonances, makes it possible to conceptualise 'occurrences at shared
borderspaces whose mutually unknown and unknowable partners-in-
difference register a shared event, but differently for each partner'
(Pollock, 2008, p. 14).

This way of imagining intrauterine beginnings is consistent with
Anzieu's 'bottom line' about the biology of female mammals. It transcends the oppositional logic of biological sexual difference while also
offering a psychology proper of prenatal/prematernal co-becoming consistent with Anzieu's psychoanalytic emphasis on 'a bodily and psychic
relationship with a mother' and the necessary early 'devotion'. The
idea of joint eventing before birth enlarges what can be thought about
prematernal experience. Because the trans-subjective stratum, with its
fragilising effects, is available for all to reopen, Anzieu's shift in the subject of maternal care from mother to people, which I raised early in this
chapter, is apposite. It was probably fortunate for Arianna's daughter
that the grandparents and father were all close by in the early weeks
when Arianna was psychologically absent. There is little doubt that
postnatal depression is not good for babies (Murray, 1992). What we
cannot say is what Arianna would have been like if her parents had not

been there, given that she felt positioned like 'still a five year old' by her mother.

Research ethics coda: What did Arianna think of the analysis?

I have been mulling over ethical questions about feeding back to participants for many years, partly prompted by comments from psycho-social colleagues who have done so (Stopford, 2004; Hoggett et al., 2010; see also Hollway and Jefferson, 2013, pp.155–157). My focus has been specifically in the context of psycho-social analysis that posits a 'defended subject'; that is, participants who have reasons not to think about some of the things that I as a researcher on subjectivity do want to think about through their cases. If the methods of data production and data analysis are psychoanalytically informed, but there is neither a therapeutic frame nor contract, what right do I have to show the result to participants who are the subject of a single case analysis (shorter and less holistic uses of data often do not raise the same ethical questions)? I have also felt in practice that decisions about feeding back results should be subject to a specific case-by-case assessment, which enables a researcher to link together all considerations before coming to a conclusion.

I eventually decided that Arianna's single case analysis, more or less as it appears in this chapter, was a suitable example for sharing with her. I had her email address. First I wrote telling her what I was writing and how her information figured, mentioning also the published article. I briefly told her the principles I used in anonymising her data and checking with her the suitability of her pseudonym and her husband's. I also said 'If you don't want to see the chapter or article – it might seem like another world now that your daughter is not a baby any longer – I understand and in that case would just want to thank you warmly for what you contributed to the project.' Arianna replied straight away:

> So wonderful and what a surprise to hear from you! I am so glad to hear that this project that started over eight years ago is progressing so well. Thank you for giving me the opportunity to participate in it. (…) I would love to have a copy of the draft – although I fear I cannot promise you that I will manage to read it and comment, since I am up to my ears with work.

I did not delay in sending the chapter draft and the next day I heard back:

> I am very busy but I could not help myself and kept reading bits and pieces of the chapter. (...) I have mixed feelings about it – not because I do not like it, I actually love it. Especially the end – 'love her baby, but hate motherhood' (...) This chapter has helped me to realise that the two are not mutually exclusive.

The mixed feelings were to do with imagining how it would feel if her daughter ever found out 'that her mother had scheduled an abortion'. Characteristically, Arianna could face imagining this, telling me about it and still generously concluding 'But in the end, I hope that it will help other people like me, who feel awful and tormented because they do not comply with society's expectations applicable to females. Thank you so much for an emotional and insightful read!' I was relieved and moved. I felt that the sharing worked ethically, that my judgement was correct about her capacity to think through the analysis sufficiently for it to be a good experience. I not only had permission but also a precious kind of validation. I replied, thanking her for her insights and generosity and went on:

> It is a relief to feel that my constructed account can be accurate enough and recognising to be thought provoking to the person whose life it is such a privilege to share. I can understand just how it feels to imagine your daughter finding out such information, and of course it is for just such reasons that we take great care with confidentiality and anonymity. But there would be no trace whatsoever back to you, just as long as you erased your copy of this draft.

And I set about anonymising my copy of the email record. I was trying to be precise when I said 'I can understand just how it feels...': Arianna and I shared the fact of being career women and mothers of one daughter, and from the time when Arianna asked me if I had children, there was a sharing of something in common, which did not disable understanding of differences (for example, when analysing Arianna's data I was not in a position of 'identifying with' her conflict about getting pregnant, nor her feelings about changes in her body). This conforms to an adult version of Ettinger's 'jointness in differentiation'/'differentiation in jointness', as well as the two-part account of object relations (Redman, 2009, see Chapter 3). Finally, on the subject of 'becoming', eight years later Arianna experienced reading my case analysis as an 'emotional read' and as 'liberating'. As I understand it, her recognition of herself in this narrative was one more (micro)event in an ongoing process of becoming a mother.

Conclusion

The strong matrixial thread of conceptualisation in this chapter is guided by three purposes: first, to explore the vicissitudes of transgressive corporeality; second, to continue the dialogue with object relations approaches with a view to appreciating their congruency with matrixial concepts, and third, but not least, to situate what can appear as the rather archaic character of matrixiality in the conditions of the contemporary Western career-orientated constructions of women.

Together the themes are addressed by asking what Arianna's example provides in relation to the danger, in Anzieu's words, that people will no longer want to look after babies. We see the baneful effects of how Arianna's subjectivity is shaped by the historical changes in gender relations that Anzieu specified (among many influences in her biography, no doubt). We see how it forecloses the possibilities of identifying with the unconditional demands of a new baby, how she dreads the 'feminine' changes in her body that suggest the maternal and are experienced in a binary with masculine-defined gender equality. Nonetheless, through conflict, psychic change is made possible, and the conflict appears precipitated by the stirrings of a trans-subjective stratum of subjectivity, proto-ethical through com-passion, foreclosed but never erased. It affords confidence that the capacity to care for babies does not get extinguished so easily, and is not the sole preserve of birth mothers (although they have a matrixial edge through the double register). In this regard, the devotion of father and grandparents, we see the value of matrixial theory's move from essentialist biology to a feminine[m], in which others are fragilised by their identifications with the baby. Arianna's conflict could be seen in a more positive light, by paying attention to the breaking through of a bond which, although fraught with worry, meant that Arianna – autonomy-dominated gender equal subjectivity and all – found a way to love her baby (while hating motherhood).

The dialogue between matrixial concepts and object relations theories (especially Winnicott here, with his impressive paediatric and psychoanalytically informed experience of new babies and their mothers) develops the theme of what happens in postnatal relations when the newly ignited trans-subjective track collides with the mother's individuated, phallic, track. In the following chapter, I explore this question further through Justine's difficulties with separation. Situating Justine (differently) in the same prevailing gender discourses, the conflict between trans-subjective and individuated tracks is articulated differently.

8
Theorising Maternal Becoming Psycho-Socially

Introduction

In Chapter 7, Arianna's relation to the discourse of gender equality was explored in terms of how, at a profound level of identity investment, she experienced being an autonomous career woman as mutually exclusive with being a 'mother type'. As her daughter grew up a little, she found she could remain career focused and this was helped by her husband, whose career was no more important than Arianna's, who loved being a hands-on father and who did a fair share of domestic work. Arianna did not, in any decisive either/or fashion, have to put motherhood before career, or sacrifice one for the other. Discourses and policies of gender equality did not fail her in this respect, but rather in being based on a male model, where being a woman-and-mother is in binary relation to autonomous self-reliance. Justine, the example in this chapter, was differently positioned.

Susan Hekman (1999, p.7) characterised the stance of early feminism as 'the erasure of difference and the pursuit of equality'. Being an erasure of women's difference from men, the goal was for women to gain equality by being as like men as they could be. This was followed historically, according to Hekman, by a second strategy, that of valorising the feminine and women's difference from men. From the point of view of Pollock's caution against a reversal strategy of phallic logic, both these strategies are mired in binaries. To identify the phallic logic is to recognise its embeddedness in the subjectivising conditions of women's lives.

Media discourses reflect this polarisation and splitting. Headlines such as 'Stay-at-Home and Career Moms Face Off on Their Choices' soon emigrated from the US 'Mommy Wars'. In the UK, debates actively engaged in by mothers themselves treated women as if they were one kind or the other, as if conflict is not experienced within mothers themselves, or as if part-time work is not a commonly preferred option (a UK poll in 2009 found that 'only 12% of mothers wanted to work full-time'[1]). Objections from voices close to government demonstrate the continuation of the same binary treatment. For example, in 2009, a UK policy report by the right-of-centre Centre for Policy Studies lamented the previous administration's stance when Harriet Harman (Labour's first Minister for Women) praised New Labour's first budget for marking the 'end of the assumption that families consist of a male breadwinner'. The Centre for Policy Studies report claimed there was a social crisis between employment and care and represented 'real women' as those 'who reject the masculine value system for one that rates caring above a career and interdependence above independence'.

The author, Cristina Odone, criticised the dominant gender equality model espoused by New Labour that 'women achieve self-realization through work'; characterised contemporary working practices as 'designed by men, for men' and opposed 'the message that to fulfil your potential as a woman, you must earn a wage packet and enjoy independent status. You must in other words be like a man (2009, p.16). If New Labour's strategy reflected 'erasure of difference' in the pursuit of gender equality and based it on a male model, this critique looks like the resurgence of Hekman's second strategy.[2] From a policy perspective, the trouble with binary thinking is the see-sawing between poles, the difficulty of thinking dialectically. From a psycho-social perspective, the defining feature of binaries is that they oversimplify because they split apart the paradoxical and contradictory characteristics of conflictual circumstances, encouraging people to identify with these stereotypes: they encourage paranoid-schizoid (either/or), rather than depressive (both/and) thinking and identifications that contribute to identity.

Justine shares with Arianna the articulation of a conflict between career and motherhood, but that is where the similarity ends: her relation to this conflict, due in large part to her material and social circumstances, is markedly different. According to the UK Office of National Statistics, Justine, subject of this chapter, would fall into the category of lone mothers with children between 0 and 4, where the percentage in employment, either full- or part-time, is 36% (as compared with 63% when in a couple) (ONS, March, 2011). In this chapter I want to explore this different relation to an ostensibly similar dilemma, as a way of analysing psycho-socially the influence of external conditions – discursive, structural and material, current and past – on Justine's becoming a mother. The following pen portrait and analysis are based on three interviews conducted by Ann Phoenix with Justine, beginning in her late pregnancy and ending when Adele was 13 months old.[3]

Justine's situation

Justine is a 24-year-old black woman of Caribbean origin,[4] third generation in London. After leaving college she had a series of jobs as receptionist and personal assistant. When she became pregnant, she had been going out with her boyfriend (also of Caribbean origin) for four years. This pregnancy followed closely on a miscarriage that had left her feeling that she was 'going crazy'. That year had been full of difficulties: she had left work because of a bad relationship with her boss, argued with her mother and moved out to spend a year living with her boyfriend at his mother's house further outside London, and argued with Michael, her boyfriend. After counselling help with the miscarriage, she began to pick up and planned getting back into work when, to the shock of both Justine and her boyfriend, she got pregnant with Adele. Michael was, she said, pleased with the pregnancy sooner than she was. She put her career on 'set back' and moved out of her mother's and younger siblings' home into temporary accommodation provided by the local authority for homeless pregnant women. Money was very tight. She would have liked to be on maternity leave, with a job to go back to.

By the time Adele was a year old, advanced in walking and talking, Justine found motherhood easier than she had expected. She had a loving and thoughtful relationship with her baby, 'I really enjoy it (…) I feel good, d'you know what I mean, I feel responsible. I look after her very well.' 'The only problem' was her baby's 'clinginess' and the criticism of her mothering that this evoked, especially from Michael. She spent a lot of time out and about with Adele and visited members of her family 'all the time'. Justine wanted to learn to drive, to study and have a job involving travelling but called these 'wishes and dreams' for the present. She contrasted her constraints with Michael's freedom to come and go.

Justine's relation to the idea of 'career' differs from Arianna's in that she never had a career, just a series of jobs in which she tended not to stay long enough to improve her situation. Because she was unemployed when she became pregnant, she was without maternity leave pay, without a job that provided her with a framework for returning to employment (something all of the higher educated women had). So there was no placeholder of a career identity waiting to be retrieved. Her life during the previous year had been in some chaos, especially after the miscarriage, which left her feeling deeply unhappy. While 35 felt like time was running out for Arianna's motherhood decision, in Justine's peer group, 24 would feel quite late. I imagine her consciously adopting the 'sensible' plan as she embraced the rather abstract notion of prioritising her 'career' but unconsciously desiring another, reparative, pregnancy. An 'accidental-on-purpose' pregnancy is what happened very quickly.[5] Although he visited most evenings, Michael was largely unavailable for childcare (unlike Vincent), as was Justine's mother (training for a delayed 'career' alongside her job, because of the interruptions occasioned by the care of her own three children), so Justine was in the position of being (almost) the sole carer of Adele.

Reflexivity

When I originally wrote a pen portrait of Justine, I was acquainting myself fully with her data for the first time. I met her only once, when she attended the social event for all the participants after the fieldwork had ended. (What I remember best was that she met up with Leanne again for the first time in years, discovering in the process that they had become mothers so close together. At the end of the occasion, I noticed with pleasure them walking away from the venue together, both pushing baby buggies, deep in conversation.) Based on Ann's reflective field notes and the interviews, I was experimenting with writing reflective notes at this stage of data analysis (to complement and develop reflective field notes). I used my own reflective awareness of what seemed to be affectively charged, to notice the following aspects of the relationship between Justine and Ann.

This is what I wrote[6]:

Justine and Ann are both of Caribbean origin; moreover Ann and Justine became mothers at roughly the same age, and Justine was the age of Ann's daughter at the time of the interview. Ann noticed that Justine did not ask where she comes from, or if she had children. Did Ann want her to, potentially to establish commonalities? In a group data analytic discussion of this case, Ann offered information supplementing her field note that indicated her desire to give Justine money, even though it is against her research principles to do so. Aware of this conflict, she asked her partner's advice and took Justine some biscuits (a practice that she did not extend to her other interviewees). To add a material perspective: of all her interviewees, Ann experienced Justine as suffering the worst financial and housing circumstances.

I thought I detected mother-daughter transferences, in both directions, between Justine and Ann. Justine was keen for Ann to return. Noting this, Ann inadvertently repeats it in two sentences at the beginning of her field note for the second interview. She is sorry at the end of the third interview. The departure is prolonged, Justine asking Ann's advice about her baby's clinginess and Ann going into an extended explanation of research findings on 'fear of strangers' and how to find out about attachment (a professional as well as a maternal positioning). On two occasions in the third interview, Ann found herself 'helping', for example, drawing Justine's attention to what she thought the baby wanted. Justine was reluctant to tell Ann that her partner gave up his earlier job and was unemployed. (Given the generalised stigma attached to unemployment, this reluctance might not have been unique to her relationship with Ann, although the way it was experienced and communicated presumably would be.) Ann notes in her second interview field note, 'As before I really liked Justine and liked what I saw of her relationship with her baby and partner.'

As I reflected on Ann's relation to Justine, it was of course appropriate to reflect on my own. On listening and then reading the transcripts, I also 'really liked' Justine and what I felt about her mothering, based on the interviews. I thought I detected how proud Ann was that the baby was so clever and advanced and I felt this too, as I listened to the audio recording. I also noticed my own com-passion with Justine's wish to get her career sorted out and 'make [herself] better'; I felt that she had the capacity to do that, and I did not want her to be thwarted by her situation. Without being there, and without sharing Justine's and Ann's ethnicity (but sharing Ann's generational and gender status and having a daughter Justine's age), I, too, seem to be involved in these affective dynamics.

In a follow-up phone call made when Adele was two years and five months old, Heather recorded that Justine 'asked how Ann was, mentioned that she had invited her to Adele's birthday party, said she was a nice lady and that she had enjoyed her company and taking part in the project'.

These pieces of evidence taken together point to the strong affective ties between Justine and Ann, ties that appear more significant when understood psychoanalytically through the idea of mother-daughter transferences (see Hollway and Jefferson, 2013, for an example of my relation to a participant in earlier research.) Although transference dynamics are not constrained by social identity categories (a male patient can transfer aspects of his paternal relationship onto a female therapist, for example), the similarity of ethnicity and age between Justine's mother and Ann would probably facilitate such a transfer. In consequence, the account of identity that becomes salient will be inflected by the interview relationship within which the account is produced. As an African Caribbean woman of approximately Justine's mother's age, as well as a university researcher, Ann would likely represent career success. Justine's experience of Ann could be richly laced with mother transferences, given her mother's wishes in this regard.

Conflict in the relation of work and motherhood

After her miscarriage, Justine had consciously decided to prioritise her career, but in saying this expressed some doubt: 'I kind of, I'd kind of made plans to start my career, well a career *of some sort* and just move on in life and think about kids later on.' As well as 'kind of' (repeated in hesitation), there is a further qualifier, 'a career of *some sort*' (italics denoting her emphasis), suggesting doubts about what she could do in order to find work that satisfied her. In fact she had not found a job before discovering the second pregnancy (also unplanned, 'I can't say we were happy'). Justine commented on the pregnancy by saying 'Once I sort of put aside the fact that I'm not going to start my career this year.' The unintentional use of a double negative ('put aside' and 'not') compounds the suggestion of her difficulty with the conflict between work and motherhood, since she said the opposite of what she intended, which would have been, 'Once I put aside the idea of *starting* a career this year' rather than '*not going to start*'. Freud (1901) called such slips of the tongue parapraxes, a communication of ideas that have been repressed as a result of unresolved conflict.

Justine's slip here appears to illustrate the internal conflict between the two identity positions, working (career) woman and mother, so freighted by their binary existence in discourses. Her troubled use of the idea of career echoes Layton's description of the liberated woman expecting to have a career, not just a job. This address has crossed a continent, an ethnicity and a class to interpellate Justine, but her relation to it is one of 'hopes and dreams' that collide with her knowledge of the realities of her previous working life; a series of clerical and reception jobs which never satisfied her enough to stay: how different from Arianna's reality of a guaranteed return to a job that she loved with a passion. Justine displaces these imaginings into a future she will have established before having a second child.

In summary, we see that, in the first interview where she is recounting to Ann the story of getting pregnant, Justine's relation to motherhood is coupled with what she says about 'career'. At a discursive level, this is not surprising because of the widespread binary of stay-at-home and career mothers. However, there is another level, that of powerful social realities that constrain Justine's agency. These I have sketched out above: in particular getting pregnant while unemployed, and having neither the family resources nor the money to acquire childcare support. These available meanings of motherhood and career, produced in a binary relation, reduce space for, and fail to contain, the experience of multiplicity and ambivalence. However, they do not act independently of Justine's real circumstances, nor of what she holds from her family past. In the following multifaceted analysis of Justine's relation to mothering, I want to keep my sights on the co-articulation of these features. I also keep in mind the workings of a matrixial track in Justine's encounter with her postnatal circumstances.

Intergenerational echoes

I have situated Justine's relation to mothering in the present, but not yet in relation to her own mother. The unthought known of mothering after birth is characterised by Laplanche (1999) as the enigmatic messages of mothers giving rise to their children's unconscious, who in their turn pass these on. In what follows, I trace, from Justine's mother, what can be understood as enigmatic messages, or internalised identifications, or the reawakened resonances of a trans-subjective stratum and find, among other things, a conflict between career and motherhood.

If we go back to Justine's double negative and take it literally ('Once I sort of put aside the fact that I'm not going to start my career this year'), she would mean that she dismissed any notion of *not* starting her career the previous year. A career is what her mother had wanted for Justine, her 'smart, bright child', as Justine says of herself. Her mother, 24 years after Justine's birth (her first child), is only now working her way up from being a poorly paid auxiliary nurse by getting training for a career in an area of healthcare that interests her. Does Justine do as her mother tells her, or as her mother did back then, or as her mother does recently? In her slip of the tongue, we are alerted not only to the difficulty of this conflict in the present, but to its past, as it manifests in Justine's relationship with her mother.

When Adele is 13 months old, Ann returns for the last time. Towards the end of the interview she asks her what Justine hopes for her daughter. Justine reflects on the mistakes that she hopes Adele will avoid.

Justine: Well I don't know. I just hope that she gets a very good education, y'know, and that, a good education, and she just I can't really...I don't know because I haven't, (.) judging from myself when you get to about 16, you just automatically don't listen [laughs] to your parents or whatever your mum has to say, you just do whatever it is you want to do whether it's good or whether it's bad, it's just not what your parents are telling you to do. So I would prefer for her to just listen to me [...] just, you know, just focus on a career base. That's what I'd like for her, focus on a career base, drive, you know, afford to, you know, be able to afford your house and that kind of thing. I don't want her to ever live like how I am now because I feel like I had the opportunity to go out there and just not be like [...] have to go homeless and that palaver. But if I had stayed at work when I, when I should have, then I wouldn't be like this; I would probably be on a mortgage thing. And kind of, yeah, I'd like her to just go that way, just different from what I did, but, you know, when she gets to 16 or before that even, who knows? I don't know. So yeah.

Ann: Alright, so you basically want her to have a different life.

Justine: Yeah, well not *totally* different. The only thing that I didn't do right was, um, when I had money just didn't save it (laughs). That's why I'm paying for it now, because I wouldn't be in this situation, I wouldn't be kind of like grovelling for um money and that sort of thing – be earning my own wage and I'd be on maternity leave or coming up to the end of maternity leave or something like that. You know what I mean, but you know, unfortunately – well it's not even that unfortunate, you know. I'm in this predicament, I'd prefer her not to be.

This passage evidences the pain of the predicament in which Justine finds herself, having subverted, by getting pregnant, her intentions to find some interesting and stable employment. This is suggested in the hesitant and contorted style of her opening response (contrasted with her more typical fluency). In the first sentence, having repeated for emphasis her wish for a good education for Adele (one that she is successfully supporting by her educational play with her daughter), Justine shifts the subject from her daughter to herself and represents herself as a teenager not doing what her mother advised. Now that she is more capable of identifying with her mother (having her own access to a maternal position), she has a different perspective on being a daughter: she now wishes that she had listened to her mother, who wanted her to 'focus on a career base'. She repeats this idea as she moves from referring to herself to referring to Adele. The sense of her wasted opportunity is powerfully conveyed by her use of the word 'ever' as she refers again to Adele's future in contrast to her situation ('I don't want her to ever live like how I am living now').

Further evidence of the pain of facing this recognition is contained in the way that, in the sentence that meets her mistake head on, she hesitates before expressing the 'should' and then the consequence of transgressing: 'If I'd stayed at work when I, when I should have, then I wouldn't be like this'. When Ann accurately sums up the implication of what Justine has just said, the recognition is too bald for Justine to accept. She needs to qualify it ('the only thing I didn't do right'), direct evidence of being faced, through another's recognition, with the regret over her 'mistake' in having a baby before she was established in a career and therefore better positioned financially. Her feelings about her financial position are conveyed in her choice of words – 'grovelling' and 'predicament' – after which she again self-protectively modifies the bleak picture by saying, 'It's not even that unfortunate', followed by what is a common move in the accounts of our sample of new mothers, namely, the way that she transfers her own wishes for a better life to her child.

The foregoing extract has a thematic structure that moves three times back and forth between two generations of daughters (Justine and Adele) and two generations of mothers (Justine's mother and herself as Adele's mother). In the first sentence Justine moves from Adele to herself as daughter and then moves back to speak as Adele's mother again, filtered through her own experience as the daughter of her mother. In 'I don't want her ever to live like how I am now' and the words that follow, Justine again effects a move from her daughter to herself (when she describes what she should have done and her actual situation) and back to her daughter ('So I'd like her to just ... '). Justine's final comment after the interviewer's intervention further describes her specific predicament and ends with another reference to her daughter in light of that ('I'd prefer her not to be'). This structure tells us something about Justine's generational location. Her account of herself growing up is not simply about an individual identity and an independent evaluation of her past life; it is freighted with the relational significance of being the clever daughter who did not do what her mother advised and who, as a result, is in the current 'predicament'. Worried that her daughter will repeat her own pattern, which looks also like the pattern of her mother, Justine echoes the maternal position of her mother, the position itself remaining relatively unmodified but its occupancy moving on one generation.

There is an objective reality to the losses Justine faces by becoming a mother – no maternity pay, no job to return to. However, for an understanding of how these affect her changing identity, it is helpful to show the way they achieve their significance beyond the difficulties of external pressures and are incorporated along with her psychic life and its history. Justine has internalised her mother's conflicts between work and mothering and the desires her mother had for her to do better. We can see these as making up the content of her mother's 'enigmatic signifiers'. As Adele's mother, she now identifies herself in her own mother's relational position – also the mother of a clever daughter – and, understanding what her mother wanted for her, experiences her wishes for Adele in this light (a good education, a career). At the same time, she is in the position of the daughter and through this position she worries that Adele will make the same mistakes as she has made. These messages will be conveyed to her daughter, for example through the important role of educational play. This is an example of the way that new mothers are generational pivots, positioned in the middle of three generations. As such, they are powerful transmitters of culture trans-generationally: in this instance the affect-laden significance of the collision between becoming a mother and educational and career success.

'His life hasn't changed much'

The gender equality model's injunction to 'be like a man' may be caricatured in the polemical right- versus left-wing politics of the Centre for Policy Studies report, above, but we saw in Arianna's case that this model of gender difference (deriving from phallic logic, according to matrixial theory) is subjectively embedded and thus had actual effects on the way she became a mother. However, Justine's relation to the gender equality model is different, not a masculine identification but a recognition of the failure of the principle of equal parenting to address her own situation because 'it's different for a man'. This became evident through her comparisons with Michael's life. In the second interview, when their baby is 4 and a half months old, Ann asks 'And how has it been for Michael since the birth? What's his life like?'

> Justine: Um, (.) I'd say, (.) well, I dunno. I'd say his life was pretty much the same. (laughs) Um (.) oh, it's different for a man (.) in my opinion. But he is the proud Dad, he spends as much time as he (.) when he's here you know [...] I don't think, I mean he's still, it's not hard for him to just get up and go, go out. Whereas it is for me. So (.) yeah, I'd say his life hasn't, it hasn't changed that much. (laughs)

Before she comes out with the answer (it is hard for her, unlike him, to 'get up and go' and his life has changed little), she takes care to demonstrate that Michael is a proud and loving father. However, she stops in mid-sentence, during a claim that seemed likely to continue as 'he spends as much time as he *can*'. She modifies this representation of his involvement in the light of her knowledge, shared with the interviewer, that he is unemployed and could spend more time with them and more time looking after Adele. She concludes, after a brief hesitation, that 'his life hasn't changed that much'. Her laughs convey considerable unease. The context here is relevant: dominant beliefs about Caribbean fathers who do not commit to one woman or one family, Justine's wish to appear in a good light to Ann, her loyalty to Michael and the hopes she has of living with him. At present, shared parenting is clearly not available to Justine and Michael, despite the fact that neither is employed. It is possible that Justine's intense bond has contributed to excluding Michael from the mother–baby couple (see below), which would reinforce their difference. Either way, from being on relatively equal terms before parenthood with regard to their autonomy, now they inhabit identities that have diverged: a connected, maternal subjectivity was called forth by motherhood during the period we encountered Justine. Michael, on the other hand, does 'just come and go', 'as he pleases'.

In the context of the availability of a gender-equal discourse of autonomy based on a masculine model, which defines a set of ideal parenting practices available to a young couple, Justine is haunted by the comparison with Michael, even while knowing that she's 'just gotta get used to it' and that she loves exclusive time with her daughter. Justine experiences conflict between motherhood and *something;*

variously described as career and an ability to come and go as she pleases. But what exactly does she want? Childcare support does not cover it, as we see below. At the end of the second interview, with Michael present, the interviewer asks: I mean do you feel that you've had enough support with being a mother?

> Justine: With being a mother, yeah. *Yeah,* I'd, I'd say, I mean (.) some-
> times I think (.) I think it's more of, *I wouldn't say jealousy,* but it's
> more of a thing like, because I can't do (.) what I wanna do, or what
> I was (.) *Oh,* it's not like I had that much of a life before *anyway.*
> Do you know what I mean? It wasn't like I was always going out and
> stuff. But I find now that *I am* restricted, that (.) I want to (laughs).
> If that makes sense. I *really want to* just (.) get out there and just *do*
> *something.* And I'm not, and the thing is, I'm not sure what (.) I'm
> not sure what it is I wanna do. Um, (2) dunno, I kind of (.) I suppose
> I get on his nerves a bit, 'cos I'm always moaning that he's always
> out and (.) stuff. And it *does* get me down sometimes, 'cos he can
> just go, come and go as he pleases, like I said before. But (.) other
> than that, I mean it's *something* that just takes getting used to. [...]
> I've just gotta get used to it, I suppose, just (.) that's about it.

After a routine affirmative response, Justine reflects on an emotion for which jealousy is not quite accurate or, perhaps, fair. The next few lines have a striking quality of rawness as, in a nuanced searching way, she tries to work out what is missing in her life, listened to by Ann (with all that Ann would represent of career success). She seems to be searching to articulate an existential dilemma that is different from the wish to be as free as she was before being a mother. Whatever is lacking seems beyond accessible language ('If that makes sense'). For example, it is not about wanting to be able to go out more, which would be a commonplace explanation. Rather, it is something profound about identity: the feeling that being a mother to Adele is not enough, but that she has nothing recognisable from her former life that would enable her to define that something more: 'I really want to just...get out there and just do something...and I'm not sure what'. Later, think-ing for a long time about what to call it, she frames it as wanting to 'be part of something more important than [2 second pause] general work'.

Alcira Maria Alizade (2006) explores this 'something' in a critique of the way that being a mother is talked of as if it becomes the whole of a woman's identity and fulfilment. She finds in mothers, a 'non-maternal psychic space', 'another psychic tendency' (2006, p.52, p.53). She sees both mothering and this other space as being vehicles for the exercise of creativity: 'Women may develop creatively both within the context of their reproductive body and outside that context' (Alizade, 2006, p.46). For all Justine's maternal passion, she is missing such a space and, trying to articulate it, finds the available language inadequate. In terms of her class and perhaps also racialised position, lived as biography, she is remote, unlike Arianna, from an adequately paid working life in which she could be part of something more important. Perhaps this is exacerbated by the binary discursive treatment of mothers and career women.

When we look beyond practicalities to identities, it appears that maternal politics are split between, on one hand, a non-gendered autonomous individual with priorities in the workplace and domestic responsibilities to organise and fulfil, and, on the other, maternal women whose life is care and nurture, especially of their own children. This binary also reflects the phallic logic described in matrixial theory. The first term of the binary refuses the particularities of the maternal under the label 'parenting', while the second term essentialises women's nurture. Both positions incite their opposite: that is the nature of dualism. It leaves no space for a psychological account of ambivalent maternal-feminine desire, such as Alizade's, differentiated from both caricatures.

Clinginess

By the third interview, Justine has decided, because of the baby's 'clinginess', to postpone finding work (and thus the need to put Adele in a nursery) until Adele is 18 months or two years old, rather than one year, as she first intended. Her baby's clinginess is the subject of family discussion and arguments with Michael (as well as being the subject of a request for advice from Ann). The following extract follows Ann's question about changes in the ways that she and her partner spend time together:

> Justine: Oh definitely. I would say there are definitely a lot more arguments as well (Ann: Right.) because he does think that I smother her (baby moans) and maybe in a way I do. But like I said, it's just because it's just the two of us the majority of the time so there's no one else to smother apart from her really.
> Ann: and the arguments are about how you're looking after her.

Justine: Yeah, well *not so much how I look after her,* just why she's so clingy. And I can't expect anything less because of the way she is and all the rest of it, but, er (baby moans) um, I don't get it just from him either. Everyone says the same thing and I am starting [baby moans] to scratch my head a bit and, okay, maybe I am smothering her a bit too much. But [...] she knows exactly what she's doing as well; she's not a silly child (baby murmurs) [...]

Kind of one of the first things we said was, you know, obviously, if we have a child, things will change (Ann: Alright.) and they have, not necessarily for the worse either, just her clinginess, that's the only downfall.

Justine goes straight to the reason for their arguments ('He [Michael] does think that I smother her'). 'Smother' suggests that her love for her baby daughter is so intense as to be problematic. Justine does not deny Michael's accusation and directly points out the reason: 'It's just the two of us.'

Justine's housing situation has had effects on her mothering in that the cramped space makes it uncomfortable for Michael to stay over as often as he might (Justine expresses the hope that he might do so when, later, she gets two-bedroom accommodation but he prefers to remain where he is). Moreover, the living space is so small that there is no convenient space for a cot (nor is there money), so that from the beginning Adele has slept with Justine. This has probably been a factor in Adele's 'clinginess', as well as in her refusal to go to sleep without Justine lying down also. The significance of these material factors is, however, informed by Justine's internal conflicts around separation and connectedness. With the words 'no one else to smother apart from her', Justine conveys the intensity of their mother–baby dyad and that it is so often unmodified by the presence of a third person (be it Michael or someone else). Yet Justine experiences special enjoyment when she and Adele are on their own together: 'I like being a Mum. I love it, um, especially when we're on our own.'

Ostensibly (informed by the phallic logic of separation), it is the baby who is clingy, and in a binary discourse of women's versus babies' needs, this usually means that the mother wants more separation, but the baby is stopping her. De Marneffe, paraphrasing Baraitser and Kristeva, disagrees, exploring the way that 'the mother experiences her desire to relate to her child as *her own desire*'. 'It is also the way her [mother's] love for her child makes her want to put herself aside, and the way that putting herself aside to care for her child *paradoxically fulfills her* (...)

(H)aving a child changes a woman's relation to herself and others in a way that has implications for how we think about the self' (De Marneffe, 2006, p.241, original emphases).

Matrixial theory, with its idea of com-passion being 'the originary joint event', explains this so that it is no longer paradoxical. Object relations theory also affords a view of feelings as not authored by individuals, such as the way 'clinginess' will move between mother and baby and doesn't belong or originate in one place. According to Winnicott, a mother's capacity for identification (which can be compromised in many ways) is crucial because it enables her 'to provide what her infant needs at the beginning, which is a live adaptation to the infant's needs'. This provision is 'the essence of maternal care' without which 'the infant does not really come into existence, since there is no continuity of being' (Winnicott, 1960, p.54). Separation from this early intersubjective unity is 'in any case, a difficult thing' according to Winnicott (ibid).

Perhaps this explains why on an occasion when Justine did appear to have the choice of some free time, she did not act on it. When Adele was about four months old, Justine got a late invitation to a cousin's poetry reading:

> I did, um, tell Michael, but he (.) he was sleeping, so obviously I didn't wanna just leave the baby with him while he's sleeping, so I had to bring her. And *that* annoyed me, because I just wanted to (.) just go and have a few hours on my own, kind of (laughs) thing, without the baby, and just to recapture that (.) that feeling.

On the face of it, her wish is clear: she wanted to go out without Adele, but her actions told a different story. For me, the provocation in Adele's account is that Michael was sleeping; that is, he was there, so she could have woken him and left Adele with him. She hesitated before coming out with this explanation, probably aware that it will not sound like a strong reason. The hesitation could also be due to dissonance between Justine's real experience (of jointness/connectedness) and surrounding opinion that she should feel OK about leaving the baby with Michael.

Whatever the contextual details, Justine's actions suggest that a dynamic operates in which Adele and Justine are almost inseparable and Michael is peripheral as a parent. To elaborate the theme of intergenerational continuity, it is worth noting Justine's childhood experience of fathers, which will inform her mothering. We know that her father already had a family before getting involved with her mother, and returned to that family, so that she saw very little of him. In practice, Justine and her siblings were brought up by their mother.

In the context of continuing criticism about Adele's clinginess, Justine later took drastic action. This time Adele was nearly 13 months old, when she and Michael left Adele with Michael's mother, so as to go out to celebrate her birthday. They dropped off Adele while the child was asleep and did not return until 2 pm the following day.

> Justine: From the time she woke up and realised she wasn't at home, she wasn't with Mum or Dad, she just wouldn't (baby shouts, words inaudible) so she wasn't happy (Ann: Right). But a lot of people just say to me I've got to do that in order for her to break out of it kind of thing, 'cos if she's always around me then she'll never really break out of it.

The acuteness of Justine's conflict is suggested by her treatment of Adele on this single occasion when she did manage to leave her, by doing so while the baby was asleep and therefore unable to mount a protest that perhaps Justine could not have tolerated. At that moment, she was avoiding identifying with her baby, who would be inconsolable until she returned, some 18 hours later. (I imagine that the inaudible words in the extract above were 'she just wouldn't *stop crying*': elsewhere, Justine tells Ann that she can't leave Adele with her own mother because she cries until she is sick.) By this time, the child's alterity, intransigently effective in refusing separation when Justine arranges it, is paradoxically having big consequences for Justine's wish for 'something more'. The older Adele gets, the more reprehensible others consider her clinginess. However, Winnicott (1963, p.87) claimed that 'gradually (in health) the need for the actual mother becomes fierce and truly terrible', a development that he situated between around six months and two years, which would tally with Adele's 'clinginess'. It followed, for Winnicott, that, therefore, 'mothers do really hate to leave their children' (ibid.). Put like this, we can see that Justine's response when she subsequently doesn't leave Adele is prompted by fragilised identifications, Justine's com-passion. Faced with Adele's predictable inconsolability, Justine gave up trying to leave Adele with any family members but was left, not only with the frustration of a life constricted by childcare, expressed in her regret that 'I can't have the free time which I think I deserve,' but also the feeling that she was in the wrong, at fault for smothering Adele. It was this opinion, based on phallic logic, which prompted her to disidentify with Adele (to foreclose her feeling-with) and pursue her (and/or Michael's) wishes for birthday celebrations.

The principle that mothers and fathers should share childcare addresses 'equal' autonomous parents who are expected to take rational decisions within the economic parameters of their lives. This is a far cry from Justine's situation, reflected in object relations and matrixial theory: Winnicott's mothers who hate to leave their children on good grounds and new mothers' double access to a fragilising 'potential for trans-subjective co-emerging and co-affecting com-passion' (Pollock 2008, p.16). Likewise, norms about when and how children should become independent based on phallic logic starting from the separation of birth, pathologise Justine and Adele's connectedness. Yet, despite the symbolic weight of these discourses, and despite the very real restrictions motherhood imposes in practice, Justine gets more pleasure from times that she and her daughter spend on their own together than anything else. It sounds also as if she is most creative in that context too:

> Especially when we're on our own, like I'm always doing silly things. I've noticed that my whole (.) personality is slowly starting to change, I have to be a lot more (.) funnier, or more creative, or just (.) something to impress her basically [...] I dunno, it's weird, I feel a bit (.) topsy-turvy.

I love this description because it describes Justine getting access to a transitional space, more playful than her former adult self. It illustrates the creativity and liberation of mothering and reminds me of Kristeva's description of 'the slow, difficult and delightful apprenticeship in attentiveness, gentleness, forgetting oneself' (1992, p.200). It shows that Justine has learned this from experience, has often managed to shrug off the abjecting binary discourses of self and other, and connect through embodied, affective experience to a transjective stratum in her experience, transforming the accompanying fragilisation into a creative new personality. 'Topsy turvy' means 'with top where bottom should be; upside down; inverted, reversed' and, figuratively, 'utterly confused or disorderly' (Shorter Oxford English Dictionary). With the benefit of matrixial theory, I can add a further meaning: topsy turvy references a trans-subjective stratum emerging from foreclosure and contributing profound and creative experiences to (co)becoming a mother.

Beyond biology?

The Centre for Policy Studies argument above provides a political example of how the binarised strategy of valorising the maternal-feminine has been dangerous, not only because it risks leaving women powerless in domestic relationships, with no independent sources of income, but because it is reducible so readily to earlier discourses based on a derogatory treatment of women's reproductive biology as their determining feature, excluding them from the public (men's) sphere. However, this still leaves the challenge of not falling into the binary models that feminism has largely offered. Most feminist academics have adopted the autonomy-based gender equality model.[7] For example, French feminist Elizabeth Badinter believes that motherhood in France is at a turning point. Having juggled paid work and motherhood for decades, French women, it appears, are expressing a desire to stay at home when they raise children. Badinter claims that this 'contravenes the model we have worked for until now [and] which makes equality of the sexes impossible and women's freedom irrelevant. It is a step backwards' (*Guardian*, 13 February 2010). Badinter, like many feminists, believes that women who stay at home are under pressure to do so from external discourses of idealised mothering [which] 'makes impossible demands on any woman who has a life outside of her child' (ibid.).

The leader of the French Green party and mother of four, Cécile Duflot, said that Badinter's examples 'completely miss the point'. It seems to me that Badinter and others 'miss the point' by interpreting women's desire to care for their own young children at home as exclusively the product of external ideological pressure. The argument is a product – once again – of binary thinking. Daphne de Marneffe pins down the misconstruals, resulting from these binaries: that mothers are living through others, that they are forsaking equality or relaxing in the joys of subsidised homemaking, and provides us with a different perspective, 'namely that caring for their children *matters* deeply to them' (2004, p.5), and she goes on to ask 'What if we were to take this seriously, to put it at the core of our exploration?' and uses this question to construct a view of maternal desire as a positive aspect of self.

The logic of these opposed feminist discourses is social versus biological. The strategy underlying the gender equality discourse is the erasure of biological difference. The way that the word 'gender' has gradually replaced 'sex' in English language cultures – often inappropriately so – exemplifies the erasure of biology, on the grounds of its essentialising political uses. However, becoming a mother does involve the 'corpo-Reality' of creation of new life through pregnancy, birth and breastfeeding. Kaja Silverman, points out how Kristeva's dimension of the corpo-Real 'is deemed to be so unthinkable, so undesirable, so dangerous in feminist thought itself that it must be expelled utterly from the hearth of feminist analysis, aligning itself thereby with masculine corporeal narcissism' (cited by Pollock, 2004, p.38).

The challenge for me, therefore, is to construct a psycho-social and embodied account not tainted with biological reductionism. The womb as an intransitive object cannot be denied: the issue is, rather, to reimagine it transitively: in matrixial theory it becomes a space of mutual encounter that ignites metramorphosis, a 'process of change in borderlines and thresholds between being and absence, memory and oblivion, I and non-I, a process of transgression and fading away' (Ettinger, 1992, p.201) characterised by 'transmissibility and relating without relations' (Pollock, 2004, p.32). The matrixial concept of 'jointness in differentiation' dissolves the problem created by the binaries of separation and fusion. This transgression of individual boundaries 'starts from the transgressive corporeality of pregnancy' (Ettinger, 2006b, p.104) but it does not end there.[8] Bearing another life within a life has affective, transjective and therefore subjectivising effects on mothering after birth as well.

A.S. Byatt, English novelist, described in terms similar to matrixial theory life after losing her son, after which she had 'lived on two time lines: the first stopped with him, the second continues without him' (Frosh and Baraitser, 2003). The first time line (the one that stopped when her son died) points to a trans-subjective track. In this light, the upheaval of becoming a mother is also about living on these two time lines (Ettinger's separate trajectories). The idea of a conflict between a mother's individual needs and the baby's needs is complicated when we propose a track or stratum that contains the other within us. This is what Kristeva proposes as a principle of her 'third' moment of feminism, a principle that transcends the binaries of identity and difference. It offers an alternative to the autonomous masculine subject, defined by 'always negotiating the other within … never completely [being] the subjects of our own experience', (op. cit.). In this perspective, our pleasures (and cares) derive from the severality within, as do Justine's in caring for Adele. If, by becoming a mother, an unthought known resurfaces – the part of ourselves that inhabits another who also inhabits us – then the autonomous individual subjectivity called into being by 21st century Western life and gender relations will no longer be pre-eminent:

what was underneath will come to the surface, but conflict remains: Justine felt 'topsy turvy'.

Conclusions

In this chapter I analysed the relation of a cluster of binaries to Justine's ambivalent and passionate experience of becoming a mother: motherhood versus career, mothers' needs versus children's needs, gender equality versus maternal-feminine difference, social versus biological, separation versus clinginess. My choice to start with a contrast between Arianna and Justine aimed to show their profoundly different *relations to* the binary of motherhood and career, although superficially they both positioned themselves as conflicted within such a discourse. Their differences had to do with their contrasting employment and domestic situations and suggested patternings of class, racialisation and employment situation. De Marneffe's treatment of maternal desire helped to explain how much her daughter's wellbeing mattered to Justine. Her dilemmas over separation and clinginess demonstrated the consequences of the binary of separation and autonomy with connectedness that, with the help of matrixial and object relations concepts, I am trying to transcend. Justine's example shows that what is claimed to precede birth (fusion or border linking and spacing) and how we conceptualise its sequelae after birth (maternal openness to trans-subjective fragilisation) matters for new mothers' relation to issues of separation and attachment. 'If psychoanalysis posits the formation of relations to the other through the cut, violence underpins the ethical' (Pollock, personal communication).

In Conclusion

9
Unfinished Business

The questions

At the beginning of the empirical project, our question was about the identity changes women experience when they become mothers for the first time. Questions of how to theorise identity, in our case its dynamic character, were also central to the wider programme within which our project was funded. Methodologically we wanted to try out more subtle and searching methods in researching identity change, which would go beyond what participants were conscious of; that is to say, psychoanalytically informed methods. Writing this book, my focus was honed to mothers' and researchers' knowing, unthought as well as thought, and knowing's relation to becoming through co-becoming, questions inspired by object relations psychoanalysis, especially that of Bion and Winnicott. Along the way, I discovered matrixial theory and began what has continued to be the challenge of integrating it through data analysis. Matrixial trans-subjectivity is only accessible to research in a form mediated by the individuation that accompanies it (all along for the mother; after birth for the child). However, its traces are decipherable and it alters the way the perinatal period and 'separation' can be thought.

It is not just participant mothers whose being is changed in the process of becoming during the research. Now I approach the end, the experience of being changed by the research is salient, something that started during the fieldwork but was only later reflected on and conceptualised: it is entirely consistent with how Bion theorises the link between knowing and becoming. Matrixial theory, especially the implications of fragilisation and compassion, meant that the 'becoming' in researcher knowing of mothers was inextricable from the ethics of

185

research relations at every stage. Despite the impossibility of capturing the maternal ineffable, I don't regret setting up the book in such terms. Playing hide and seek with the ineffable has been revealing and anyway serves as a reminder that something arcane (hidden and secret) lies beyond whatever it is I have managed to reach and have reached in readers.

Using the whole sample

I discarded at least two whole-sample analyses in the course of writing this book. As a psycho-social methodologist, I want to show that a whole-sample analysis can be achieved beyond the paradigm of statistical generalisation or comparative analysis of pre-set sub-samples. I had approached the analysis in that vein, selecting exemplary contrasting cases and spreading out via cluster analysis, elaborating and refining through conceptual development. I took care to bear in mind differences within clusters and similarities across, so as not to oversimplify.

The first whole-sample analysis never found its way in to the book: too long (too long-winded), too 'bottom up', to arrive at a concise or cogent whole, although fascinating in its detailed examination of similarities and differences. It provided me with a further layer of familiarity with the whole data set. The attempt that did, temporarily, reach the book was prompted by a particular example, Sylvia (whose data still feels like unfinished business), to orientate my analysis around the theme of family in maternal identity formation. 'Family' provided a less inter-subjective (mother–baby) object of analysis and reflected the central characteristic of 'generation' in becoming mothers: a new generation replaces an older one; daughters become mothers, her parents (and his) become grandparents and so on. It seems to me that the object of analysis one selects ('family', 'becoming') is central in shaping the appropriate balance between 'psycho' and 'social', in the process of conducting trans-disciplinary analyses: it is not possible to pay equal attention to everything.

That chapter was removed after a reader advised me it didn't quite fit. Although I agreed with the reasoning, removing it exacerbated my feeling of unfinished business, which I noticed in my struggle with trying to cram further ideas into the conclusion or into chapters that were already long and whose coherence I should not compromise). Following my own methodological advice, I reflected on what was beneath the surface of this unfinished feeling – with help.[1] The most insistent unfinished business seems to be about my belief that I should use the whole sample for a formal analysis because the diversity of our sample was carefully thought out (and laboriously recruited by Heather Elliott). Our research design was fashioned in order to tell us something beyond single cases, which indeed it does.

I needed to use the whole sample, yes. But what constitutes use? Can I allow it to count that I am using my knowledge of the whole sample in everything I notice in any given case; that every conceptual innovation, link or theoretical refinement is based on the prolonged and intensive period in which I have come to know these 19 women? And when I say 'know', can I apply my own distinction – central to this book – between knowing about and knowing of, such that I recognise that I have processed, digested, taken in, learned from the experience of and been changed by, the research encounters with these 19 women? Although not all to the same extent.

The answer to these questions should be yes, because that is the implication of my espoused, psychoanalytically informed, epistemology. It is similar, I think, to what Lorenzer meant by scenic understanding; a holistic, affective kind of knowing that changes the knower. As Bion would point out, the end point of such a train of thought is uncertain: for example, what does the above mean for how I bring this scenic knowing to conscious awareness and pin it down in language and print, as here? Everything I have said about objectivity through subjectivity becomes relevant. And just to make it more complicated, when I talk about the whole that I am drawing on, I cannot limit that to the whole set of data; rather it includes the myriad encounters whereby it has come to mean what it means, encounters that include my own biography. I find it difficult even to give an account of how I 'selected' the cases that appear prominently in this book. The cases I chose at various points made me curious about some thread of intelligibility that presented itself because of my conceptual interests; for example, anxiety, inside–outside and the encounter with 'reality', the gender binary, the uncertain move from daughter to mother, intergenerational transmission. They each afforded me a different journey of discovery, which also changed over time.

Mothers' becoming

At the beginning of this book, the idea of identity change or transition predominated, drawing from the framing of the original research proposal. The concepts of subjectivity and subjectivising were in frequent use too. Now I highlight 'becoming', a word that figured in the acronym we all used for the project (BaM – becoming a mother). The concept builds bridges to affect theory and emphasises the interminable dynamic quality of being. Matrixal theory conceptualises the origins of becoming as co-becoming. We all – women and men, mothers and not-mothers, have access to the originary com-passion of becoming-infant life, due to our prenatal matrixiality. The privilege and potential trauma of becoming a mother is to re-experience this in a new temporal register, as an adult; that is, with a coexisting individuated track of subjectivity. A new mother needs access to both these at once: she must tune in to the archaic communications of her baby and, as an adult with life-giving responsibility, think and act on the baby's behalf.

This demand manifests as the *'angoisse'*, and contributes to what Cathy Urwin refers to as post-partum 'existential loneliness' (2007, p.248). Having others who can tap in to the same reserves – especially a new mother's own parents and the baby's father – is profoundly important, as is the holding and containing structure of 'family'. However, the different intensity of the upheaval and variations in balance of positive and negative expressions of *angoisse* within the sample are instructive. As well as being biographically linked, they are socio-culturally patterned. For example, the white, higher-educated ('middle-class') women in the sample had already left their families of origin years before and were widely separated from them geographically. They lived with their partners beforehand and unerringly assumed, married or not, a form of household based on this parental unit and the new baby. All the Bangladeshi women lived with their families of origin until they married. At that point, a few moved in with just their husbands but most moved in with the husband's families (perhaps including other sons and their families). This varied little with higher education. On moving out, their continued proximity to the husbands' parents was a priority and to the women a valuable bonus.

Characteristic of white and black participants without higher education was the pattern of starting out with the new mother's family of origin, moving into independent council accommodation if and when available, staying close and being in daily contact: moving out and starting a family was part of the task of growing up, but this did not mean separation. This relational framing of the new mothers' identity transitions was not only vertical (to their parents) but also horizontal (to their siblings, especially sisters). When De Marneffe says 'in the old days, women lived out their years in dense webs of female relationships' (2004, p.17), I want to qualify by noting greater continuities over time for working-class women as well as the effects of changes in gender relations (which have been most marked for middle-class women). A case like Jenny's illustrates what I would rather classify as the dense web of *family* relationships, because it easily accommodates fathers, brothers and grandfathers. The position of babies' fathers was patterned in ways close to the above: more marginal in the white and black working-class grouping in contrast to the centrality of the maternal family of origin. By contrast, the baby's father was the central link where the mothers were living in their husband's family of origin.

Sketching out such patterns is one theme in the socio-cultural framing of mothers' becoming and could be repeated with other objects of analysis, such as employment and consequences like maternity leave. Such analyses reference the importance of setting in all its layered meanings. Detailed analysis of mothers' *relation to* these factors can, however, only be achieved at the level of single-case analysis.

Mothers' knowing

It is possible to take a similar patterned approach to mothers' knowing. One of our original research questions was about participants' relation to sources of learning and expertise about becoming mothers. There were patterned differences across the sample here too. I am reminded of another piece of unfinished business: a comparative analysis I wrote of Sarah's and Becky's relation to expert knowledge, these two selected for their contrasts. That analysis became the basis for a whole sample-based analysis of pattern that showed up difference in educational level, with its correlation to class. That analysis was moved in, out, around and back several times as the book took different shapes. It didn't fit, for example, with an early 'tidy' plan to select the six interview and observation cases and structure the book around these (logical but not what emerged). It felt important and still does, probably because Bion's 'learning from experience' proved a valuable conceptual tool for making sense of the differences. The idea of learning from experience is, in turn, important because of the connections between knowing and becoming in Bion's account. In a nutshell (and at the risk of oversimplification), the kind of learning that results in 'knowing of', the kind where learning acts by changing the learner/knower, was more accessible to those without higher education. It was a greater struggle for those with higher education, many of whom – to some extent – had learned to depend on the accrual of a stock of knowledge, in this case sources of expertise about pregnancy and early motherhood. For example, Sarah's desire to control her journey into motherhood occasioned her exhaustive research to this end ('I'd never actually thought to ask what contraction pains felt like. I guess that's the only question I didn't ask'). 'Knowing about' can act as a way of shoring up established investments against the uncertainty of unbidden (uncontrolled) learning from experience, heightening psychic conflict. This contrasted with Becky's rejection of all sources of expertise except her mother. She had outstanding confidence in her own emergent knowledge ('it's my body'). I analysed a long and beautiful extract in which Becky described how she learned the best way to settle her baby. It was replete with details that would have done justice to a well-trained infant observer. Interestingly, Becky drew on the postnatal continuities with what she had learned about her baby's rhythms prior to birth. Becoming the mother who could read her son's bodily communications (identify with his projected internal states) and the one who knew best how to respond to them in the service of his wellbeing was an important thread in her maternal becoming.

The whole sample could be situated with reference to a continuum running from learning from experience (knowing of) to searching out expert knowledge (knowing about). However it is important to recognise that these are not mutually exclusive and there are ways of learning from expert information that go beyond the accumulation of a stock of knowledge with which to defend against uncertainty. Nonetheless this continuum did appear to do meaningful work to think about variations in the sample.[2] 'Knowing of' was more typical of early school leavers, young women who were content to prioritise becoming mothers over less satisfying life trajectories and regarded their mothers as reliable exemplars. This applied across ethnicities.

Like Sarah, many of the other higher-educated working women with career trajectories who organised their lives with precision and flare, did not like the feeling of being out of control, and this was likely to affect their relation to getting to know their babies, whose rhythms are innocent of clock time. In the perspective of matrixial theory, women who are established on their differentiated phallic track may nonetheless draw on the original modality of co-feeling, re-registered during pregnancy, but reaching back to their own unsymbolisable beginnings. However, to be available for this is to be fragilised; it means being confronted by psychic change and can therefore engender trauma and attempts at foreclosure of these feelings.

When I imagine communicating with new mothers or intended new mothers, the unfinished business emerges by asking myself what I would say to my daughter and her peer group of career women. The core aspect of becoming a mother – your relation with your baby – cannot be planned for; you cannot control it in advance. You can, however, begin to play, to enjoy, to have imagined conversations during pregnancy. You can try to retune into that elusive, unsettling other track of knowing, like an old-fashioned medium-wave radio where a foreign channel fascinatingly fades in and out as you are trying to listen to a chosen, familiar, programme. This is the knowing that involves being in the unique moment and taking the time to 'listen' – to notice with your intuitive emotional responses as the instrument – to what the baby is communicating unawares; to reflect on it, while not knowing for sure, and act provisionally. In other words you can be prepared to learn from new experience. This is the core of mothers' knowing. Theoretically speaking, it is the territory of reverie, container-contained, communicative projective identification. The matrixial territory of com-passion provides its inextricable link to ethics.

...and knowing mothers through research

Methodologically speaking, *with one important distinction*, the above principles about mothers' knowing are relevant to researchers' relations to participants and data. The distinction is that these processes in research are working among adults, so there is symmetry in relation to the co-existence of matrixial and phallic tracks, whereas in relation with the baby – yet to become individuated – the asymmetry of adult care, based on its dual track nature, is central. For example, Rabiya and I were mutually exercising both responsibility and compassion in relation to each other (Chapter 4). The use of infant observation as a research method has provided a resource whose value I can hardly overestimate. It did not need much modification because it already had a history of adapting psychoanalysis outside clinical practice. Not surprisingly, given my emphasis on learning from experience, it was the experience of joining the observation seminars and taking this practice out into field and data analysis that underpinned some momentous changes in me as a researcher.

Bits

Writing a book is, of course, a part of research and hence part of the politics of knowledge. One consequence of Bion's emphasis on emergence and living with uncertainty is traceable in the way I have written this book, the shape it has (uncertainly) taken and the way I try to deal with the residual bits at this final stage.

I have numerous files into which I have placed 'bits'. These electronic files consist of what just needed to be written down, and/or writings that took a wrong tack, didn't fit coherently, exceeded the eventual confines of what I could fit in. They were leads that I wanted to follow, without knowing where they would take me and if I could use them. I had the vague assumption that I would go back to them and check them for valuable parts, but I shudder at the thought (worse still, the pages of handwritten notes, haphazardly filed: 'Add', 'Remember', 'Use'). To do this would, I think, feed the fantasy that I can cover everything; sort out every remaining question. There was, for example, a large file that examined the theoretical connections between object relations and matrixial relations and started to consider where this left the concept of unconscious intersubjectivity. I still want to show how compatible they are, through exploring the fast-changing relations of the two tracks, matrixial (trans-subjective) and phallic (individuated) in early first-time motherhood. Two readers commented critically on my tendency to go into theoretical mode; one felt hit over the head by these passages, the other (younger) one wondered if it harked back to my formation in a culture of critical treatments of grand theory and ventured the adjective 'nerdish'. (How grateful I am to those who spared the time, and for their forthrightness!)

Using the expanded mental space afforded by these other minds, I was able to make a link to a feeling of discomfort I've had for a while when I use the term 'argue': when I find myself using that term I hesitate. Is this how I want to proceed (probably not)? I want to show, not tell; for example, this is what containment looks like in ordinary research encounters, or an example of noticing and following through on a provocation while engaged with data analysis. What is a good balance between showing and theoretical telling is of course uncertain, provisional, and depends on a given specific instance. The pedagogic principle underlying my emphasis on showing through data examples is one further instance of privileging 'knowing of'. It is based on my intention that readers be able to learn from being affected by the re-told experience on which data analysis is based. Whereas theoretical argument that gets too far removed from the data is liable to feel parched of life, I have tried to link theory closely with examples that can be identified with, as well as to use a more vivid style of writing. I hope it's made a difference.

Notes

1 Knowing Mothers, Researching Becoming

1. ESRC RES-148-25-0058 'Identities in Process: Becoming Bangladeshi, African Caribbean and White Mothers', 2005–2008. Wendy Hollway, Ann Phoenix, Heather Elliott, Cathy Urwin, Yasmin Gunaratnam.
2. A published version of this poem, spoken by an actor who had familiarised herself with the audio record of Juhana's voice, is freely available on the internet (Hollway, 2013c).
3. I chose her pseudonym because in Urdu Juhana means 'young girl'.
4. See Urwin, Hauge, Hollway and Haavind (2013) for an elaboration of this theme in a different Bangladeshi case study.
5. Two volumes (both Wetherell, 2009) collect together information from every project.
6. Three dots in round brackets denotes omissions from a cited published text. Three dots in square brackets denotes omissions from a data extract.
7. See Hollway, 2010b, p.216, for an account of the different theoretical connotations between identity and subjectivity and an explanation of my usage.
8. In many disciplinary traditions, ranging from cognitive science to philosophy, art and social theory, a distinction is made between different ways of knowing. In cognitive science and neuropsychology, these kinds of knowing are defined spatially in terms of different sides of the cerebral cortex (left brain/right brain) (for example, Schore, 2010) and the right brain is dominant early in life. The right brain is often pigeon-holed as the seat of intuitive or creative thinking, the left of logic. Damasio (2000), based in neurology, conducts a broad ranging critique of the inadequacy of a cognitive approach to consciousness. Ehrenzweig (1967) developed a theory of art through his distinction between differentiated and undifferentiated thinking, emphasising the need for both. Aristotle used the term phronesis (Flyvbjerg, 2001), meaning practical wisdom, attained from experience, in contrast to both episteme and techne. Apart from Aristotle, these distinctions all exist in the shadow of Enlightenment glorification of rationality and the consequent suspicion of intuition.
9. The second tranche of funding was a Fellowship: ESRC RES-063-27-0118 'Maternal Identities, Care and Intersubjectivity: A Psycho-social Approach', 2008–2010.
10. In a special issue of the journal *Infant Observation* (Urwin, 2007), Cathy Urwin introduces the observation side of the study in detail. This is followed by the six observers' case write-ups.

2   Empirical Psycho-Social Research: Design and Psychoanalytically Informed Principles

1. Others include especially the project team working alongside us at the Open University, led by Rachel Thomson (Thomson et al., 2011; Thomson et al., 2012); also, for example, the work of Daphne de Marneffe (2004), Lisa Baraitser (2009) and Imogen Tyler (2000).
2. This informs professional ethics, whether in social care or research. Because the ethical thing to do necessarily depends on the specific situation, in all of its complexity, ethical practice cannot be predetermined. The most helpful course of action will only be worked out by retaining the capacity to think in circumstances that may lend themselves to just the opposite.
3. This was at the Centre for Advanced Studies in Oslo (2010–2011). At various times, Ann Phoenix, Cathy Urwin and Rachel Thomson were also group members.
4. I have noticed, in supervising those using interview methods, a reluctance to give up asking specific questions closely related to the research question itself for fear of not getting enough relevant information. The problem is that then the questions are themselves likely to be overloaded (unintentionally) with prompts and expectations as to what the researcher is looking for, so there is a tendency to produce expected or sought after answers to research questions.

3   The Reality of Being a Young Mother: Agency, Imagination and Objectivity

1. Tom Wengraf (2013) explores critical realism in the context of psycho-social studies, focusing on researching 'variable agency' through the related biographical narrative interpretive method (BNIM).

4   Weird Beyond Words: The Transgressive Corporeality of Pregnancy and Compassion-Based Ethics

1. Pollock has been foremost in bringing Ettinger's work to an Anglophone readership and my debt to her profound grasp of Ettinger's work is apparent in this chapter.
2. It is construed variously as an unpleasant obligation ('responsibility for the Other is the good; it is not pleasant, it is good'; as guilt ('the self is bound to the other in a relation of guilt in which the self bears the burden of the Other's subjectivity the Other's freedom and the Other's mortality', and persecution (that 'I am first and foremost hostage of the other, that I am persecuted because I cannot escape the priority of the Other over me in terms of my responsibility' (all cited in Marcus, 2010).
3. Herethics is Julia Kristeva's term: 'herethics; heretical, feminine and ethical' (Kristeva, 1977, p.185). Baraitser, who cites this definition, continues 'it is an ethics that challenges the autonomous subject, as it is founded on the indeterminacy of pregnancy' (2008, p.102).

4. In the Lacanian tradition, the concept of the Real suggests the impossibility of accessing a non-symbolic part of subjectivity. Ettinger modifies this impossibility: 'Extrapolating the latest revisions Lacan made to his theory of the Real and phantasy towards what seems its potential yet subversive continuity, Bracha Ettinger has been working to give form to a subjacent, sub-symbolic stratum of subjectivization that, nonetheless, has the effect of altering or expanding the symbolic itself' (Pollock, 2004, p.10).
5. Ettinger uses 'stratum' and 'track'. The former alludes to what has been laid down separately and coexists relatively separately; track has more mobile connotations: moving from past to future via the encounters of present actuality and its processing. 'The trans-subjective track', Ettinger says, 'is reached by self relinquishment and is characterized by a subjectivity that surpasses personal limits' (2006a, p.221).

5 How Does Zelda Know and How Is Zelda Known? Psychoanalytically Informed Data Analysis

1. From a narrative perspective, a similar idea, that we cannot expect the participant to tell it like it is, gives rise to the 'hermeneutics of suspicion' (Josselson, 2004).

6 Scenic Writing and Scenic Understanding

1. Only recently has Lorenzer's work been available to an Anglophone readership. See two special issues: *Psychoanalysis, Culture and Society*, 2010 and *Forum: Qualitative Social Research*, 2012. My direct quotations from Lorenzer reference the German text. Thanks to Mechthild Bereswill, Christine Morgenroth and Peter Redman for a partial translation into English.
2. Aspects of earlier pen portrait style are still evident in my introductory portrayals, for example Justine, Chapter 8. This reflects the time of writing and my aims for that analysis.
3. Jung's collective unconscious refers to an innate and original symbolism, shared by all.
4. Unsurprisingly, psycho-social perspectives on the use of transference outside the clinic are influenced by different ways of theorising unconscious processes (Frosh, 2010); Special issue of *Psychoanalysis, Culture and Society*, 2008). I use a capacious definition of unconscious processes, from the unsaid to the unthinkable, partly because Bion has done so much to expand early Freudian usage and also because it is appropriate to my non-clinical concerns.
5. See Bereswill, Morgenroth and Redman (2010, p.240ff) and Morgenroth (2010) for accounts and examples of Lorenzer's group data analytic method.
6. 'Hoodies' refers to young men in groups who supposedly wear jackets with hoods in order to conceal their identities from surveillance cameras while they carry out antisocial or criminal activities. The observation took place at a time when hoodies were being widely and emotively publicised in the British media in terms of the way they were perceived as threats to law and order.

7. I am grateful to the observer, Ferelyth Watt, who used this extract in the *Infant Observation* special issue from the project (Watt, 2007).
8. In Margaret Rustin's experience 'often a whole seminar group can be seized by immense worry about the intrusive potential of the observational setting' (Rustin, 1989, p.9).
9. At this point, the data analysis has moved a long way from the original situation, in time, in membership and purpose. Thomson, Moe, Thorne and Nielsen, members of the aforementioned Oslo group, explore the ideas of travelling affect and travelling data, a term used to convey the 'overriding significance of *recontextualising* material in new times and places, and with different audiences' (Thomson et al., 2012, p.311).
10. The same principle (only more than two) that informs the use of groups for data analysis, as in Lorenzer's depth hermeneutic method (Morgenroth, 2010).
11. We should not reify 'the social unconscious': it is a transitive object, in other words, concept dependent (Bhaskar, 1998, p.198). See Chapter 8 for further explication.
12. Both joining and differentiating is how Ettinger describes the border operating in the metramorphic encounter.

7 'I'm Not the Mother Type': Gender Identity Upheaval

1. Typified by Nancy Chodorow's *Reproduction of Mothering* (1978), and Jessica Benjamin's *The Bonds of Love* (1988).
2. When reflection on this note is informed by the idea of transference-countertransference dynamics, I am prompted, not only to notice the conflictual nature of Arianna's relation to work, but also to inquire into my own relation to career and how it might be a presence in the interview relationship. Arianna was very interested to learn that I had one child, a daughter, and identified with me as a career woman. While recognising our similarities, I felt quite differentiated from her conflictual feelings around pregnancy and early motherhood.
3. On the day I revised this chapter, a morning radio news programme, discussing the near-absence of women orchestra conductors, referred to a male conductor blaming the fact on women's brains turning to mush when they have babies: women/mothers as the other of phallic meaning indeed.
4. Obstetricians are frequently reported as saying that fertility declines rapidly from age 35 and that women should not therefore leave motherhood too late.
5. See Hollway (2012a) for an elaborated discussion (using Arianna's case) of Winnicott's 'primary maternal preoccupation', his idea of new mothers' 'flight to sanity' and matrixial concepts.
6. I have extracted at length here, attempting to convey a raw quality of almost madness (remembered) in Arianna's talk by retaining repetitions, hesitations, unfinished ideas and the collapse of grammar. See also Sarah, Chapter 4. Notably the baby, who is on her knee, is not unmoved by this peroration. In matrixial perspective, how would she not be?

7. Ettinger's use of 'transjective' is like projection and introjection while reject-ing the phallic nature of the grammar, which separates the subject and object of an act of '-jecting' (from jacere 'to throw').

8 Theorising Maternal Becoming Psycho-Socially

1. A YouGov poll finding cited in Odone (2009), a Centre for Policy Studies report 'What Women Want'.
2. In the 1980s and early 1990s, valorising the feminine was expressed in an emerging North American feminist psychology that saw women and moth-ers in terms of connectedness and relationality in opposition to autonomy and separateness (for example, Jordan et al., 1991; Gilligan, 1993). As we saw in the previous chapter, a later generation of young (probably child-less), high-achieving American women did not recognise the close connection between women and relationality; their identities, like Arianna's, were settled in masculine-shaped, career-based 'defensive' autonomy.
3. A more detailed pen portrait and a differently orientated analysis can be found in Hollway (2010a).
4. This vignette deviates from some of the principles in Chapter 6, where I am critical of using just the kinds of social identity categories deployed here. When I considered changing its style (the original was written some time ago), I realised that it met my needs in this context, namely to present some relevant social information in a condensed way so that I could move on to the events I want to focus on. It is also relevant that there is no observation data for Justine.
5. Outside the Bangladeshi subsample (who were all married and who – it seemed – did not routinely use contraception), the label 'unplanned' for pregnancies was very common (more common than 'planned'). The phrase 'accidental-on-purpose' came to mind because it captures well so many of these pregnancies.
6. The notes that follow are also published in Hollway (2010a).
7. However, new work, for example De Marneffe (2004, 2006), Baraitser (2009), O'Reilly (2007, 2007), has escaped this trend, voices in what O'Reilly identifies as a new 'matricentric feminism'.
8. A matrixial approach also makes sense of Justine's feeling of going crazy after she lost her first pregnancy (even though this was at about two months, that is before the 'quickening'), powerfully felt by Justine as loss but for which she had no language. Becky expressed a similar devastation, also after an 'unplanned' first pregnancy which was closely followed by another 'unplanned' pregnancy.

9 Unfinished Business

1. Echoing the principle of the importance of recruiting the help of other minds with whom to think, I thank Rachel Thomson for a crucial joint thinking session that came at the right time.
2. It resembles somewhat Joan Raphael Leff's typology of mothers as regulators and facilitators (1983; 1986), later adding reciprocators and conflicted.

References

Alford, F. (2002) *Levinas, the Frankfurt School and Psychoanalysis*. Middletown, CN: Wesleyan University Press.

Alizade, A. M. (2006) 'The non-maternal psychic space', In A. M. Alizade (ed.) *Motherhood in the Twenty-first Century* (pp. 45–58). London: Karnac.

Anzieu, D. (1990) *A Skin for Thought: Interviews with Gilbert Tarrab*. London: Karnac.

Archer, M. (1998) 'Realism in the social sciences', In M. Archer, R. Bhaskar, A. Collier, T. Lawson and A. Norrie (eds) *Critical Realism: Essential Readings* (pp.189–205), London: Routledge.

Balint, E. (1993) *Before I was I*. London: Free Association Books.

Baraitser, L. (2008) 'On giving and taking offence', *Psychoanalysis, Culture and Society*, 13(4), 423–427.

Baraitser, L. (2009) *Maternal Encounters: The Ethics of Interruption*. London: Routledge.

Benjamin, J. (1988) *The Bonds of Love*. London: Virago.

Benjamin, J. (1995) *Like Subjects, Love Objects: Essays on Recognition and Sexual Difference*. New Haven: Yale University Press.

Bereswill, M., Morgenroth, C. and Redman, P. (2010) 'Special issue: "Alfred Lorenzer and the depth-hermeneutic method"', *Psychoanalysis, Culture and Society*, 15(3), 221–250.

Bhaskar, R. (1998) 'Philosophy and scientific realism', In M. Archer, R. Bhaskar, A. Collier, T. Lawson, and A. Norrie (eds), *Critical Realism: Essential Readings* (pp. 16–47). London: Routledge.

Bick, E. (1964) 'Notes on infant observation in psychoanalytic training', *International Journal of Psycho-Analysis*, 45, 628–645.

Bion, W. (1959) 'Attacks on linking', *International Journal of Psycho-Analysis*, 40, 308–315.

Bion, W. (1962a) *Learning from Experience*. London: Karnac.

Bion, W. (1962b) 'A theory of thinking', *International Journal of Psycho-Analysis*, 43, 306–310.

Bion, W.R. (1967) *Second Thoughts*. London: Heinemann (Maresfield reprints).

Blackman, L., Cromby, J., Hook, D. and Papadopoulos, D. (2008) Editorial. 'Creating Subjectivities', *Subjectivity*, 22, 1–27.

Bléandonu, G. (1999) *Wilfred Bion. His Life and Works, 1897–1979*. Trans. C. Pajaczkowska. London: Free Association Books.

Bollas, C. (1987) *The Shadow of the Object: Psychoanalysis of the Unthought Known*. London: Free Association Books.

Bollas, C. (1989) *Forces of Destiny. Psychoanalysis and Human Idiom*. London: Free Association Books.

Bordo, S. (1987) *The Flight to Objectivity: Essays in Cartesianism and Culture*. New York, Albany: SUNY Press.

Britton, R. (1998) *Belief and Imagination. Explorations in Psychoanalysis*. London: Routledge.

Bueskens, P. (2014) 'Introduction', In P. Bueskens (ed.) *Mothering and Psychoanalysis: Clinical, Sociological and Feminist Perspectives* (pp. 1–72) Bradford, Canada: Demeter.

Chodorow, N. (1978) *Reproduction of Mothering*. London: University of California Press.

Clarke, S. and Hoggett, P. (eds) (2009) *Researching Beneath the Surface*. London: Karnac.

Damasio, A. (2000) *The Feeling of What Happens: Body, Emotion and the Making of Consciousness*. London: Random House.

Davies, B. and Harré, R. (1990) 'Positioning: The discursive production of selves', *Journal for the Theory of Social Behaviour*, 20(1), 43–63.

De Marneffe, D. (2004) *Maternal Desire: On Children, Love and Inner Life*. New York: Little Brown.

De Marneffe, D. (2006) 'What exactly *is* the transformation of motherhood? Commentary on Lisa Baraitser's paper', *Studies in Gender and Sexuality*, 7(3), 239–248.

Dench, G. and Gavron, K. (2006) *The New East End*. London: Profile Books.

Despret, V. (2004) 'The body we care for: Figures of anthropo-zoo-genesis', *Body & Society*, 10, 111–134.

Devereux, G. (1967) *From Anxiety to Method in the Behavioural Sciences*. The Hague: Mouton.

Edwards, J. (2008) 'Early splitting and projective identification', *Infant Observation*, 11(1), 57–65.

Ehrenzweig, A. (1967/1970) *The Hidden Order of Art*. London: Paladin.

Elliott, H. (2011) 'Interviewing mothers: Reflections on reflexivity and closeness in research encounters', *Studies in the Maternal*, 3(1).

Elliot, H., Gunaratnam, Y., Hollway, W. and Phoenix, A. (2009) 'Practices, identification and identity change in the transition to motherhood', In M. Wetherell (ed.) *Theorizing Identities and Social Action* (pp. 19–37). London: Palgrave.

Elliott, H., Ryan, J. and Hollway, W. (2012) 'Research encounters, reflexivity and supervision', *International Journal of Social Research Methodology*, 15(5), 433–444.

Ettinger, B. L. (1992) 'Matrix and metramorphosis', *Differences*, 4(3), 170–208.

Ettinger, B. L. (1997) 'The feminine/prenatal weaving in matrixial subjectivity-as-encounter', *Psychoanalytic Dialogues*, 7(3), 367–405.

Ettinger, B. L. (2006a) 'Matrixial trans-subjectivity', *Theory, Culture and Society*, 23(2/3), 218–222.

Ettinger, B. L. (2006b) 'From proto-ethical compassion to responsibility: Besidedness and the three primal mother-phantasies of not-enoughness, devouring and abandonment', *Athena*, 2, 100–135.

Ettinger, B. L. (2010) '(M)Other re-spect: Maternal subjectivity, the *Ready-made mother-monster* and The Ethics of Respecting', *Studies in the Maternal*, 2(1).

Finlay, L. (2003) 'Through the looking glass: Intersubjectivity and hermeneutic reflection', In L. Finlay and B. Gough (eds) *Reflexivity: A Practical Guide for Researchers in Health and Social Sciences* (pp. 105–119). Oxford: Blackwell.

Flackowicz, M. (2007) 'Daughter, mother, wife: Transitions from ideals to the real family', *Infant Observation*, 10(3), 295–306.

Flax, J. (1993) *Disputed Subjects: Essays on Psychoanalysis, Politics and Philosophy*. London: Routledge.

Flyvbjerg, B. (2001) *Making Social Science Matter: Why Social Inquiry Fails and How it Can Succeed Again*. Cambridge: Cambridge University Press.

Fox Keller, E. (1985) *Reflections on Gender and Science*. London: Yale University Press.

Freud, S. (1901) 'Slips of the tongue', In *The Psychopathology of Everyday Life* Standard Edition, Volume 6 (pp. 53–105). London: Random House (Vintage edition, 2001).

Freud, S. (1922) 'Identification', In *Group Psychology and the Analysis of the Ego*, Standard Edition Volume 18 (pp. 105–110). London: Random House (Vintage edition 2001).

Froggett, L. and Hollway, W. (2010) 'Psychosocial research analysis and scenic understanding', *Psychoanalysis, Culture and Society*, 15, 281–301.

Frosh, S. (2010) *Psychoanalysis Outside the Clinic*. London: Palgrave Macmillan.

Frosh, S. and Baraitser, L. (2003) 'Thinking, recognition and otherness', *The Psychoanalytic Review*, 90(6), 771–789.

Frosh, S. and Emerson, P. (2005) 'Interpretation and over-interpretation: Disputing the meaning of texts', *Qualitative Research*, 5(3), 307–324.

Gallop, J. (2002) *Anecdotal Theory*. Durham, NC: Duke University Press.

Gentile, J. (2007) 'Wrestling with matter: Origins of subjectivity', *Psychoanalytic Quarterly*, LXXVI, 547–583.

Ghent, E. (1990) 'Masochism, submission, surrender: Masochism as a perversion of surrender', In S. Mitchell and L. Aron (1990) *Relational Psychoanalysis: The Emergence of a Tradition* (pp. 211–242). Hillsdale, NJ and London: Analytic Press.

Gilligan, C. (1993) *In a Different Voice*. Cambridge, MA: Harvard University Press.

Groarke, S. (2008) Psychoanalytical infant observation: A critical assessment', *European Journal of Psychotherapy and Counselling*, 10(4), 299–321.

Grotstein, J. (2007) *A Beam of Intense Darkness. Wilfred Bion's Legacy to Psychoanalysis*. London: Karnac.

Gunaratnam, Y. (2013) 'Roadworks: British Bangladeshi mothers, temporality and intimate citizenship in East London', *European Journal of Women's Studies*, 20(3), 1–15.

Hall, S. (1988) Minimal Selves. In: *Identity: the Real Me*. ICA Documents 6, 44–66. Institute of Contemporary Arts.

Hanly, C. (2004) 'The third: A brief historical analysis of an idea', *Psychoanalytic Quarterly*, LXXIII(1), 267–290.

Harris Williams, M. (2010) *Bion's Dream: A Reading of the Autobiographies*. London: Karnac.

Heimann, P. (1950) 'On counter-transference', *International Journal of Psycho-Analysis*, 31, 81–84.

Hekman, S. (1999) *The Future of Differences: Truth and Method in Feminist Theory*. Cambridge: Polity.

Henriques, J., Hollway, W., Urwin, C. Venn, C. and Walkerdine, V. (1998) *Changing the Subject: Psychology, Social Regulation and Subjectivity*. 2nd Ed. London: Routledge.

Henwood, K. (2008) 'Qualitative research, reflexivity and living with risk', *Qualitative Research in Psychology*, 5(1), 45–55.

Hinshelwood, R. D. (1991) *Dictionary of Kleinian Thought*. London: Free Association Books.

Hoggett, P. (2008) 'What's in a hyphen? Reconstructing psychosocial studies', *Psychoanalysis, Culture and Society*, 13(4), 379–384.

Hoggett, P., Beedell, S., Jimenez, L., Mayo, M. and Miller, C. (2010) 'Working psycho-socially and dialogically in research', *Psychoanalysis, Culture and Society*, 15(2), 173–188.

Hollway, W. (2006) *The Capacity to Care: Gender and Ethical Subjectivity*. London: Routledge.

Hollway, W. (2007) 'Afterword', *Infant Observation*, 10(3), 331–336.

Hollway, W. (2008) 'The importance of relational thinking in the practice of psycho-social research: Ontology, epistemology, methodology and ethics', In S. Clarke, P. Hoggett, and H. Hahn (eds) *Object Relations and Social Relations* (pp. 137–162). London: Karnac.

Hollway, W. (2010a) 'Conflict in the transition to becoming a mother: A psychosocial approach', *Psychoanalysis, Culture and Society*, 15(2), 136–155.

Hollway, W. (2010b) 'Relationality: The intersubjective foundations of identity', In M. Wetherell and C. Mohanty (eds) *Sage Handbook of Identities* (pp. 216–232) London: Sage.

Hollway, W. (2011a) 'In between external and internal worlds: Imagination in transitional space', *Methodological Innovations Online*, 6(3), 50–60.

Hollway, W. (2011b) 'Psycho-social writing from data', *Journal of Psycho-social Studies*, 4/5(1–2) http://hls.uwe.ac.uk/research/Data/Sites/1/journalpsycho-socialstudies/jan2011/issue5_vol1.pdf.

Hollway, W. (2012a) 'Infant observation: Opportunities, challenges, threats', *Infant Observation*, 15(1), 21–32.

Hollway, W. (2012b) 'Rereading Winnicott's "Primary Maternal Preoccupation" ', *Feminism and Psychology*, 22(1), 20–40.

Hollway, W. (2013a) 'Locating unconscious "societal-collective" processes in psychosocial research', *Organisational and Social Dynamics*, 13(1), 22–40.

Hollway, W. (2013b) 'Objectivity', In Thomas Teo (ed.), *Encyclopaedia of Critical Psychology*, Dordrecht: Springer.

Hollway, W. (2013c) ' "Mum's over the Moon": Rough verse and surprise of the real: Notes and audio performance', *Studies in the Maternal*, 5(1).

Hollway, W. and Froggett, L. (2012) 'Researching in between subjective experience and reality', *Forum: Qualitative Social Research*, 13(3), Art.13.

Hollway, W. and Jefferson, T. (2013) *Doing Qualitative Research Differently: Free Association, Narrative and the Interview Method.* 2nd ed. London: Sage.

Horney, K. (1967) 'The flight from womanhood' (1926), In *Feminine Psychology* (pp. 54–70). New York: Norton.

Hughes, T. (2008) *'The Spoken Word'.* British Library Sound Archive.

Hunt, J. (1989) *Psychoanalytic Aspects of Fieldwork.* Qualitative Research Methods Series, 18. California: Sage.

Instant Atlas (2007) THIS borough – Tower hamlets local information. *Geowise.* Available from: http://www.instantatlas.com/downloads/LBTH.pdf.

Jervis, S. (2009) 'The use of self as a research tool', In S. Clarke and P. Hoggett (eds) *Researching Beneath the Surface* (pp. 145–166). London: Karnac.

Jordan, J., Kaplan, A., Miller, J., Stiver, I. and Surrey, J. (Eds) (1991) *Women's Growth in Connection.* New York: Guilford Press.

Josselson, R. (2004) 'The hermeneutics of faith and the hermeneutics of suspicion', *Narrative Inquiry*, 14(1), 3–10.

Klein, M. (1952[1988]) 'The origins of transference', In *Envy and Gratitude and Other Works 1946–1963* (pp. 48–56). London: Virago.

Klein, M. (1963[1988]) 'On the sense of loneliness', In *Envy and Gratitude and Other Works 1946–1963* (pp. 300–313). London: Virago.

Kristeva, J. (1975[2002]) 'Desire in language', reprinted in K. Oliver (ed.) *The Portable Kristeva* (pp. 93–115). New York: Columbia University Press.

Kristeva, J. (1977[1991]) 'Stabat mater', In T. Moi (ed.) *The Kristeva Reader* (pp. 160–186). Oxford: Blackwell.

Kristeva, J. (1992) *Black Sun: Depression and Melancholia*. New York: Columbia University Press.

Kristeva, J. (2005) '*Motherhood Today*', www.kristeva.fr/motherhood.html, accessed 15th April 2014.

Laplanche, J. (1999) *Essays on Otherness*, edited by J. Fletcher. London: Routledge.

Lawrence, W. G. (2010) *The Creativity of Social Dreaming*. London: Karnac Books.

Layton, L. (2004) 'Relational no more', In J. A. Winer, J. W. Anderson, and C. C. Kieffer (eds) *Psychoanalysis and Women (The Annual of Psychoanalysis, XXXII)* (pp. 29–42). Hillsdale, NJ: Analytic Press.

Layton, S. (2007) 'Left alone to hold the baby'. *Infant Observation*, 10(3), 253–266.

Leithäuser, T. (2012) 'Psychoanalysis, socialization and society – the psychoanalytical thought and interpretation of Alfred Lorenzer', *Forum: Qualitative Social Research*, 13(3), Art.17.

Levinas, E. (1985) *Ethics and Infinity: Conversations with Philip Nemo*. Pittsburgh, PA: Duquesne University Press.

Levinas, E./ Etttinger, B. (2006) 'What would Euridyce say? Emmanuel Levinas in conversation with Bracha Lichtenberg Ettinger', *Athena*, 1, 137–145.

Little, M. (1986) 'On basic unity (primary total undifferentiatedness)', In G. Kohon (ed.) *The British School of Psychoanalysis* (pp. 136–153). London: Free Association Books.

Loewald, H. (1980) *Papers in Psychoanalysis*. New Haven, CT: Yale University Press.

Lorenzer, A. (1977) *Sprachspiel und Interaktionsformen* (Language Games and Interaction forms). Frankfurt/M: SuhrKamp.

Lorenzer, A. (1986) 'Tiefenhermeneutische Kulturanalyse', In Alfred Lorenzer (ed) *Kultur-Analysen: Psychoanalytische Studien zur Kultur* (pp. 11–98). Frankfurt/M: Fischer.

Manley, J. (2010) 'The slavery in the mind: inhibition and exhibition', In G. W. Lawrence (ed.) *The Creativity of Social Dreaming* (pp. 65–82). London: Karnac.

Marcus, P. (2010) *In Search of the Good Life: Emmanuel Levinas, Psychoanalysis and the Art of Living*. London: Karnac.

Mason, J. (2008) 'Tangible affinities and the real life fascination of kinship', *Sociology*, 42(1), 29–45.

McLeod, J. and Thomson, R. (2009) *Researching Social Change: Qualitative Approaches*, London: Sage.

Meltzer, D. (1986) *Studies in Extended Metapsychology. Clinical Applications of Bion's Ideas*. London: Karnac.

Miller, L. (1989) 'Introduction', In L. Miller, M. Rustin, M. Rustin and J. Shuttleworth (eds) *Closely Observed Infants* (pp. 1–4). London: Duckworth.

Miller, L., Rustin, M., Rustin, M.J. and Shuttleworth, J. (eds) (1989) *Closely Observed Infants*. London: Duckworth.

Mitchell, S. A. and Aron, L. (eds) (1999) *Relational Psychoanalysis: The Emergence of a Tradition*, Hillsdale, NJ: The Analytic Press.

Morgenroth, C. (2010) 'The research relationship, enactments and "counter-transference" analysis: On the significance of scenic understanding', *Psychoanalysis, Culture and Society*, 15(3), 267–280.

Murray, L. (1992) 'The impact of postnatal depression on infant development', *J. Child Psychology and Psychiatry*, 33(3), 543–561.

Odone, C. (2009) *What Women Want*, UK: Centre for Policy Studies.

Oeser, F. (2010) 'Social dreaming to creativity', In G. W. Lawrence (ed.) *The Creativity of Social Dreaming* (pp. 9–24) London: Karnac.

Ogden, T. H. (1983) 'The concept of internal object relations', *International Journal of Psycho-Analysis*, 64(2), 227–241.

Ogden, T. (1989) *The Primitive Edge of Experience*. New York: Jason Aronson.

Ogden, T. (2009) *Rediscovering Psychoanalysis: Thinking, Dreaming, Learning and Forgetting*. London: Routledge.

O'Reilly, A. (ed.) (2007) *Maternal Theory. Essential Readings*. Bradford, Canada: Demeter.

Peirce, C. (1903) *Complete Papers of Charles Sanders Peirce*, Vols 1–8. C. Hartshorne and P. Weiss (eds) (1966) Cambridge MA: Harvard University Press.

Phoenix, A. (1990) *Young Mothers?* Cambridge: Polity Press.

Pluckrose, E. (2007) 'Loss of the motherland: The dilemma of creating triangular space a long way from home', *Infant Observation*, 10(3), 307–318.

Polanyi, M. (1958) *Personal Knowledge: Towards a Post-critical Philosophy*. London: Routledge.

Pollock, G. (2004) 'Thinking the feminine: Aesthetic practice as introduction to Bracha Ettinger and the concepts of matrix and metramorphosis', *Theory, Culture and Society*, 21(5), 5–65.

Pollock, G. (2008) 'Mother trouble', *Studies in the Maternal*, 1.

Raphael-Leff, J. (1983) 'Facilitators and regulators: Two approaches to mothering', *British Journal of Medical Psychology*, 56, 379–390.

Raphael-Leff, J. (1986) 'Facilitators and regulators: Conscious and unconscious processes in pregnancy and early motherhood', *British Journal of Medical Psychology*, 59, 43–55.

Raphael-Leff (1991) 'The mother as container: Placental process and inner space' *Feminism & Psychology*, 1, 393–408.

Raphael-Leff, J. (1993) *Pregnancy: The Inside Story*. London: Karnac.

Redman, P. (2009) 'Affect revisited: Transference-countertransference and the unconscious dimensions of affective, felt and emotional experience', *Subjectivity*, 26, 51–68.

Redman, P., Bereswill, M. and Morgenroth, C. (2010) 'Special issue on Alfred Lorenzer, "Introduction"', *Psychoanalysis, Culture and Society*, 15(3), 213–220.

Richardson, L. (1992) 'The consequences of poetic representation: Writing the Other, writing the Self', In C. Ellis and J. M. Flaherty (eds) *Investigating Subjectivity: Research on Lived Experience* (pp. 125–137). London: Sage.

Rose, N. (1990) *Governing the Soul: The Shaping of the Private Self*. London: Routledge.

Roseneil, S. (2006) 'The ambivalences of Angel's "arrangement": A psychosocial lens on the contemporary condition of personal life', *Sociological Review*, 54(4), 847–869.

Roseneil, S. (2009) 'Haunting in an age of individualization, subjectivity, relationality and the traces of the lives of others', *European Societies*, 11(3), 411–430.

Rustin, M.J. (1989) 'Encountering primitive anxieties', In L. Miller, M. J. Rustin, M. Rustin, and J. Shuttleworth (eds) *Closely Observed Infants* (pp. 7–21). London: Duckworth.

Salling Olesen, H. (2012) 'The societal nature of subjectivity: An interdisciplinary methodological challenge', *Forum: Qualitative Social Research*, 13(3), Art.4.

Salling Olesen, H. and Weber, K. (2012) 'Socialization, Language, and scenic understanding. Alfred Lorenzer's contribution to a Psycho-societal Methodology', *Forum: Qualitative Social Research*, 13(3), Art.22.

Schore, A. (2010) 'The right brain implicit self: A central mechanism of the psychotherapy change process', In J. Petrucelli (ed.) *Knowing, Not Knowing and Sort of Knowing: Psychoanalysis and the Experience of Uncertainty* (pp. 177–201). London: Karnac.

Sevenhuijsen, S. (1998) *Citizenship and the Ethics of Care*. London: Routledge.

Sowa, A. (2002–2003) 'Sustained thinking and the realm of the aesthetic in psychoanalytic observation', *Infant Observation*, 5(3), 24–40.

Spillius, E. (1988) 'Introduction' to section 3 'On thinking', In E.B. Spillius (ed.), *Melanie Klein Today* (pp. 153–159) London: Routledge.

Stenner, P. (2008) 'A. N. Whitehead and subjectivity', *Subjectivity*, 22, 90–109.

Stopford, A. (2004) 'Researching postcolonial subjectivities: The application of relational (postclassical) psychoanalysis to research methodology', *Critical Psychology*, 10, 13–35.

Symington, J. and N. (1996) *The Clinical thinking of Wilfred Bion*. London: Routledge.

Thomson, R. (2007) 'The qualitative longitudinal case history: Practical, methodological and ethical reflections', *Social Policy and Society*, 6(4), 571–582.

Thomson, R., Hadfield, L., Kehily, M. J., and Sharpe, S. (2012) 'Acting up and acting out: Encountering children in a longitudinal study of mothering', *Qualitative Research*, 12(2), 186–201.

Thomson, R. and Kehily, M. J. (2011) 'Troubling reflexivity: The identity flows of teachers becoming mothers', *Gender and Education*, 23(3), 233–245.

Thomson, R., Kehily, M. J., Hadfield, L. and Sharpe, S. (2011) *Making Modern Mothers*. Bristol: Policy Press.

Thomson, R., Moe, A., Thorne, B. and Nielsen, H. B. (2012) 'Situated affect in travelling data', *Qualitative Inquiry*, 18, 310–322.

Thorp, J. (2007) 'The search for space in the process of becoming a first-time mother', *Infant Observation*, 10(3), 319–330.

Tyler, I. (2000) 'Reframing pregnant embodiment', In S. Ahmed, J. Kirby, C. Lury, M. McNeil and B. Skeggs (eds) *Transformation: Thinking Through Feminisms* (pp. 288–302). London: Routledge.

Urwin, C. (1985) 'Constructing motherhood: The persuasion of normal development', in C. Steedman, C. Urwin and V. Walkerdine (eds) *Language, Gender and Childhood*. London: Routledge.

Urwin, C. (2007) 'Doing infant observation differently? Researching the formation of mothering identities in an inner London borough', *Infant Observation*, 10(3), 239–252.

Urwin, C. (ed.) (2007) 'Becoming a mother: Changing identities. Infant observation in a research project', *Infant Observation*, 10(3), 231–234.

Urwin, C. (2011) 'Infant observation meets social science', *Infant Observation* 14, 3, 341–344.

Urwin, C. (2012) 'Using surprise in observing cultural experience', In C. Urwin and J. Sternberg (eds) *Infant Observation and Research: Emotional Processes in Everyday Lives* (pp. 93–103). London: Routledge.

Urwin, C. and Sternberg, J. (eds.) (2012) *Infant Observation and Research: Emotional Processes in Everyday Lives*, London: Routledge.

Urwin, C., Hauge, M-I., Hollway, W., Haavind, H. (2013) 'Culture as a process lived through the person: Becoming a Bangladeshi mother in London', *Qualitative Inquiry*, 19(6), 470–479.

Venn, C. (2014) ' "Race" and the disorders of identity: Rethinking difference, the relation to the other and a politics of the commons', *Subjectivity*, 7(1), 37–55.

Watt, F. (2007) 'Mixed feeds and multiple transitions – a teenager becomes a mother', *Infant Observation*, 10(3), 281–294.

Wengraf, T. (2013) 'Critical realism and psycho-societal method: Researching variable agency by using BNIM', available from tom@tomwengraf.com.

Wetherell, M. (ed.) (2009) *Identity in the 21st Century*. London: Palgrave.

Wetherell, M. (ed.) (2009) *Theorizing Identities and Social Action*. London: Palgrave.

Wetherell, M. (2010) 'The field of identity studies', in M. Wetherell and C. Mohanty (eds) *The Sage Handbook of Identities* (pp. 3–26). London: Sage.

Winnicott, D. W. (1984[1956]) 'Primary maternal preoccupation' In *Through Paediatrics to Psychoanalysis: Collected Papers* (pp. 300–305) London: Karnac Books.

Winnicott, D. W. (1960) 'The theory of the parent-infant relationship', In D. W. Winnicott (ed.) (1990) *The Maturational Processes and the Facilitating Environment* (pp. 37–55). London: Karnac.

Winnicott, D. W. (1963) 'From dependence towards independence in the development of the individual', In D. W. Winnicott (ed.) (1990) *The Maturational Processes and the Facilitating Environment* (pp. 83–92). London: Karnac.

Winnicott, D. W. (2005[1971]) *Playing and Reality*. London: Routledge.

Woograsingh, S. (2007) 'A single flavour of motherhood: An emerging identity in a young Bangladeshi woman', *Infant Observation*, 10(3), 267–280.

Index

Abortion, 63, 67, 142, 143, 152, 160
action, 3, 22, 43, 63, 67, 68, 111, 112, 113, 121, 124, 127, 134, 151, 177, 178, 192
Adowa, 33
affect, xi, 14, 19, 23, 26, 29, 31, 32, 43, 47, 51, 53, 56, 71, 73, 74, 75, 91, 97, 111, 113, 122, 130, 134, 149, 153, 167, 168, 172, 181, 185, 186, 194
affective flows, 55, 72, 135
agency, 26, 57, 62, 63, 66, 68, 69, 71, 72, 73, 75, 83, 149, 169, 192
Alford, F., 88
Alizade, A.M., 174, 175
alpha (α), 112, 149
  elements, 112
  –function, 49, 112, 120
alterity, 88, 102, 110, 113, 119, 121, 154, 157–9, 178
ambivalence, 14, 16, 28, 92, 94, 139, 169
anguish (angoisse), 102, 103, 119, 121
anonymise/anonymity, 97, 159, 160
anxiety, 15, 27, 43, 50, 53, 73, 101, 102–9, 110, 111, 115, 116, 119, 121, 129, 130, 155, 185
  Cartesian, 73
  Zelda's, 102–9
Anzieu, D., 139–40, 141, 151, 158, 161
Archer, M., 57, 69
Arianna, 27, 35, 142–61, 163, 164, 165, 166, 169, 172, 175, 182, 194, 195
Aron, L., 72
asymbolic, 113
autonomous, 15, 16, 110, 140, 148, 149, 153, 163
  individual/subject, 23, 27, 82, 88, 141, 150, 152, 154, 156, 181, 192

autonomy, 82, 87, 99, 141, 150, 152, 161, 173, 180, 182, 195
  defensive, 141, 149, 195
Azra, 33

Badinter, E., 180
Balint, E., 71, 129
Baraitser, L., 20, 21, 75, 83, 84, 87, 88, 92, 102, 111, 158, 176, 181, 192, 195
Becky, 36
becoming (excluding the phrase/becoming a mother), 3, 16, 17, 21, 23, 25, 26, 30, 45, 69, 72, 74
  maternal, xi, 22, 185–7
  of being, 21
  see also co-becoming
Benjamin, J., 87, 140, 194
Bereswill, M., 122, 130, 134, 193
beta (β), 112
  elements, 112
Bhaskar, R., 69, 70, 194
bias, 31, 74
Bick, E., 19, 47
binary, 15, 57, 67, 74, 75, 85, 87, 102, 128, 135, 140, 150, 161, 163, 164, 168, 169, 175, 176, 179, 180, 182, 185
  merger and separation, 102
  women's versus babies' needs, 176
  see also non-binary
biographical, 26, 44, 128, 186, 192
Biographical Narrative Interpretive Method (BNIM), 192
biology, 85, 87, 98, 141, 161
  beyond, 157–9, 180–2
Bion, W.R., 22, 23, 26, 27, 31, 49, 56, 69, 79, 92, 93, 96, 101, 102, 104, 109–10, 112, 113, 115, 116, 117, 120, 121, 123, 128, 129, 133, 134, 135, 148, 149, 183, 185, 187, 189, 193

frequency, 53, 80, 94
Freud, S., 79, 85, 96, 109, 110, 113,
    117, 152, 157, 168, 193
friends, 15, 30, 37, 38, 51, 54, 60,
    61, 62
Froggett. L., 34, 122, 123, 130, 132
Frosh, S., 75, 111, 181, 193
frustration, 15, 17, 66, 93, 99, 105,
    117, 178
fusion, 102, 119, 120, 158, 181, 182

Gallop, J., 21
Gavron, K., 18
gender, 21, 87, 139, 162, 167, 175,
    180, 185
  difference, 27, 28, 139, 163, 164,
      172–5
  equality, 27, 28, 99, 139, 140, 141,
      148–9, 157, 161, 163, 164, 172,
      180, 182
  relations, 24, 82, 161, 181, 187
  settlement, 150
generalisation, 44, 45, 53, 56, 129, 187
generation, 17, 28, 140, 165, 167, 171,
    172, 177, 184, 195
Gentile, J., 57, 62, 66, 68, 69, 72
Ghent, E., 74
Gilligan, C., 195
grandfather, 59, 187
grandmother, 14, 34, 37
Groarke, S., 48
Grotstein, J., 79
guilt, 63, 81, 94, 107, 192
Gunaratnam, Y., 40, 99, 191

Haavind, H., 34, 191
Hafna, 35
Hall, S., 20
Hanly, C., 62
Hannah, 36
Harré, R., 71
Harris Williams, M., 79
hate, 66, 110, 178
  H, –H, 110
  motherhood, 160
Hauge, M-I., 34, 191
Heimann, P., 129
Hekman, S., 157, 163, 164
Henriques, J., et al, 74, 141

Henwood, K., 31
hermeneutic, 111, 193
  depth, 123, 194
Hinshelwood, R.D., 113, 129
history, 20, 23, 73, 102, 134, 172, 189
Hoggett, P., 74, 75, 129, 135, 159
holistic, 23, 56, 61, 122, 123, 131, 136,
    159, 185
Hollway, W., 25, 31, 34, 35, 36, 37, 38,
    39, 40, 43, 44, 46, 49, 50, 80, 86,
    122, 123, 128, 130, 132, 155, 191,
    194, 195
Horney, K., 85
Hughes, T., 3, 123
Hunt, J., 31
hyphen, 75, 135

identification, 47, 50, 71, 91, 99, 113,
    117, 134, 161, 164, 169, 177, 178
  masculine, 172
  projective, 22, 27, 74, 79, 101, 102,
      112–15, 120, 129, 189
  two-part, 71
Identities and Social Action
    programme, 17, 20, 23
identity
  categories, 124–6
  change, x, 13, 17, 20, 22, 23, 27, 29,
      43, 44, 51, 127, 183, 185
  gender, 139
  investment, 16, 24, 98, 141, 163
idiom, 3, 26, 105, 107, 126, 127
imagination, 30, 57, 63, 66, 67, 68–73,
    74, 122, 123, 124, 126, 127–8, 129
in between, 22, 86, 124, 127–8, 136
individual, 19, 27, 30, 57, 58, 62, 71,
    72, 75, 83, 87, 91, 92, 96, 97, 109,
    113, 122, 128, 131, 135, 140, 155,
    172, 177, 181
  autonomous, 99, 141, 150, 152, 175
ineffable, x, xi, 22, 74, 80, 81, 95, 98,
    101, 184
intergenerational, 169, 185
  continuity, 13, 14, 17, 177
intermediate space/area of
    experiencing, 57, 68, 70, 75, 123,
    127, 131
  see also in between

projection, 66, 73, 107, 113, 152, 157, 195
projective identification, *see* identification, projective
provocation, 27, 130–1, 132, 134–5, 177, 190
psyche, 102, 112
psychic space, non-maternal, 174–5

qualitative, 22, 25, 26, 29, 31, 32, 46, 56, 69, 111, 125, 127, 193

Rabiya, 38, 92–5, 99, 189
'race', 21, 134, 135
Raphael-Leff, J., 45, 84, 195
realism, critical, 57, 69–73, 75, 192
   naïve, 62
reality, 15, 26, 57, 58, 61–9, 70, 71, 72, 73, 74, 93, 15, 115, 119, 123, 126, 127, 132, 134, 169, 172, 185
   concrete social, 127, 128, 130
   facing, 61–7
   unyielding, 72
Redman, P., 71, 72, 122, 134, 160, 193
reflection, 19, 26, 31, 46, 47, 48, 50, 52, 56, 57, 90, 100, 111, 117, 118, 194
   see also field notes, reflective
reflexivity, 31, 46, 125, 166–8
relation to, 3, 20, 26, 28, 30, 43, 44, 51, 53, 56, 57, 62, 63, 65, 68, 71, 72, 75, 87, 92, 99, 107, 116, 121, 126, 135, 139, 149, 152, 161, 163, 164, 165, 167, 168, 169, 172, 177, 182, 183, 187, 188, 189, 194
relational, 17, 21, 51, 62, 80, 84, 85, 87, 88, 109, 121, 122, 124, 127, 129, 140, 141, 172, 186, 195
   female, 141
   psychonalysis, 87, 140
representation, xi, 24, 71, 109, 112, 127, 173
   scenic, 125
resonances, 22, 86, 98, 119, 158, 189
reverie, 22, 25, 27, 96, 101, 102, 113, 114, 123, 128–30, 136, 189
Richardson, L., 123
Rose, N., 24
Roseneil, S., 30, 141

rough verse, 3, 26, 123
Rustin, M.J., 129, 194
Ryan, J., 46, 47, 50, 55

Salling Olesen, H., 122, 123, 127
sample, 3, 15, 17, 18, 21, 22, 24, 28, 30, 31, 32–43, 45, 47, 48, 93, 94, 125, 141, 142, 171, 184–5, 186, 187, 188, 195
   whole sample, 184–5
sanity, 155–7, 194
Sarah, 39, 82–4, 85, 92, 99, 187, 188, 194
scan, 51, 63, 64, 67, 68, 69, 70, 81, 82, 105, 106, 143
scene/scenic understanding, 4, 22, 23, 27, 61, 62, 74, 122, 123, 127–8, 129, 130, 131–4, 133, 134, 135, 136, 185
   composition, 27, 130, 134
   writing, 122, 123, 124
Schore, A., 191
scientificity, 74
separation, 28, 73, 79, 80, 81, 85, 87, 89, 98, 99, 102, 120, 148, 149, 158, 162, 176, 177, 179, 181, 182, 183, 186
Sevenhuijsen, S., 92
sexual difference, 85, 141, 148, 149, 150, 158
Sharmila, 39
Silma, 39, 44
single case, 26, 27, 33, 96, 101, 159, 185, 187
situated, 20, 31, 66, 89, 122, 123, 135, 169, 188
social identity categories, 26, 123, 124, 125, 126
societal-collective, 134, 135, 136
societal-cultural, 27, 128, 134
sonic, 86, 119
Sowa, A., 109, 117
space, *see* borderspace; confidential space; intermediate space; mental space; psychic space; transitional
speech marks, 127
Spillius, E., 69
split, 31, 86, 90, 105, 123, 141, 164, 175

splitting, 39, 101, 105, 107, 108, 119, 163
Stenner, P., 74
Sternberg, J., 49
Stopford, A., 159
stratum, 82, 86, 89, 90, 91, 99, 101, 102, 120, 128, 149, 151, 155, 161, 169, 179, 181, 193
see also track
subject, 23, 43, 46, 57, 65, 68, 71, 72, 73, 82, 83, 84, 85, 86, 88, 89, 91, 92, 99, 101, 102, 119, 120, 139, 149, 151, 153, 154, 155, 158, 159, 161, 162, 169, 179, 181, 182, 183, 190, 193
subjectivity, 15, 19, 20, 21, 23, 24, 26, 31, 50, 57, 62, 68, 69, 71, 73, 74, 75, 79, 83, 85, 86, 87, 89, 92, 99, 102, 120, 122, 125, 140, 141, 148, 149, 154, 155, 157, 161, 173, 181, 185, 186, 191, 192, 193
subjectivising (subjectivizing), 149, 151, 153, 157, 163, 181, 185, 193
supervision, 47, 49–50, 111
support, 5, 7, 14, 15, 22, 26, 31, 34, 36, 38, 39, 43, 45, 47, 49, 50, 62, 64, 65, 68, 103, 108, 111, 114, 118, 130, 140, 157, 169, 171, 174
Sylvia, 40, 50, 184
symbolic/symbolization, xi, 27, 49, 72, 83, 85, 88, 89, 109, 112, 113, 118, 120, 129, 133, 134, 135, 148, 179, 193
non-/un, 22, 122, 129, 188, 193
presymbolic, 23
Symington, J.&N., 117

Tavistock Centre, 19, 47
temporal register, 152, 153, 186
thinking, 15, 19, 21, 27, 47, 57, 63, 65, 66, 67, 68, 69, 70, 93, 115, 117, 164, 180, 191
Bion's theory of, 31, 56, 109–13, 121
Thomson, R., 19, 31, 34, 45, 46, 49, 192, 194, 195
Thorp, J., 33
tolerate, 93, 112, 114, 117, 129, 178
Tower Hamlets, London borough of, 17, 18, 21, 24, 32, 141

traces, 86, 99, 119, 134, 149, 153, 155
track, 99, 120, 149, 150, 151, 162, 169, 181, 188, 190, 191, 192, 195
see also stratum
transcript, 44, 48, 51, 54, 126, 146, 167
transference-countertransference, 113, 132, 193, 194
mother-daughter transference, 167, 168
transgenerational, 172
transgression, 86, 101, 181
transition, 15, 20, 32, 141, 185
identity, 3, 17, 125, 186
transjective, 121, 158, 179, 181, 195
transmission, 153, 185
trans-subjective/ity (transsubjective), 22, 23, 27, 72, 79, 80, 82, 85, 86, 88, 91, 92, 99, 101, 102, 119, 120, 139, 149, 151, 153, 154, 155, 158, 159, 161, 162, 169, 179, 181, 182, 183, 190, 193
see also transjective
traumatic, 35, 39, 43, 46, 105, 108, 109
triangulation, 26, 43, 48, 54, 56, 65, 107
see also other minds
truths, 48, 62

unbidden, 99, 135, 136, 188
uncertainty, 20, 93, 95, 114, 115, 125, 129, 130, 147, 154, 188, 189
unconditional demands, 161
unconscious, 18, 19, 31, 43, 50, 53, 67, 71, 88, 89, 92, 96, 113, 120, 122, 128, 129, 130, 134, 135, 149, 150, 151, 152, 166, 169, 190, 193, 194
repressed, 96
societal-collective, 134
societal-cultural, 134
supra-individual, 135
undifferentiatedness, 119, 123
unemployed, 34, 37, 134, 165, 167, 169, 173
unicity of being, 139
unknowable, 102
unsignifiable, 148

Printed and bound by CPI Group (UK) Ltd, Croydon, CR0 4YY